RETURNS TO THE FIELD

RETURNS TO THE FIELD

MULTITEMPORAL RESEARCH
AND CONTEMPORARY
ANTHROPOLOGY

Edited by
SIGNE HOWELL AND
AUD TALLE
AFTERWORD BY
BRUCE KNAUFT

INDIANA UNIVERSITY PRESS
Bloomington & Indianapolis

This book is a publication of

Indiana University Press
601 North Morton Street
Bloomington, Indiana 47404-3797 USA

iupress.indiana.edu

Telephone orders   800-842-6796
Fax orders   812-855-7931

Library of Congress Cataloging-in-Publication Data

Returns to the field : multitemporal research and contemporary
anthropology / edited by Signe Howell and Aud Talle; afterword by
Bruce Knauft.
    p. cm.
   Includes bibliographical references and index.
   ISBN 978-0-253-35676-5 (cloth : alk. paper) — ISBN 978-0-
253-22348-7 (pbk. : alk. paper) 1. Anthropology—Fieldwork. 2.
Anthropology—Research. 3. Anthropology—Longitudinal studies. I.
Howell, Signe. II. Talle, Aud, [date]
   GN34.3.F53R48 2012
   301.072′3—dc23
                                          2011021671

1 2 3 4 5   17 16 15 14 13 12

CONTENTS

PREFACE

The anthropologists writing in this volume address a topic of great relevance to the practice of ethnographic fieldwork, which has received remarkably little attention: what we call multitemporal fieldwork. This is the practice of returning to the same group of people on many occasions over a long period of time. In August 2006 we arranged a workshop in Oslo to which we invited speakers with this kind of long-term fieldwork experience to critically examine their experience. In order to sharpen the focus we selected anthropologists who had done fieldwork with minority populations. The seminar turned out to be very successful. We found that we shared many similar experiences and reflections. We therefore decided to take our conversation one step further by arranging a panel at the American Anthropological Association Meeting in 2007. In the intervening period the participants made written comments on our discussions in Oslo, and continued to think further about the topic; and we invited Terry Turner, Peter Metcalf, and David Holmberg to join our group. The AAA session went so well that we decided to make the papers into a book. We, the editors, identified a number of themes that we asked the participants to address in their papers for this volume.

In the introduction we address these themes and elucidate some methodological and analytical issues that we have identified as springing out of the practice of multitemporal fieldwork, so as to set the scene for the ethnographically grounded chapters that follow. Bruce Knauft, an active participant both in Oslo and at the AAA session, opted to write an afterword to the volume. For this reason, we do not provide a systematic introduction to each of the chapters, but highlight aspects from them as these are appropriate to the general discussion.

We count ourselves lucky to have experienced first-hand ways of life that, in most cases, are gone forever. As we look back on the times we have spent in the field, it is hard to escape a very personal sense of nostalgia. At the same time, this book provides several examples of people refusing to become passive victims, demonstrating cultural resilience and resistance to many imposed restrictions on their way of life, transforming the negative into something positive.

We wish to extend our thanks to the Department of Social Anthropology, University of Oslo, for providing financial support to arrange the original seminar.

Oslo, November 2010

RETURNS TO THE FIELD

RETURNS TO THE FIELD

Introduction

SIGNE HOWELL AND AUD TALLE

To say that ethnography is *like* initiation is not to recommend that the researcher should actually undergo the process by which a native attains the wisdom of the group . . . The metaphor of initiation evokes, rather, the deepening of understanding that accrues to long-term field research with repeated visits throughout the anthropologist's career.

—*James Clifford*

Most anthropologists are agreed that models of society which leave out time are inadequate: they are too far from reality to be illuminating theoretically . . . Our concern is not whether to study change in society but *how* to study it . . .

—*Monica Wilson*

FIELDWORK AND ANTHROPOLOGY

Ethnographic fieldwork performed according to the ideal of participant-observation has been the hallmark of anthropology since the time of Franz Boas in the United States and Bronislaw Malinowski in the United Kingdom. The famous statement by Malinowski in his introduction to the *Argonauts of the Western Pacific* that the ultimate goal of ethnographic fieldwork is "to grasp the native's point of view, his relations to life, to realize *his* vision of *his* world . . . the hold which life has on him" (1922, 25, original emphasis) has never lost its appeal for new generations of anthropologists setting out on their first fieldwork. And, despite the rather naïve assumption about "the native's point of view" and our ability to represent it in a straightforward manner, extended ethnographic fieldwork continues to be crucial for anthropological theorizing. It gives rise to knowledge not readily available through the more common social science methods of interviews, questionnaires, and statistical data. To insist on the uniqueness of our disciplinary legacy and practice is especially pertinent in today's intellectual climate, in which a number of other disciplines in the social sciences and humanities increasingly proclaim to be doing "ethnography" or "fieldwork" as part of qualitative research methodology. When one examines what this means in practice, we feel certain that most anthropologists would experience unease; such a statement rarely implies the immersion into local life that anthropologists mean by the terms.

This appropriation of "fieldwork" elsewhere—and also of the concept of culture—is rather ironic, given that recent anthropological debate has questioned their validity. The critique of culture dominant in the 1990s made ethnographic fieldwork in remote parts of the world a contested scholarly activity (see Borneman and Hammoudi 2009; Clifford and Marcus 1986; Marcus and Fischer 1986; Marcus 1998). Much of the anthropological writing of the past seemed to be rendered irrelevant when characterized as ethnographic realism[1] (Marcus and Fischer 1986). Just as other disciplines discovered culture and used it in their studies, the concept of culture was deconstructed to such an extent that it was abandoned altogether in influential anthropological circles (e.g., Borofsky 1994; Clifford 1988; Marcus and Fischer 1986). Uncertainty could be observed among students as fieldwork in former colonial areas became, for a variety of reasons, regarded as politically incorrect (for elaborations on this see among others Clifford and Marcus 1986; Marcus 1998). At the same time, and probably related to the critique, "anthropology at home" became more popular—accompanied by an increase in the use of interviews and questionnaires at the expense of participant-observation.

One purpose of this book is to put extended fieldwork back on the anthropological map as not only legitimate, but both essential and desirable in the pursuit of knowledge about social and cultural forms (see also Borneman and Hammoudi 2009). Not only extended field-work, but also that undertaken in unknown and alien places carries its own methodological value insofar as it forces anthropologists to perceive the world they study through a lens of unfamiliarity. As we redirect the insights we have gained back on our own world, we can see this in a fresh light. It is, we argue, only through this comparative dimension as a methodological practice that anthropology will maintain its special place in the human sciences.

We wish to extend the argument about the centrality of fieldwork in anthropology to one aspect that has received little attention, namely what we call multitemporal fieldwork. By this term we mean many returns to the same place across the years, but not necessarily in a systematic chronological pattern. We claim that these many en-gagements over time assist us in achieving a semblance of the Ma-linowskian aim of understanding the "native's point of view," and in addition make it possible to follow social processes at close range. The contributors to this volume all share a commitment to fieldwork, and also share in the belief that multitemporal fieldwork enhances our knowledge in many ways: about the people we study, about pat-terns of social and cultural life, about ourselves, and about the cen-tral tenets of anthropological theory.

Furthermore, what the contributors to this book also have in com-mon is that each of them has been studying a minority group. We chose this focus because we ourselves, the organizers, have studied minority groups, and also because minority groups in modern na-tion-states are relatively easily definable as separate communities. They tend to be peripheral to the majority populations with whom they share citizenship, they experience a common identity, and they have had to face severe challenges to their way of life over a short period of time—often coinciding with the anthropologists' engage-ment with them.

The objectives of this volume are threefold. First, we seek to ex-plore how multitemporal fieldwork gives rise to a different, more pro-found, understanding of continuity and change. Second, we wish to explore how some of these minority populations have met the challenges imposed upon them from external forces of change. Finally, we reflect on how the passing of time becomes a factor in anthropological analysis.

MINORITIES UNDER PRESSURE

Although dispersed across several continents (South America, Africa, Siberia, South Asia, Southeast Asia, Oceania), the minority groups discussed in this volume share many commonalities by virtue of having experienced a repressive colonial past. The establishment of new nation-states after colonial rule, however, continued and intensified earlier trends of exploitation and modernization and rendered many of these groups even more vulnerable. A new dependence upon a monetized economy led to several shifts in economic activities—for example, increased agricultural activities directed at the sale of produce rather than domestic consumption, the exploitation of the natural environment in new ways in order to generate income, and intensified labor migration. Such changes, in turn, have affected gender and generational relations as well as systems of governance and local politics. All this has seriously challenged peoples' understanding of their own identity as individuals and as members of social groups.

As subjects of research, small-scale minority groups could once be defined relatively easily. Over time, however, the very same societies are becoming entangled in wide-ranging fields of interaction and points of reference stretching far beyond their own localities in many ways, challenging anthropological devices of description and analysis. Given the fact that these minority populations have undergone important, and at times dramatic, changes as a result of the intense large-scale processes into which they are drawn during the period of our engagement with them, charting these changes becomes particularly urgent.

Our decision to invite only researchers who had worked with minority groups was initially a pragmatic one. We had worked among such people and needed to frame the discussion, but as we got to know each other we realized that we had much in common beyond purely analytical concerns. We also share an emotional involvement with the people we have studied, based to a large extent on our experience of having witnessed a period of much unwelcome, sometimes painful, change. We have observed at first hand the vulnerability of minority groups in their encounter with global trends and state politics, and we, the anthropologists, found ourselves drawn in directions beyond the strictly disciplinary. Our interaction with the people we study has matured and intensified, due not least to the many return visits. In the process, what began as a scholarly activity aimed at understanding the workings of a particular social and cultural system has drawn the researchers into multiple moral and political dilemmas that have transcended professional concerns. Concern about minority issues, and categories such as Fourth or Indigenous World, were only just taking shape when we started our fieldwork, but have since become widely recognized. Fieldworkers cannot ignore the implications of such trends as we continue our ethnographic relationships. The struggle of marginalized groups for self-determination and cultural identity in the world today may easily turn into a common cause for the researcher and the people alike (see in particular Holmberg, Hviding, Metcalf, Turner, and Vitebsky this volume).

The minorities described in this book belong to what today is called the Indigenous World. This is a politicized category that increasingly is embedded in human rights discourses and global politics (IWGIA 2008). During the last twenty years, extensive lobbying by human rights activists, representatives of the people themselves, and last but not least anthropologists has put the indigenous issue on the agenda of powerful organizations such as the UN, the International Labour Organization and the World Bank (www.worldbank.org/indigenous).

Thus, as we see it, the diachronic approach documented in this volume springs simultaneously from a professional vantage point of observing social processes and from a moral commitment emanating from prolonged contact with threatened peoples. The fact that these groups are minorities living in close proximity to powerful majority populations whose agendas may not coincide with their own needs and desires adds urgency to the anthropological project. Has the escalating vulnerability of minority groups within colonial and postcolonial nation-states contributed in any way to our long-term involvement with such populations? In other words, is there a connection between the minority status of the people studied and multitemporal fieldwork? We think there may be.

As will be evident in the chapters of this volume, continuous engagement with the field means involvement in others' destinies. Professional and personal lives become intertwined in multiple and unpredictable ways. Turner, for instance, has successfully accompanied Kayapo political leaders on their travels to enlist support for their fight to retain rights over their traditional territory inside the Amazon forest. He acted as recording secretary to their political activism, an activity that enabled him not only to give something back to those who had accepted him into their midst but also to use the events as "ethnographic windfalls." Metcalf has tried, with little success according to his own evaluation, to engage the attention of the general public in the North, not least the British, in the plight of the Upriver People of Borneo. Vitebsky was enlisted by both the Sora (Orissa, India) and the Siberian Eveny to perform tasks they felt he was better equipped to succeed in than they in their fight against external bureaucratic forces. Hviding assisted in, among other things, writing applications for funds to establish ecotourism resorts in the Solomon Islands. He has also translated native stories and legends into four local languages. And finally, Holmberg traces his involvement in the dramatic transformation of the Tamang from a minority on the margins three decades ago to a vibrant community with indigenous status in the present political landscape of Nepal.

RESTUDIES VERSUS MULTITEMPORAL STUDIES

The most common form of sustained ethnographic fieldwork is undertaken as one period of eighteen to twenty-four months in connection with one's doctoral degree. The material obtained at that time

becomes an endless source for subsequent writing. A number of anthropologists have, however, found the opportunity to make a return visit after a period of fifteen to twenty years and written about
the changed situation they encountered. To return to one's original
fieldsite is not unusual in anthropology—quite the contrary. To do
so even many times is a common research strategy. However, few
have taken the opportunity to theorize this scholarly practice.[2]

Before we discuss the characteristics of multitemporal fieldwork
in some detail, we consider a few classical texts that deal with restudies. In his book *Social Change in Tikopia: Restudy of a Polynesian
Community after a Generation* (1959), Raymond Firth makes the distinction between what he calls a "dual-synchronic study" (a comparison of two "ethnographic presents") and a "diachronic study" (a
continuous study of events through time). He emphasizes that the
former allows the researcher to capture differences and similarities
between two separate periods of time, but notes also that this will not
necessarily open up for an analysis of trends of change as it evolves
over time. The latter, he says, would involve "assumptions about regularities in the interim period" (1959, 22). His distinction—between
dual-synchronic and diachronic—is similar to the one that we are
concerned with in this volume, and it is precisely by having undertaken what we call multitemporal fieldwork and reflecting upon that
practice that we seek to make good the inevitable limitations of a
single return visit.

Another well-known example of a restudy is that of Kenneth Read,
whose first fieldwork took place between 1950 and 1952, but whose
seminal study on the Gahuku-Gama of New Guinea did not appear
until 1965. Read returned briefly in 1981 and 1982 and wrote mov-
ingly about the dramatic changes that had taken place in the interim
(Read 1986). As an anthropologist, Read is unusual for his time in
that both accounts are very personal and reflexive. His return visits
were, he says, "too brief to undertake anything that might reason-
ably be called systematic or intensive research" (ibid., xv), but he
found that his place in the social order was reactivated immediately
and that his relationships with the people he had known took on a

much more profound quality. They opened up to him and gave him access into much that previously had been only dimly discerned, let alone understood. This in turn made Read examine himself, trying to understand not only how all the changes that had occurred had affected the people, but, more challenging personally, how they affected the status of his own knowledge and understanding obtained during his first fieldwork, and how he himself was a changed person. This experience is not uncommon for those who return after some period of time; in some way or other, the authors in this volume grapple with similar thoughts.

More recently, upon Bruce Knauft's return to the Gebusi in the Highlands of New Guinea after sixteen years, he found the changes so dramatic as to make their way of life virtually unrecognizable (Knauft 2002). Knauft's restudy seeks to understand the Gebusi's engagement with modern institutions (political, economic, religious), and he uses the empirical situation he encountered to theorize the processes of how remotely located peoples develop their own ways of being and becoming modern. He states that he would never have been able at the time of his first fieldwork to predict the changes that had occurred, and he would not have been able to glean from the second fieldwork what life had been like sixteen years earlier (2002, 23). Had he been back several times during that period, however, the chances are that he would have been better equipped to do both, and also possibly to make the change seem less unfathomable.

Quite a few anthropologists who have worked in Africa have returned for one or more restudies. One of the pioneers was Monica Wilson. The theme of her resulting restudy monograph (1977) is how a society organized to serve the interests of men and elders has increasingly been turned around to reward young men and women. This is a familiar observation, but precisely because the developments she charted can be duplicated in many parts of Africa, it demands special attention. Monica Wilson's point is not simply that the changes are obvious and widespread; rather, based on her early fieldwork supplemented by archival work, she shows how changes in kinship over an almost one-hundred-year period demonstrate the complexity in social trends, even in a society as small in scale as that of the Nyakyusa-Ngonde. In other words, little, if anything, can be taken for granted.

If we turn to multitemporal fieldwork, there are also many examples of multiple returns to the same field locale, but few that put a focus upon the methodological and analytical implications of the many return visits. Pat Caplan, for instance, returned to Mafia Island off the Tanzanian coast several times and used time effectively as a factor in her analysis through an account of a personal narrative of one informant (Caplan 1997). While she demonstrates the value of long-term friendship in anthropological analysis, she does not problematize temporality as such. Longitudinal fieldwork has been more common in American anthropology. There the discipline developed along somewhat different lines from the British, French, and other European traditions. The legacy of Boas, who returned to the Kwakiutl twelve times and whose ethnography aimed "to be a written record of an alien way of life that was true to that way of life and omitted no essential" (quoted in Codere 1966, xi), meant not only that American Indians were made the object of study of new generations of anthropologists, but also that being on their doorstep, as it were, the anthropologists were able to return again and again for shorter or longer periods to the same groups or regions. Moreover, whole anthropology departments tended to get involved in such longitudinal studies. The edited volume *Long-term Fieldwork in Social Anthropology*, by George Foster, Thayer Scudder, Elizabeth Colson, and Robert Kemper (1979), addressed the issue of ongoing research in the same locality. It thus formed part of a particular American tradition of large-scale teamwork by students and teachers who would return to the same community year after year (usually during the summer vacations), such as the Harvard Chiapas project, the Navajo study, and the Kalahari project (see also Kemper and Royce 2002). The projects were conceived more as fact-finding missions—often testing hypotheses—and as training-grounds for graduate students, and less as open-ended inductive research. Certainly, these projects resulted in vast amounts of important ethnographic material, but they provoked little reflection on method or on the epistemological consequences for their findings of that particular approach

In France, the best-known example of similar long-term collaborative field research was that undertaken by Marcel Griaule and his associates with the Dogon of Mali during the 1930s, '40s, and '50s (Clifford 1983; van Beek 1991). Again, this led to much insight and valuable information that otherwise would have been lost to the anthropological community; in particular, their study of Dogon religion and symbolism is hardly surpassed in the attention paid to detail. Because Dogon religious knowledge was circumscribed by secrecy and its possession closely tied to power and status, Griaule was at the mercy of his interlocutors as to what they were willing to impart. As he returned again and again, their confidence in him increased, and he was slowly let into the deeper recesses of esoteric knowledge. However, Griaule and his colleagues did not subject their method to any kind of sustained critique (Clifford 1983, 135–138).

More recently, a number of anthropologists—too many to mention—have returned to their African and Asian fieldsites again and again, but few reflect on the practice of returning. One exception is an edited volume that sets out to debate the significance of fieldwork in anthropological research (Dresch, James, and Parkin 2000). All the authors have long-term experience from their chosen fieldsites with several return visits. In fact, they regard the return visit as part of *doing anthropology* (ibid., emphasis added). Nevertheless, despite a number of thought-provoking observations made about the benefits of constantly returning, this is not a theme as such of the volume.

In an article debating spatial practices of the Mursi in southern Ethiopia, David Turton makes multitemporality analytically central. His repeated visits forced him to abandon initial assumptions about territorial boundedness and historical stability of the Mursi as an isolated minority group (2005, 259). In other words, his revisits made him appreciate past events in light of present findings and inspired him to launch on an analysis of place-making, using Appadurai's concept of locality, as a temporal process. This is thus a case where new insight arose directly as the result of repeated return visits. We find similar explorations about the intersections between spatial and temporal dimensions in the chapters of this book. Barnard, for instance, in discussing his experience with Bushmen in southern Africa over time, makes the point that he has expanded his geographical field from just the Naro, among whom he did his original fieldwork, to include a number of neighboring groups, arguing that this regional comparison makes more sense and enables him to cast new light on the Naro themselves.

Yet another well-known ethnographic example of repeated returns to the field is Elizabeth Colson's work in Zambia (e.g., Colson 1984, 2010). In an article on the social history of HIV/AIDS among the Gwembe Tonga in southern Zamibia, where she has repeatedly returned for over half a century, Colson describes local reactions and interpretations of a global epidemic as these have developed from the beginning in the early 1980s (or earlier) until today. Her microhistoric description follows closely people's etiological understanding and disease management in conjunction with the development of the epidemic. The long-term perspective facilitated by repeated returns and being present when something occurs adds considerable quality and validity to the anthropologist's story. Without the "[fieldwork] moment" (James 2000), Colson's account would probably have been far less convincing and suggestive. What comes out clearly in Colson's study is the persistence of moral values in people's lives and how the Gwembe continue to adhere to these over time and despite changing circumstances (Colson 2010). Several authors in this volume have made similar observations of continuity in change (Hviding, Howell, Talle, and Morphy and Morphy).

James Clifford, in the quote above, captures the positive connection between frequencies of contact with the field and an insider perspective. His use of initiation implies the deeper understanding that he suggests this gives rise to. Multitemporal fieldwork, we argue, further opens up particularly fruitful spaces for anthropological reflection both on fieldwork methodology and disciplinary precepts, as well as on the performance of personal and scholarly identity. The restudy type of research, which could be termed comparison *of* times, or dual-synchronic (Firth 1959; Garbett 1967), leaves a long time gap with little or no observational knowledge of what has been taking place in the community between field visits. Multitemporal field-work, by contrast, gives rise to a more processual understanding—a description *through* time—in which one is enabled to witness the many events that provoke change or resistance to change, as well as the false starts, as it were, of change. However, restudies, or dual-synchronic studies, may alert the researcher more acutely to contrasts between different times of observation (Rudie 1994).

CHANGE AND CONTINUITY

Communities and the contexts in which they exist change over time. This is nothing new. However, change in many minority communities, often located at the margins of the nations to which they belong, is more rapid and more extreme than is the case with the majority populations among whom they live. All the contributors to this volume describe how the minority communities they first studied as young anthropologists have changed dramatically during the twenty to thirty years that they have been involved with them. This is largely attributable to changes in the communities' relationship with the outside world. Being vulnerable minorities, they are unable to defend themselves effectively against external interferences, and, as the nation-states to which they belong modernize, the minorities are pulled into the wider world. This affects internal organization; it affects people's perception of themselves and their life worlds. From Melanesia through Asia to Africa and the Amazon, the case studies here demonstrate this in various ways and with different emphasis. To have been able to follow developments during such turbulent times gives the anthropologists a privileged vantage point in their quest for making sense of the changes and people's reactions to them.

People's reactions to new events may be placed in a historical trajectory with some degree of confidence. Many examples of this are described in this volume. Holmberg, for instance, shows how, while some lament the "loss" of culture, traditional dress is skillfully remixed into "new distinctively Tamang cultural productions." Morphy and Morphy demonstrate that funerary practices among the Yolngu of northeast Arnhem Land retain their central sociological position despite major upheavals resulting from being marginalized, but that their actual performance takes on new ramifications as a result of modern technology. Turner shows that the Kayapo kinship system retains its core principles in ways that he would not have predicted. Vitebsky, by constrast, shows how the Sora in India have succumbed to proselytizing Pentecostal missionaries, but also how one man wished to learn about the old shamanistic practices from Vitebsky himself, who had studied and recorded many such séances and local exegeses during his initial fieldwork. Having witnessed what he calls devastating changes among the Upriver People of Malaysian Borneo, Metcalf examines the experience of nostalgia for the past not only by the people he lived among, but also his own. He has observed with impotent sorrow the disintegration of longhouse communities and the social organization that made life there meaningful, largely due to extensive logging and the introduction of wage-labor and cash, to be replaced with life in poverty—economic as well as cultural and moral—at the outskirts of new towns. Howell shows that the Chewong, faced with similar external pressures, struggle to maintain the moral relevance of their animistic ontology that links humans and animated natural species in a world in which money is making rapid inroads into the constitution of relationships.

In the midst of fieldwork, how is the anthropologist to distinguish the transitory from the durable, cultural change from cultural persistence? asks Sally Falk Moore (1986). This is precisely where multi-temporal fieldwork comes into its own, and there are many examples in this book of how the anthropologist is confirmed in discerning persistent (core) value and practices. Talle found that female circumcision holds as strong a sway over women today as it did thirty years ago. Howell shows that a deep-seated egalitarian ethos persists among the Chewong despite opportunities for increasing social stratification. Just as interestingly, we can discern new practices that are transformed and incorporated in keeping with existing practices, as for instance in the case of Maasai evangelization.

Albeit in different ways and for different reasons, most of the authors consider the existence and significance of what one may call core values, dominant symbols, or persistent value schema, elucidating how phenomena manifest central assumptions about the nature of things. Actual practices and ideas may change over time, but those that hold a particularly powerful semantic and moral position, constituting a basis for meaningful social action, may best be discerned through a long-term perspective.

To witness the moment when something actually happens affords a fuller understanding than to be told about it some time later. There are examples of how "being there" at decisive moments enabled the anthropologist to explore the relevance of new practices and values. Some changes in a way of life are irretrievable, as Metcalf shows for Borneo, while other societies seem to be on the verge of momentous change at one moment only to reject it at a later stage, as Turner argues in describing Kayapo local organization. Likewise, Howell points out that whereas in 2004 several Chewong women and girls had converted to Islam and regularly attended prayer meetings dressed in the attire of Malaysian Muslim women, by 2006 this practice had ceased altogether, leaving no trace other than the unattended Muslim prayer hut. Had she not been there to observe the practice and returned two years later, she would have been completely unaware of these events. Or had she not returned, she would have assumed that Islam had replaced Chewong animistic religion. This example may be viewed as a demonstration of the resilience, indeed triumph, of core values when faced with outside forces that seem more powerful.

The accounts of fieldwork in this book make it clear that the multitemporal fieldwork strategy allows for close observation of gradual change and gives rise to cumulative knowledge. Many bear witness to some kind of continuity of core values (Hviding, Howell, Morphy and Morphy, Vitebsky), although we can never predict what the future will hold. Others demonstrate surprising and unpredictable turns of events.

THE BACKWARD AND FORWARD GAZE

Multitemporal fieldwork gives rise to a multitude of ethnographic *presences* which, in turn, leads in our writing to a combination of several ethnographic *presents*. Repeated returns to the same locale with perhaps, but not necessarily, a different topical research focus—the optic of analysis—give rise to continual reflexivity on the part of the anthropologist. Old questions are looked at anew in the light of personal as well as local history—just as new developments locally are placed in the same trajectory (for example Morphy and Morphy, Talle, Metcalf, Howell, Hviding, and Barnard, this volume). Can one argue that this series of fieldwork presences, these diverse moments of ethnographic eyewitnessing and participant observation, give one a privileged position for understanding how people react to new opportunities and the choices they make in order to handle them? All the anthropologists in this volume argue in the affirmative; the advantage of observations over a long period of time both sharpens and broadens the lens of observation. This is due as much to the empirical situations they have participated in as to changes in their own personal life cycles, and to changes in the discipline (Colson 1984; Rudie 1994).

Not only do the communities we study change over time, responding to internal and external developments and challenges, but the anthropologists as individuals equally change. We become older, we go through a range of rites of passage that affect our perceptions of self and other—from student to university professor, from single to married, and in most cases we become parents. In this way our lives parallel those of our friends and informants from our initial fieldwork. But the discipline of anthropology has similarly changed during the past twenty to forty years, giving rise to new trends and new relevancies; and we, as anthropologists, respond to these, though not always perhaps as critically as warranted (Bourdieu 2003). In his chapter on his more than thirty-year engagement with Bushmen groups, Barnard deals with this question explicitly. He shows how developments in kinship studies and in hunter-gatherer studies have changed during this period, and that these changes have affected the way he sees them. Likewise, Talle's reading of pain literature after having studied female circumcision in Somalia made her reflect on earlier observations among the Maasai. Howell's new-found interest in economic anthropology and the anthropology of hunters and gatherers is a direct result of the changes that she has been observing as a consequence of the introduction of a money economy. Thus, our disciplinary gaze goes through a number of changes and transformations as we focus and refocus our anthropological preoccupations, in the field, at our desk, and, not least, in the classroom.

Most anthropological fieldwork has traditionally been inductive and open-ended, and knowledge has been acquired through attempts at immersion in the field situation. More often than not it was an existential encounter between the lone anthropologist and the unknown people in an unfamiliar setting. Not infrequently there were few or no previous studies of the society in question, and the ethnographer became his or her own archivist (Parkin 2000b, 107). Such is the case with several of the contributors to this volume (Turner, Vitebsky, Howell, Holmberg, Knauft)—something that in itself raises important issues regarding one's cumulative understanding.

First ethnographer or not, as we keep returning we alternate between certainty and uncertainty about our "data" as we read and reread our field notes and ponder known events afresh in light of new fieldwork. Most of the authors in this volume comment upon this development of their relationship with the people they study as well as with previous interpretations and understandings. If asked, most anthropologists will say that, undoubtedly, repeated fieldwork over a long period of time will give rise to enhanced understanding. One's language skills improve, one's access to people's lives becomes ever more relaxed, one is able better to contextualize events—new and familiar—and grasp complexities more easily; but, paradoxically, it is also the case that the more one learns and the more one observes, the more the picture becomes less clear. In our experience, clear patterns are more easily discernible during the relatively early stages of fieldwork than after many years. This does not mean that the early perception is wrong—or right; only that complexity tends to muddy the waters. Different contexts give rise to different meanings, and as we experience a multitude of contexts, we need to sort out the multiplexity of seemingly similar occurrences. Like other fieldworkers, the frequently returning anthropologist must rely on verbal reports from those who have been present during her absence and whose personal agendas will vary widely. With the advantage of having known her interlocutors intimately over time, she may more easily contextualize the accounts of events that took place during her absence and may have a better chance of disentangling the various agendas.

Several of the anthropologists in this volume have done long-term fieldwork with more than one group (Barnard, Howell, Vitebsky), and they consider how each setting gave rise to different experiences. Not only did the sociocultural conditions differ, eliciting different bases for relating to people, but the anthropologists themselves experienced their own situations—personal and professional—as different in each case. Not least, on the second time around they had matured in their professional outlook, and they were more experienced as fieldworkers. Having worked in two or three different communities, they gain insight from each that is of relevance for the other, lending considerable authority to the comparative exercise (Howell, Vitebsky).

Sequential ethnographic presences relatively close in time constitute processes, as one merges into the other. While restudies tend to conceptualize time in a linear stretch—from one point in time to another—multitemporal fieldwork facilitates a more cyclical and reflective understanding of temporality in anthropological analysis. This comes out clearly in Hviding's chapter dealing with the Marovo of Solomon Islands. His long-term perspective on Marovians erases and distorts distinctions between past and present, and, as the author himself aptly formulates it, "the present does not appear as a radical rupture with a 'traditional' past."

Perhaps we may think of multitemporal fieldwork as a process that includes the time *not* spent in the field; when we read and reread our earlier fieldnotes between each visit and ponder the significance of recently observed events and utterances in light of these; when we teach and read and get new inspiration from recent debates in the discipline (Dresch et al. 2002; Turton 2005). These acts provide new chances to improve the strategy for our next visit, but at the same time they require openness and truthfulness as regards our earlier findings and interpretations. In this respect, multitemporal fieldwork is a risky project. We are brought face-to-face with our own observations, memory, and understanding, and this demands a high degree of reflexivity.

Repeated moments of observation at close intervals minimize the effect of inaccurate memory on the part of informants as well as the anthropologist. Recurring returns also mean heightened mental as well as actual proximity to the field, and possibly even a narrowing of "experience-near" and "experience-distant" ways of knowing, between observation and interpretation, so to speak (Geertz 1973). In multitemporal fieldwork the flow of time becomes an integral part of our analysis, in the sense that it both integrates our data and frames our interpretation. We see that things have come and gone. We see when something new starts and, from this we may get a sense of the rate of change. Just as in physics, where three observations are necessary in order to measure acceleration, but only two to measure velocity, so one needs (minimally) three visits in order to assess rate, and quality, of social and cultural change.

Another way to put it is that we learn the grammar and syntax of social life. This we learn not just by observing and participating in the present, but because all our senses become sensitized to past events and we may be able to anticipate future happenings. This gives rise to another positive effect of multitemporal fieldwork, namely how it provides opportunities for serendipity: "making discoveries by accident and sagacity of things not in quest of" (Shorter Oxford English Dictionary). At stake is one's sagacity as an ethnographer, a faculty developed through experience and increasing local knowledge. In this way it enables one to grasp the significance of the unexpected, to see connections those less informed would not draw (see Holmberg's use of contingency this volume). But perhaps we should not be so instrumental—or teleological—in our deliberations. Perhaps we should ponder the acquisition of implicit knowledge that we gain through our prolonged relationship with the people that we study, the existence of which we are not consciously aware, but which nevertheless guides our writing and search of truth through time.

*   *   *

In his Marett Lecture more than fifty years ago, Evans-Pritchard asserted that "social anthropology is a kind of historiography, and therefore ultimately of philosophy and art." This, he said, "implies that it studies societies as moral systems and not as natural systems, that it is interested in design, not process, and that it therefore seeks patterns and not scientific laws, and interprets rather than explains" (1962 [1950], 26). We agree wholeheartedly in all but one of these points. We believe that anthropology is also about process. In this book we show that those who have had the privilege of making multiple return visits to their fieldsites have not only deepened their understanding, but also widened the scope of their anthropological practice in subtle and creative ways.

NOTES

The first epigraph for the chapter is from James Clifford, 1983, *The Predicament of Culture: Twentieth-Century Ethnography, Literature, and Art*, Cambridge, MA: Harvard University Press, at 144. The second is from Monica Wilson, 1977, *For Men and Elders: Change in the Relation of Generations and of Men and Women among the Nyakyusa-Ngonde People 1875–1971*, London: International African Institute, at 21.

1. While this label may be appropriate to some of our ancestors, careful reading of many early ethnographies does not support such a characterization.

Rather, the authors often display a modest attitude to the information they have obtained and the dangers of generalization upon scant knowledge.

2. Elizabeth Colson writes that at the time of writing "some fifty or more long-term studies are in existence, and it is normal to think that a first study is only one stage of the anthropologist's long-term involvement with a particular people" (1984, 2).

REFERENCES

Borneman, John, and Abdellah Hammoudi, eds. 2009. *Being There: The Fieldwork Encounter and The Making of Truth.* Berkeley: University of California Press.

Borofsky, Robert. 1994. Introduction. In Robert Borofsky, ed., *Assessing Cultural Anthropology.* New York: McGraw-Hill.

Bourdieu, Pierre. 2003. Participant Objectivation. *Journal of the Royal Anthropological Institute.* 9:281–294.

Caplan, Pat. 1997. *African Voices, African Lives: Personal Narratives from a Swahili Village.* London: Routledge.

Clifford, James. 1983. Power and Dialogue in Ethnography: Marcel Griaule's Initiation. In George W. Stocking, Jr., ed., *Observers Observed: Essays on Ethnographic Fieldwork.* Madison: University of Wisconsin Press.

———. 1988. *The Predicament of Culture: Twentieth-Century Ethnography, Literature, and Art* Cambridge, MA: Harvard University Press.

Clifford, James, and George E. Marcus. 1986. Introduction. In James Clifford and George E. Marcus, eds., *Writing Culture: The Poetics and Politics of Ethnography.* Berkeley: University of California Press.

Codere, Helen, ed. 1966. *Franz Boas: Kwakiutl Ethnography.* Chicago: University of Chicago Press.

Colson, Elizabeth. 1984. The Reordering of Experience: Anthropological Involvement with Time. *Journal of Anthropological Research* 40(1): 1–13.

———. 2010. The Social History of an Epidemic: HIV/AIDS in Gwembe Valley, Zambia, 1980–2004. In Ute Luig and Hansjörg Dilger, eds., *Morality, Hope and Grief: Anthropologies of AIDS in Africa.* London: Berghahn Books.

Dresch, Paul, Wendy James, and David Parkin, eds., 2000. *Anthropologists in a Wider World,* New York and Oxford: Berghahn Books.

Evans-Pritchard, Edward E. 1962 [1950]. Social Anthropology: Past and Present. In *Essays in Social Anthropology.* London: Faber and Faber.

Firth, Raymond. 1959. *Social Change in Tikopia: Restudy of a Polynesian Community After a Generation.* London: George Allen and Unwin.

Foster, George, M. Thayer Scudder, Elizabeth Colson, and Robert V. Kempert, eds. 1979. *Long-term Field Research in Social Anthropology*. New York: Academic Press.

Garbett, George K. 1967. The Restudy as a Technique for the Examination of Social Change. In D. G. Jongmans and P. C. W. Gutkind, eds., *Anthropologists in the Field*. Assen: Van Gorcum 6 Comp. N.V.

Geertz, Clifford. 1973. *Interpretation of Cultures: Selected Essays*. New York: Basic Books.

International Work Group for Indigenous Affairs. 2008. *IWGIA Yearbook 2008*, www.iwgia.dk.

James, Wendy. 2000. Beyond the First Encounter: Transformations of "the Field" in North East Africa. In Dresch, James, and Parkin, eds., *Anthropologists*.

James, Wendy, and David Mills, eds. 2005. Introduction. In Wendy James and David Mills, eds., *The Qualities of Time*. Oxford: Berg.

Kemper, Roy V., and Anya Peterson Royce. 2002. Introduction. In Roy V. Kemper and Anya Peterson Royce, eds., *Chronicling Cultures: Long-term Field Research in Anthropology*. New York: AltaMira Press.

Knauft, Bruce, 2002. *Exchanging the Past: A Rainforest World Before and After*. Chicago: The University of Chicago Press.

Malinowski, Bronislaw. 1922. *Argonauts of the Western Pacific: An Account of Native Enterprise and Adventure in the Archipelagoes of Melanesian New Guinea*. London: Routledge and Kegan Paul.

Marcus, George E. 1998. *Ethnography through Thick and Thin*. Princeton: Princeton University Press.

Marcus, George E., and Michael M. J. Fischer. 1986. *Anthropology as Cultural Critique: An Experimental Moment in the Human Sciences*. Chicago: University of Chicago Press.

Moore, Sally Falk. 1986. *Social Facts and Fabrications: Customary Law on Kilmanjaro, 1880–1980*. Cambridge: Cambridge University Press.

Parkin, David. 2000a. Fieldwork Unfolding. In Dresch, James, and Parkin, eds., *Anthropologists*.

———. 2000b. Templates, Evocations and the Long-term Fieldworker. In Dresch, James, and Parkin, eds., *Anthropologists*.

Read, Kenneth E. 1965. *The High Valley*. New York: Columbia University Press.

———. 1986. *Return to the High Valley: Coming Full Circle*. Berkeley: University of California Press.

Rudie, Ingrid. 1994. *Visible Women in East Coast Malay Society: On the Reproduction of Gender in Ceremonial, School and Market*. Oslo: Scandinavia University Press.

Turton, David. 2005. The Meaning of Place in a World of Movement: Lessons from Long-term Field Research in Southern Ethiopia. *Journal of Refugee Studies* 18(3): 258–280.

van Beek, Walter E. A. 1991. Dogon Restudied: A Field Evaluation of the Work of Marcel Griaule. *Current Anthropology* 32: 139–167.

Wilson, Monica. 1977. *For Men and Elders: Change in the Relation of Generations and of Men and Women among the Nyakyusa-Ngonde People 1875–1971.* London: International African Institute.

PART 1

CHANGE AND CONTINUITY IN

LONG-TERM PERSPECTIVE

1 | Forty-five Years with the Kayapo

TERENCE TURNER

In the forty-five years I have worked with them, the Kayapo people of Central Brazil have lived an epic of successful resistance, creative cultural self-transformation, and political accommodation to coexistence with Brazilian society and the global economic system. It was for me a fantastic piece of luck that I was able to begin working with them just a few years before the dramatic series of events that marked the beginning of this process (and only four to ten years after all but one of the then extant Kayapo communities had agreed to give up raiding Brazilian settlements and accept peaceful coexistence with the Brazilian state). I have thus been able to witness, and to some small measure take part in, the entire process of what may be called the Kayapo *reconquista*. From a recently pacified, mostly monolingual population of barely 2,000 persons distributed among nine villages with no legally demarcated territory and an uncertain future as a pauperized marginal minority when I first arrived among them, they have emerged during the period of my fieldwork as the most culturally dynamic and politically effective indigenous people in Brazil, with recognized territorial reserves totaling almost 150,000 square km, roughly equivalent to the area they occupied at the time of their first contacts with Brazilians at the beginning of the nineteenth century, before the Portuguese and Brazilians began to penetrate their country. Their present population—about 7,200, distributed in twenty-six villages—is rather larger than it was at that time (Turner 1992b).

MY FIELDWORK IN THE CONTEXT OF KAYAPO HISTORY

I first visited the Kayapo in 1962 as a graduate student doing research for my doctoral dissertation. From then until October 2007 I have made twenty-one trips back to the Kayapo, about one per year since 1989. I have also served as a traveling companion and translator for Kayapo groups or individual leaders on trips outside Kayapo territory to France, the United Kingdom, the United States, Canada, and various urban centers in Brazil. These trips have contributed unique insights into Kayapo ways of seeing the world and themselves, and I consider them to have been part of my research. In all, I have done research in eight Kayapo communities, in two of them on repeated visits over periods of forty and forty-five years, respectively. My first fieldwork with the Kayapo of Gorotire and Kubenkranken villages lasted fourteen months. Since then my stays in Kayapo communities have ranged from five months to one week.

In 1962 the extant Kayapo villages were scattered over an area that had not yet been penetrated by Brazilian settlers or extractivists. The villages were widely separated, relatively large (several with around three hundred people) politically and socially autonomous units. My first ethnographic research focused on their social and political organization, described in abstraction from their historical and contemporary relations with the regional society and the Brazilian state. In analyzing my field data I sought to explain how the social system, framed in these synchronic terms, reproduced itself, and at a higher level to locate my account in a comparative model of the Ge and Bororo systems then being researched by my dissertation director, David Maybury Lewis, and the members of the Harvard–Museu Nacional Central Brazil Project (Turner 1979a, 1997b).

The basic insight on which I based my analysis was that the communal institutions of Kayapo, and more generally of Central Brazilian

Butchering a deer, 1962. PHOTOGRAPH BY JOAN BAMBERGER.

society—age sets, ceremonial associations, and political groups associated with men's houses or central spaces in the circular village—embodied, in their structures and the rites of passage they conducted, the transformations of family relations that made up the developmental cycle of the matriuxorilocal households that constituted the segmentary units of all of these societies; and that the focus of this system of transformations is the exploitative relationship of senior adults as wife's parents to their daughters' husbands. The analysis and comparative model I developed on the basis of these ideas were presented in my doctoral dissertation and my contributions to the collective volume of the Central Brazil Project, *Dialectical Societies* (Turner 1965, 1979a, 1979b).

The relative isolation of the Kayapo villages from intensive contact with Brazilian society, which formed the pragmatic context of my relatively orthodox social anthropological analysis of village-level social structure, however, was dramatically changed in the late 1960s and early 1970s as a result of the drive by the military government that had seized power in 1964 to open up the Amazon to settlement and economic development. The damage this soon began to inflict on the native peoples of the region exploded into an international scandal in 1968, with sensational if inaccurate reports of "genocide" in the British press.

The first major threat to the Kayapo was not slow to materialize after the first wave of reports of invasions of indigenous territory in 1968. In 1970 the federal government launched a covert operation to sever the northern 20 percent of the National Park of the Xingú, where a major Kayapo village was located, from the rest of the park and sell off the land to private speculators and would-be settlers. This involved secretly building a road, BR-80, through the park with a crossing at the Xingú consisting of a ferry-raft hauled by a tugboat brought overland for the purpose. The Kayapo responded to this double-cross by sending a party of men to swim out and sink the tugboat by chopping a hole in its side. When the Brazilians installed a motorized ferry, the Kayapo killed the ferry operator and his family and took over the operation and maintenance of the ferry themselves, charging tolls to Brazilian users. As Brazilian ranchers arrived with their families and employees to clear plots of land and build ranch houses in tracts they had bought in the stolen area, they were confronted in each case by superior numbers of armed Kayapo and given the choice between leaving immediately with what they could carry or shooting it out and being wiped out along with their houses. Stubborn would-be proprietors were duly assaulted and eliminated. Other Brazilian interlopers such as hunters and Brazil nut gatherers were similarly dealt with. By 1990 no Brazilians were left alive in the sequestered territory, and the Brazilian government, recognizing a fait accompli, made it an official Kayapo reserve (Turner 1991a, 1992b, 1993).

Then, in the early 1980s, settlers and placer gold miners began to invade the eastern Kayapo area near the village of Gorotire. One fair-sized group of would-be settlers, about twenty in number, was killed in an encounter with an armed Kayapo patrol; another, slightly smaller group perished in a similar confrontation with Kayapo in the sequestered Xingú territory. In 1985 two large gold mines, with about two thousand miners who were illegally established on what had been informally recognized and accepted as Kayapo territory, were assaulted and captured by Kayapo. The mines were accessible only by air. The Kayapo, in surprise attacks, seized the landing strips. While painted and feathered warriors brandishing traditional war-clubs cowed the miners, who offered no resistance, other Kayapo equipped with rifles and shotguns ringed the airstrips with firing positions. Using the miners' short-wave radio, they broadcast an ul-timatum to Brasilia: agree to demarcate the entire eastern Kayapo territory and deed ownership of the mines to the Kayapo or no planes would be allowed to land or take off and the miners would be cut off from their sole source of food and other supplies. After a tense standoff that lasted ten days, the government caved in to the Kayapo demands, on condition that the Kayapo would keep the mines open under their administration for at least two years, taking a 10 percent share of the value of the gold produced. In 1991 the Brazilian govern-ment recognized the eastern Kayapo area where the captured gold mines, along with Gorotire and four other Kayapo villages, were lo-cated. Then, in 1993, after a spectacular campaign of European con-certs by the rock star Sting, accompanied by the Kayapo chief, war leader, and baritone Rop-ni, raised the necessary funds, the govern-ment recognized the huge Mekranoti area to the north of the re-cently conceded reserve of Capoto-Jarina on the Xingú. Since then, tough and persistent negotiation by Kayapo leaders with Brazilian authorities has led to the recognition of five additional reserves. In sum, the Kayapo reconquista of their territory has been achieved through an astute combination of diplomacy, low-intensity warfare, alliances with both domestic and foreign governmental and nongov-ernmental organizations (NGOs), and flamboyant mass demonstra-tions and other forms of self-representation that have caught the at-tention of national and global media (Turner 1991a, 1993, 2000).

ETHNOGRAPHY AND ACTIVISM: RESISTING AND RETHINKING

Ethnographers studying Amazonian societies found themselves called upon to record and report on the damage being done to the societies and environment of the peoples with whom they were working. For many, including myself, the situation seemed to call for activist engagement in defense of indigenous peoples and their rights. In the beginning there were many discussions among anthropologists about how or whether to reconcile activism and advocacy with academic anthropology and scientific objectivity. Soon, however, indigenous peoples themselves began to force the reframing of the terms of these discussions by their own resistance struggles and the changes in Brazilian government policy this success helped to bring about, together with support from NGOs, anthropologists, and some of the media (Turner 1991b). This was true above all of the Central Brazilian peoples with whom I and others of the Harvard–Museu Nacional project had been working, notably the Xavante but most spectacularly the Kayapo. Like many other anthropologists at the time, I had initially conceived of activism as a political defense of societies we had described and theorized in the ethnographic present. Their ongoing interaction with Brazilian society (I speak here of the Kayapo case) did not form an integral part of my ethnographic project, largely because they did not seem to me to have the political and cultural (or ideological) capacity to deal with the challenge on their own terms.

The success of the Kayapo resistance, however, the ways it drew upon the strengths of their social and cultural system, and the way that system was showing itself able to absorb and adapt to the effects of coexistence with the national society, now came to appear, to me at least, to call for ethnographic investigation and theoretical analysis in its own right. This in turn seemed to me to point to the necessity of integrating an ethnographic and theoretical understanding of indigenous resistance with programs of practical activism in defense of indigenous rights, on the one hand, and with the partial but nevertheless valid insights of the older anthropological approach with its perspective limited to the "ethnographic present" (Turner 1991a, 1991b).

Ethnographic study of the Kayapo struggle for political autonomy, social survival, and cultural expression in the real-time present, however, seemed impossible to confine within the conceptual limitations of value-free "participant observation." Given that this struggle and the changes it comprised formed part of the objective ethnographic situation I was attempting to record, and that my presence and actions constituted, willy-nilly, part of the intrusive social and cultural system with which the Kayapo were struggling to come to terms, I felt that I was in any case part of the process I was attempting to observe. I could see, moreover, that the Kayapo were drawing upon their social organization, values, and cultural forms in creative ways to deal effectively with the challenges they were facing. I saw that I could contribute in various ways as a resource person to their struggle. Given that the Kayapo people, at least the many of them that I had come to know personally, were strongly committed to defending their way of life and clearly felt that it still constituted the source of the values and forms of consciousness in terms of which they oriented their lives, I felt it was ethically incumbent on me to do what I could to help. I thus became more self-consciously engaged in a combination of ethnography and activism, no longer conceived in conventional terms as "participant observation" but as a more active process of "observant participation" (Turner 2006c; Turner and Fajans-Turner 2006).

FILM, VIDEO, AND AN ETHNOGRAPHY OF REPRESENTATION

My first efforts at ethnographic study of Kayapo resistance and cultural adaptation to the new historical conditions of coexistence with Brazil under the developmentalist military regime took the form of ethnographic film—beginning in a small way with the BBC series *Face Values* in 1976 and with a fuller focus on resistance in the two films I made with Granada TV International's *Disappearing Worlds* series in 1987 and 1989. These two films marked a turning point in my ethnographic career in several respects. Up until 1987 I had made only three trips to the Kayapo. Since 1989 I have traveled to, or with, Kayapo at least once a year until now. I also became excited by the possibilities of film, and video, not just as ethnography but as a way to reach a broader public, and most intriguingly (for me anyway) as a potential vehicle for the ethnographic subjects to take control of the means of representation and become their own ethnographers and publicists.

In 1990 I obtained a grant from the Spencer Foundation and founded the Kayapo Video Project and Video Archive. This provided video cameras and training in basic camera skills, editing facilities and assistance in using them, and space for an archive for the storage of rushes and video masters (both the latter thanks to the cooperation of the Centro de Trabalho Indigenista of São Paulo). Kayapo camerapersons began shooting videos of their own cultural reality, including ceremonies, political meetings, and encounters with Brazilian officials. They quickly realized that turning the video camera on Brazilian reporters and cameramen at demonstrations or the Constitutional Assembly in 1988 was not merely a means of recording these events but, for Brazilians and international media, itself became the most sensational event to be recorded. As such, the video camera has become an integral part of public Kayapo political encounters with Brazilian officialdom. As an ethnographer, I discovered that keeping the shot record for Kayapo video camerapersons and editors in the role of assistant editor as they made their editing decisions in the cutting room was a revealing way of studying the process of constructing representations—a sort of objective correlative of the process of concept formation—and as such a unique ethnographic tool in its own right (Turner 1992a). I have written in various places about what I have learned in this way, but here I want to make just one point about what I think the Kayapo have learned, or perhaps absorbed would be a better word, from the use of the video camera and the making of their own videos: the self-conscious objectification of the cultural forms through which they order their experience of their own social and historical actions (Turner 1991a, 2002).

MULTIPLE RETURNS AND THE BUILDING OF TRUST

As I have returned over the years to the same communities, or to others where people I knew in different villages in earlier periods of fieldwork are now living, I have found that I have become regarded as a more or less permanent fixture of the Kayapo landscape. I have long been relatively fluent in the language, and stories about me at different ages (bachelor youth, young married man, father, elder) have circulated throughout Kayapo country, so that I find that I have become known even to people whom I have never met. My support of Kayapo resistance has become part of my reputation, so that nowadays Kayapo call on me to help out with actions or projects requiring a level of trust unimaginable in my first fieldwork visits. Some of these actions and projects represent ethnographic opportunities unavailable to me at earlier stages of my relationship with the Kayapo. For example, over the last four years the Western Kayapo have organized two general meetings to mobilize opposition to the government's plans to build hydroelectric dams on the Xingú River. The first of these brought together non-Kayapo indigenous groups from the Upper and Middle Xingú; the second united representatives of all the Kayapo villages. The Kayapo leaders who organized these meetings invited me to be present at them and act as recording secretary, in which capacity I was asked to draft a summary of the proceedings afterwards to serve as a press release. Needless to say, the speeches and ritual aspects of these events have been, for me, an ethnographic windfall, which I have sought to describe in articles published in *Anthropology News* and *Anthropology Today* in collaboration with my co-author, my daughter Vanessa Fajans-Turner (Turner and Fajans-Turner 2006a, 2006b).

INTER-ETHNIC CONFLICT, COMMODITIES, AND INTERNAL TENSIONS

The Kayapo struggle to defend and retake control of their territory went hand in hand with attempts by some leaders to acquire power and wealth by making deals with Brazilian extractivists—loggers, placer gold miners, and in one case the giant iron-mining company the Companhia do Vale do Rio Doce. In exchange for permission to mine or log on land now controlled by their communities, these leaders extracted payments—royalties or kickbacks—from the entrepreneurs or companies involved, ostensibly for deposit in communal bank accounts in Brazilian towns located near the reserve borders. The leaders of the communities most heavily involved with such contracts, such as Gorotire and Kikretum—a few traditional chiefs and a handful of younger men, mostly sons or nephews of the chiefs, who had received some education and thus become enabled to deal with Brazilian businessmen and institutions such as banks or the offices of the Federal Indian agency, FUNAI—were quick to exploit the leverage that the successful reassertion of control over their traditional territory provided to negotiate mining and logging concessions with Brazilian extractivist entrepreneurs (Turner 2000).[1]

This pattern was replicated in several other villages, notably Kikretum, and also in the large Kayapo reserve called the Kayapo Indigenous Territory. In the town of Redenção, the leaders of Gorotire actually occupied and took over the regional FUNAI office in the mid-1990s, creating a permanent external base for their political and economic dominance of their home village (they were expelled in July 2007 by a team of FUNAI administrators sent to clean up the financial and administrative chaos they had created).

It cannot be emphasized too strongly that the successful Kayapo defense of their territory and communities from being invaded and overrun by developers has been the fundamental condition of the continuity of Kayapo culture and society. At the same time, however, these successes were accompanied by changes in social, political, and economic relations that gave rise to new tensions within Kayapo society and between the Kayapo and elements of the surrounding regional, national, and global society. The new wealth and the political power based in the new territorial control and resulting relations with Brazilian governmental and private economic agencies were unevenly distributed among communities over space, unevenly over time between periods in the development of the same communities, and unevenly as between different social strata within the communities. Certain Kayapo leaders took advantage of their newly recognized legal control of their lands to make deals with Brazilian loggers and miners, allowing them to operate on Kayapo reserves in exchange for kickbacks. They established bank accounts and, to administer them and take care of the mining and logging concessions, acquired residences in Brazilian towns close to the reserves. These deals between some Kayapo leaders and Brazilian entrepreneurs led to intense friction with many ordinary citizens of Kayapo communities, both because of the failure to distribute the income from the deals equitably to the population as a whole, and because everyone could see that the effects of logging, mining, and ranching on the local forest and riverine environment were eroding the quality of life of the villagers (Turner 1996). Some of the young urbanizing leaders managed to win election to local municipal councils and to acquire considerable wealth in money and commodities. They retained Brazilian servants and bodyguards, cars, and even in a few cases private airplanes (these were nominally owned by communities but effectively controlled by a leader). A nascent "new class" of inter-ethnic mediators thus developed, composed of the first generations of young men to learn Portuguese and become able to take over the jobs of negotiating with Brazilian merchants, loggers, and miners and to manage their communities' bank accounts (Turner 2000).

The result was the development of a new form of "class struggle" in the communities most affected. In some respects, these conflicts appeared as intensified versions of the inter-generational conflicts endemic in the traditional age set and extended family household organization, but with the additional stresses resulting from the differentiation of the "new class" of "young leaders" from the general stratum of younger men, the new forms of monetary and commodity wealth, and the potentially irreversible environmental damage inflicted by extractivist enterprises and development projects. The latter were driven by the need for infinite capital accumulation, a specifically economic motivation alien to Kayapo culture and previous experience, so that Kayapo political leaders were slow to recognize the nature and scale of the threat they posed of irreversible damage to their environment and resource base.

Some of the income from the logging and mining contracts was distributed to the general populace of the home villages of the young leaders who negotiated the contracts. These brought in large amounts of money (used for shopping trips to Brazilian towns) or Brazilian commodities, the most conspicuous of the latter being Brazilian-style houses of tile and concrete with corrugated iron or fiberglass roofs, clothing suitable for shopping expeditions to Brazilian towns, radios with cassette recorders, medical supplies, hunting weapons, and metal tools and cooking utensils. Such commodities, held as private personal property, became coveted signs of status, especially for younger men and women, for whom the new commodity wealth, with its prestigious associations with the wealth and power of Brazilian society, appeared as an alternative route to higher communal prestige, circumventing their subordinate position in the traditional extended family hierarchy and communal age-associations associated with the men's house.[2] The new forms of commodity wealth available at the village level, however, fell far short of what the young leaders with their new power base in Brazilian towns outside the boundaries of the reserve were able to acquire (Turner 2009).

The resulting tensions led to open conflict and threatened secession in the Kayapo communities most affected. In 1994 the younger adult men's age set of the village of Gorotire, revolted by the environmental effects of gold mining and the social effects of the unequal distribution of the proceeds, confronted the senior men and leaders of the community with an ultimatum: join us in an assault on the big mining operation of Santidio, where we will capture and drive out the two thousand miners and destroy the mining equipment and buildings, or we will carry out the attack ourselves and then secede with our families from Gorotire and found a new village. The senior men reluctantly joined the attack, as did some men from the village of Kikretum and elements of the federal police, who took the opportunity to support the termination of an illegal invasion of indigenous land. The assault was a complete success. The miners meekly surrendered without a shot and were obliged to hike eighty kilometers through the forest to the nearest road while the Kayapo raiders wrecked the mine. Public opinion in the other Kayapo communities at around the same time turned definitively against mining and logging concessions, and with the exception of a few small logging operations they have ceased to operate in Kayapo territory (Turner 1996). This transformation of political policy towards nonsustainable forms of extractive industry, in large part the result of pressure from the normally subordinate younger men against the "young leaders" with their new bases of power outside the communal political struc- ture of village society, has been repeated in different forms in several communities. It represents a historic turning point in Kayapo social and political consciousness.

SOCIAL AND CULTURAL CHANGE AND STRUCTURAL RESILIENCE: A QUANTITATIVE APPROACH

Whether and to what extent these new developments might have been accompanied by changes in fundamental aspects of Kayapo kinship and social organization—specifically, the complex of age sets and ceremonial organizations associated with the men's house and the structure of the matriuxorilocal extended family household, the site of the key exploitative relationship between mother- and father- in-law and daughter- and son-in-law—emerged as the basic ethno- graphic focus of my continuing work with the Kayapo. Methodologi- cally, the question assumed the specific form of whether quantitative and/or structural changes in extended family and household struc- ture, and associated shifts in the system of communal groupings that served to model and reproduce it, had occurred that could be analytically linked to the changing forms of commodity wealth and class-like relations brought on by the new sources of economic and political power from beyond the village. In ethnographic terms: in those Kayapo villages with the greatest influxes of money and com- modity wealth (exemplified most fully by Gorotire and Kikretum), would the younger, inter-ethnically mobile adults, more interested and more able than their elders to acquire money and Brazilian com- modities and the status associated with them, attempt to opt out of the traditional extended family residential pattern in which they would be obliged to remain subordinate to their parents-in-law (in the case of a man) or parents (in the case of a woman)? Would they, in other words, tend to set up neolocal households that might better suit their identities as semi-Brazilianized persons and better enable them to protect their hoards of private commodity property? Would such a shift in domestic group structure be reflected in changes in the communal age set and men's house system supposedly developed to maintain and renew it?

With these questions in mind, and with the purpose of testing my original interpretation of the systemic relationship between the matriuxorilocal extended family household as the segmentary unit of Kayapo society and the men's house–centered complex of communal political and ceremonial groupings, I turned to a statistical analysis of the fifteen household censuses, accompanied by descriptions of the communal age-associations and ceremonial organizations of the same villages, that I have conducted over the forty-five years I have worked with the Kayapo. These genealogical household censuses include two series of successive observations of the same two communities (five censuses at roughly ten-year intervals in one case, and four censuses at intervals of between twelve and thirteen years on average in the other). I include in the latter series a census taken in 1954 by Alfred Metraux that I found among his fieldnotes in the archive of the Laboratoire in Paris (Turner 2005). The communities included in this set of studies represent both extremes of the scale of relative wealth in Brazilian money and commodities and political involvement with Brazilian regional institutions and Federal agencies.

This is perhaps an appropriate point to note that multitemporal field research also obviously affords the possibility of multisite research, where the same variables can be observed in combination with different (or in some cases identical) circumstances. For purposes of comparison, a combination of the two is clearly the optimal research design.

The following is a very brief summary of my census study results. With one exception, all the communities in the study, including all the previous stages of the two communities studied over time, possessed matriuxorilocal extended family households as the predominant form of segmentary structure. All these communities also possessed men's houses and a full complement of men's and women's age sets and associations, thus supporting my hypothesis that this set of collective institutions functions to reproduce the matriuxorilocal structure of the extended family households. I also found that as I had hypothesized, those communities in closest proximity to Brazilian settlements, and having the most intense interaction with Brazilian extractivists and town life, tended to have fewer persons per household, and thus less extensive extended families living under the same roof. I also discovered, however, to my considerable surprise, that in these communities a tendency had developed to group neolocal houses belonging to women from the same extended family into matriuxorilocal clusters, which are called "the same house." I further found that if these clusters are counted as integral ("the same") extended family household, the rate of matriuxorilocal residence in these "acculturated" villages is essentially the same as that in the more remote villages with less Brazilian contact. I concluded that the Kayapo had successfully maintained their social structure, based on the relationship of the matriuxorilocal extended family household and the system of communal institutions associated with the men's house, by combining and coordinating two opposing types of structural change: diminishing the size of individual households, thus accommodating the tensions arising from the increasing importance of Brazilian commodity ownership, while promoting the grouping of matrilaterally related houses to form integral matriuxorilocal clusters.

The single exception to this pattern appeared to be a perfect negative case for the hypothesis: the village of Piaraçu, which possessed neither Kayapo-style extended family households nor a men's house or the superstructure of collective age groups that constitutes the organizational framework of every other Kayapo village. Piaraçu was founded in 1971 as a guard post at the Xingú ferry crossing of the new highway built by the Brazilians in conjunction with their invasion of Kayapo territory in 1970, after the Kayapo captured the ferry. The Kayapo originally established it as a toll-collecting post for the ferry, and later added a truck and outboard motor repair shop, under the leadership of a charismatic young Kayapo man who made himself an expert mechanic but had little interest in traditional Kayapo family structure or ceremony. He divorced his Kayapo wife and took a wife from a non–Ge-speaking people, the Kayabi. Neither speaks the other's language. They seem to get along happily enough, but it is not a conventional Kayapo extended family household. His own married daughter lives with her husband in a separate house. Roughly half of the population of the village consisted of families from other non-Kayapo speaking indigenous peoples of the region (mostly Kayabi and Juruna). Kayapo who settled at the post had to return to their home villages to take part in ceremonies. On my return to Piaraçu in 2009, however, I found to my surprise that it was in the process of remaking itself as a conventional Kayapo village. The Kayabi population had been obliged to leave on the grounds that their alcoholic chicha drinking parties were incompatible with Kayapo teetotalism, and a new wave of Kayapo immigrants had established a number of new matriuxorilocal extended family households, which now constituted a clear majority in the village. I was invited to sit with the adult men in a circle of chairs that had been assembled in the clearing in the middle of the village—an incipient men's house. A group of adolescent youths, I noticed, had set up their own little circle of chairs on the periphery of the larger men's circle—an embryonic age set division like that of ordinary Kayapo men's houses. I have been told that since my visit most of the inhabitants of Piaraçu have built a new circular village with a men's house a short distance from the disorganized jumble of houses of the original toll station and truck repair station. Piaraçu, in short, has turned out to be the exception that proved the rule of the resilience of Kayapo social organization.

My initial hypothesis that house size would be found to vary inversely with the intensity and scale of economic and social contacts with regional Brazilian society was also borne out by the census data from the two largest and richest villages, Gorotire and Kikretum. These are the two villages with the heaviest exposure to Brazilian commodities and the greatest infusions of money from logging and mining contracts. In both, the average size of individual households was significantly smaller than in the poorer, more remote villages. In the latter it is normal to find two, three, or more nuclear families formed by the daughters and sons-in-law of an older woman or pair of sisters under the same roof. In the two richer villages, by contrast, the houses, most of which are built of masonry in the Brazilian style, tend to contain only one couple of parents-in-law and one other family comprising a married daughter and son-in-law. Additional married daughters tend to live in separate houses that cluster around their common mother's house and continue to be spoken of collectively as "the same house."

The history of the two large communities, Gorotire and Kikretum, provides an illuminating context for the variations in domestic group composition and communal political structure documented by my series of household censuses and inventories of collective groups. The influx of money and Brazilian commodities from contacts with placer gold miners and (somewhat later) loggers, and the new possibilities for personal and social identity construction presented by the establishment of more stable and accessible interaction with regional Brazilian society, beginning in the early 1970s, added to the rising pressure of the sharply increasing population on the existing stock of houses at Gorotire. Both senior and junior couples with families felt increasingly crowded in extended family houses of the traditional format, which provided inadequate secure space for storage of their hoards of Brazilian-style clothes and possessions. They welcomed the arrangement with a logging enterprise negotiated by the chiefs in about 1970 to rebuild the existing houses of the village as Brazilian-style masonry cottages. These, however, proved inadequate to accommodate the demand for additional family housing. In 1974, the population of Gorotire sought to alleviate the pressure by building an extension of the village with twelve new houses and space for many more in the traditional round configuration. The village, however, split soon afterward as a result of a violent conflict between its three principal leaders. Over one hundred of the followers of the chief who had provoked the fight by attacking his two colleagues seceded, following him to settle at the new community of Kikretum.

The fission of the community, and the immediately preceding construction of the village extension, made available an increased number of new or newly empty houses, many of which were occupied by nuclear families from existing extended family houses. As a result, I found, in my census of 1978, that the number of extended family households at Gorotire had fallen below 50 percent of the houses in the village, the lowest rate of matriuxorilocal residence encountered in any case in the study. Ten years later, however, I found that the new neolocal households formed at that time had almost all become matriuxorilocal extended families as their own daughters married and brought their husbands to live with them in their maternal homes.

The population of Gorotire rose sharply despite the schism, due in part to immigration by Kayapo from other communities attracted by Gorotire's greater wealth and access to commodities. This has resulted in the construction of more new houses. Some of the new construction has been impelled by the tendency, noted above, for the essential matriuxorilocal pattern to reassert itself in the form of clusters of neolocal households formed by the married daughters of a woman built close to their mother's house, with the cluster as a whole being referred to as "the same house." Taking these new data into account, the rate of matriuxorilocal residence at Gorotire was by 2003 as high (88 percent) as it is in the most remote and commodity-poor village (Kamaú, with 90 percent, as of 2007).

The weakening of the matriuxorilocal extended family postmarital residence pattern in some communities such as Gorotire and Kikretum thus appeared, in the perspective of repeated restudies, to be temporary and partial. The lasting effects of increased access to money and commodity wealth in these communities have been limited to a statistically significant diminution of average individual household size, but at Gorotire this has not led to a significant lessening of the basic rate of matriuxorilocal residence in the more recent censuses, because it has been offset by the increase in the number of clusters of neighboring houses containing members of a single matriuxorilocal extended family. At Kikretum, the relatively low rate of matriuxorilocal residence coincided with two recent secessions, leaving empty houses available for reoccupation, and the fact that the village was about to begin building a circular extension of the existing village along the lines of Gorotire's project a quarter-century ago. The Kikretum data thus appear to constitute a repetition of the Gorotire pattern (Turner 2005).

In sum, the factors responsible for the diminution of the average number of families and persons per house and the alternative social values associated with them seem to have been, or to be once again in the process of being, coopted and accommodated within the dominant matriuxorilocal pattern institutionalized in the men's house system of communal age-associations and continually reproduced by the communal ceremonies. This system remains in full force in both communities, and it continues to embody and inculcate the fundamental pattern of generational and gender inequalities and exploitation that constitutes the essential framework of Kayapo social organization at both the domestic and communal levels. My original hypothesis of the interdependence of the extended family household and communal group structure is thus supported by both the positive cases and the (temporarily) negative case (Piaraçu) in my series of village studies.

My theoretical representation of the structure of Kayapo society, however, has undergone fundamental ontological and epistemological changes from its initial form as a synchronic snapshot of a Kayapo community at one moment in its history (i.e., in an "ethnographic present"). Rather, my concept of Kayapo social organization has become one of a dynamically covarying set of relations that assumes different forms at discrete moments in a diachronic process. My notion of this pattern has shifted in the process from that of an ahistorical, ideal-normative structure, assumed to correspond to average regularities in ethnographic data "on the ground", as in Durkheimian and Anglo-Structuralist anthropology, to a focus on quantitative variations in tension with relatively invariant factors, forming shifting patterns in historical time. To return to the historical account of the Kayapo struggle to defend and reclaim their territory—a struggle that has framed my ethnographic career as it frames this presentation—it can be seen that the continuing vitality, the effective invariance so to speak, of Kayapo social structure with its system of communal institutions and ceremonial organization is the direct corollary of the political, military, and diplomatic success of this struggle. This protracted and continuing success has validated the forms of communal organization and mobilization that have served the Kayapo people as the master schema of their collective actions as political and historical agents.

"YOU ALWAYS COME BACK"

As a general methodological conclusion, I would offer my Kayapo analysis as an example of why attempts to get beyond formal normative descriptions of social organization to the documentation of material sociological dynamics as manifested in quantitative rates or shifting statistical frequencies require multiple revisits (ideally more than two, to the same sites if possible). As a case in point, on my second visit to Gorotire, I found that the village had just gone through a disruptive schism that had caused a number of extended-family households to break up and the critical function of the men's house as a dormitory for uninitiated boys and bachelor youths to fall into abeyance. As a result, the rate of matriuxorilocal extended family residence as a proportion of total households was at its lowest for any Kayapo village except Piaraçu (a special case, which for much of its existence lacked a men's house and age set system, for reasons I have explained). If I had not returned again, as I did (twice) after a couple of decades had elapsed, I might well have concluded, wrongly, that Gorotire's exceptionally long-lasting and intense contact with Brazilian society, with its resulting relatively high level of commodity consumption, had proved to be irreversibly destructive of the traditional Kayapo household and men's house structure. As

Terence Turner and Vanessa Fajans-Turner in Gorotire, 2003.
PHOTOGRAPH BY BETI BAMBERGER.

my two later revisits revealed, this was not the case: both of these apparent trends were subsequently reversed as the traditional structure reasserted itself. More importantly, I would have missed the real story of Gorotire's successful accommodation of relatively intense economic interaction with Brazilian society within the frame of the traditional Kayapo social system, through the innovative combination of diminishing average house size and the increased size and frequency of clusters of single-family houses considered as the equivalents of single matriuxorilocal extended-family households, as I have described.

In personal terms, observing and participating in the remarkable history of Kayapo political, social, economic, and cultural transformation through multiple temporally and spatially separate field studies has brought concomitant transformations in my theoretical perspective and my role as anthropologist. These transformations have formed part of my own personal development as I have aged, married (twice), and had children. Both my wives and my children have accompanied me to the Kayapo, and my older daughter, Vanessa, has actually carried on research of her own with them. This became the basis of her undergraduate thesis and two articles that she and I wrote and published together as co-authors (Turner and Fajans-Turner 2006a, 2006b). My multitemporal research with the Kayapo has thus extended itself into a multigenerational process, transcending the limits of my own personal temporality, just as the historical career of the Kayapo that I have been observing for so long now encompasses successive generations (Turner 2006c). Kayapo men and women I knew as children have aged and produced their own children, who in turn have become adults and leading actors in the drama of their people's historic encounter with the modern Brazilian nation and the world system. This parallelism has not escaped the Kayapo. While I have been absorbed in sorting out the continuities and changes in their social history, they have been interested observers of the continuities and changes in my own life, such as my divorce from my first wife, my second marriage, and the birth of my children (leading to my belated promotion, as they saw it, to the age grade of mature men). An important aspect of our mutual relationship over the years has been their recognition that, as one elderly leader who remembers my first arrival in 1962 recently put it, "You always come back."

NOTES

1. FUNAI is the Brazilian federal government's Indian agency, the National Foundation for the Indian (Fundação Nacional do Indio). FUNAI's relationship with the indigenous peoples of Brazil has been intensely ambivalent since its establishment in the 1960s. It does much good and has many devoted and skilled staff members, but it is also plagued with corruption, administrative inefficiency, and inadequate budgeting, and it is constantly under pressure from

other departments of the federal, state, and local governments to promote their environmentally destructive development projects at the Indians' expense. The result is that the Indians often see it as part of the problem and treat it as an adversary.

2. The Kayapo traditionally held items of everyday use, such as tools, baskets, and indigenous-style houses as personal property. They also have a distinct category of "valuables" (/nêkrêtch/) that are exchanged between certain categories of relatives, but are not considered to be interchangeable with Brazilian commodities and money (Turner 2009).

REFERENCES

Turner, Terence. 1965. *Social Structure and Political Organization among the Northern Cayapo.* PhD diss., Harvard University, 1965.

———. 1979a. The Ge and Bororo Societies as Dialectical Systems: A General Model. In David Maybury-Lewis, ed., *Dialectical Societies.* Cambridge: Harvard University Press, 147–178.

———. 1979b. Kinship, Household and Community Structure among the Northern Kayapo. In David Maybury-Lewis, ed., *Dialectical Societies.* Cambridge: Harvard University Press, 179–217.

———. 1991a. Representing, Resisting, Rethinking: Historical Transformations of Kayapo Culture and Anthropological Consciousness. In George Stocking, ed., *Post-Colonial Situations: The History of Anthropology,* vol. 7. Madison: University of Wisconsin Press, 285–313.

———. 1991b. De cosmologia para ideologia: Resistencia, adaptação, e consciencia social entre os Kaiapo. In E. Viveiros de Castro, ed., *Pesquisas Recentes em Amazonia.* Campinas: Editora UNICAMP. Reprinted 1993 under altered title, "De cosmologia a historia: resistencia, adaptação e consciencia social entre os Kayapo." In Eduardo Viveiros de Castro and Manuela Carneiro da Cunha, eds., *Amazonia: Etnologia e Historia Indigena.* São Paulo. Universidade de São Paulo (43–66). English translation, 1993. From Cosmology to Ideology: Resistance, Adaptation and Social Consciousness among the Kayapo. In T. Turner, ed., Cosmology, Values, and Inter-ethnic Contact in South America, *South American Indian Studies* 9:1–13. Bennington, Vt.: Bennington College Press.

———. 1992a. Defiant Images: The Kayapo Appropriation of Video. *Anthropology Today* 8 (6): 5–15.

———. 1992b. Os Mebengokre Kayapo: De communidades autónomas ao sistema inter-etnica. In M. Carneiro da Cunha, ed., *Historia dos Indios no Brasil.* São Paulo: Companhia das Letras, 311–338.

————. 1993. The Role of Indigenous Peoples in the Environmental Crisis: The Case of the Brazilian Kayapo. *Perspectives in Biology and Medicine* 36 (3): 526–545.

————. 1996. An Indigenous Amazonian People's Struggle for Socially Equitable and Ecologically Sustainable Production: The Kayapo Revolt against Extractivism. *Journal of Latin American Anthropology* n.s. 1 (1): 98–121.

————. 2000. Indigenous Rights, Environmental Protection and the Struggle over Forest Resources in the Amazon: The Case of the Brazilian Kayapo. In Jill Conway, Kenneth Keniston, and Leo Marx, eds., *Earth, Air, Fire and Water: The Humanities and the Environment.* Boston: University of Massachusetts Press, 145–169.

————. 2002. Representation, Politics, and Cultural Imagination in Indigenous Video: General Points and Kayapo Examples. In Faye Ginsburg, Lila Abu-Lughod, and Brian Larkin, eds., *Media Worlds: Anthropology on New Terrain.* Berkeley: University of California Press, 75–89.

————. 2005. A Fifty-year Comparative Genealogical Household Census of Kayapo Communities: Theoretical and Political Implications. Paper presented to the annual conference of the Society for the Anthropology of Lowland South America, June 2005.

————. 2006a. (With Vanessa Fajans-Turner.) Interethnic alliances among indigenous and Brazilian "Peoples of the Xingú." *Anthropology News* 46 (3): 27, 31.

————. 2006b. (With Vanessa Fajans-Turner.) Political Innovation and Interethnic Alliance: Kayapo Resistance to the Developmentalist State. *Anthropology Today* 22 (5): 3–10.

————. 2006c. Anthropology as Reality Show and as Co-production: Internal Relations between Theory and Activism. In Steve Sangren and Dominic Boyer, eds., *For a Critique of Pure Culture: Special Issue in Honor of Terry Turner. Critique of Anthropology* 26 (1): 15–26.

————. 2009. Valuables, Value and Commodities among the Kayapo of Central Brazil. In Fernando Santos-Granero, ed., *The Occult Life of Things: Native Amazonian Theories of Materiality and Personhood.* Tucson: University of Arizona Press.

2| "Soon We Will Be Spending All Our Time at Funerals"

Yolngu Mortuary Rituals in an
Epoch of Constant Change

FRANCES MORPHY AND HOWARD MORPHY

> Future ethnologists will have a lot to do since you cannot
> accomplish the study of an entire civilization in one lifetime:
> we are leaving a work in progress. That is what ethnography is.
>
> —*Jean Rouche*

As researchers engaged with the Yolngu of northeast Arnhem Land, we are very conscious of being part of a work in progress—not only because the task at any one point in time is so enormous, but also since Yolngu society, like all societies, is in a constant state of change. The primary ethnographic data for this chapter cover the thirty-five years of our own long-term fieldwork among the Gumurr Miwatj (eastern) Yolngu, beginning in 1973. In addition we are fortunate to be able to build on an outstanding ethnographic heritage that dates from the first years of intensive European occupation of Yolngu country. The research of W. Lloyd Warner in the late 1920s, Donald Thomson between 1935 and 1944, and Ronald and Catherine Berndt in the 1940s, '50s, and '60s, and the work of our contemporaries and near contemporaries Warren Shapiro, Nicolas Peterson, Nancy Williams, Ian Keen, and Janice Reid have created an exceptional record of the last eighty years of Yolngu society. There are now several younger scholars in the field, or just out of it, whose work promises to carry the record into the next century, and increasingly Yolngu scholars themselves are adding to the tradition.

Here we focus on changes in Yolngu mortuary ceremonies. In his fieldnotes of 29 July 1937 Donald Thomson wrote, "If a man could but follow all that takes place when a yarkomirri [*yäkumirri*, important; lit. name-having] man dies he would understand almost all of the culture of these people" (Peterson 1976, 97). Today Yolngu mortuary rituals are equally informative, both about the changes that have occurred in the interim and about the dominant values of contemporary Yolngu society. As representations of social structure and religious beliefs they show remarkable continuities over time, yet they also show many influences from the outside world—borrowings from Pacific Island cultures and from Christianity, the use of photographs and motor vehicles, and so on.

CHANGE, CONTINUITY, AND THE
RELATIVE AUTONOMY OF SYSTEMS

Observed over a period of more than thirty years, Yolngu society has been in a state of almost constant change, affected by its encapsulation within the settler Australian state with its concomitant and perpetual changes in government policy settings (F. Morphy 2008), the introduction of new technologies, and economic transformation. A long-term historical perspective, encompassing both the observations of earlier ethnographers and our own over the span of our adult lives, allows us to see a society responding creatively and contingently to new circumstances and opportunities, but one in which life is often on the edge of being out of control, where the expression of values in new ways has had unintended consequences.

It is tempting to see contemporary mortuary rituals as a hybrid adjustment, with history sedimented productively in expressive culture. In the recent annals of Australian Aboriginalist anthropology two paradigms currently hold sway. One is the dominant "intercultural" view, in which everything in the lives of Aboriginal people is seen as co-produced by the encompassing settler society (Hinkson and Smith 2005; Merlan 1998). In the words of Francesca Merlan, the scene is "not one of autonomy, but of still unequal, intercultural production" (1998, 181). The other appeals to the politics of resistance (Cowlishaw 1988), seeing Aboriginal lives as constructed in opposition to or in resistance to the demands of the encapsulating society. Our position, arrived at gradually through our long-term observation of Yolngu institutions over time, steers what might be construed as a middle course.

Hybridity theories, of which the intercultural approach is an exemplar, tend to do a disservice to local historical processes and to continuities in dominant value trajectories and principles of structuration that give a degree of coherence within change and that radically influence the ways in which new technologies and institutions are incorporated within local systems. We find it more productive and revealing to adopt a theoretical model in which social systems and systems of value are construed as having the property of relative autonomy (H. Morphy 2007, 2011). This approach "privileges neither 'adaptation' nor 'resistance' as modes of interaction with other systems, and allows such interactions to have effects on a system and its trajectory without compromising its relative autonomy" (F. Morphy 2008, 121).

CONTINUING THEMES AND CHANGING EVENTS

If Donald Thomson the time traveler were to awake suddenly seventy years on to hear the sounds of a Yolngu burial ceremony at Yilpara on Blue Mud Bay, they would be totally familiar to him and he might at first think that little had changed. Yolngu mortuary rituals comprise the same song cycles and dance sequences, and the same intonations of important *yäku*, as would have been performed in his time—subject only to the inevitable processes of change that occur

Frances Morphy with Milyin Mununggurr, her Yolngu language teacher, and Leon White, a school teacher, at Wandawuy, 1976. PHOTOGRAPH BY HOWARD MORPHY.

Howard Morphy with Mick Magani at Gatji, 1974. PHOTOGRAPH BY FRANCES MORPHY.

in any performance tradition. However, when he came out of his tent and looked more closely at the context he might be surprised that the performance he had once seen enacted during the disinterment of bones from a grave now accompanies the transfer of a coffin from a funeral shade to the back of a Toyota Land Cruiser.

We have excellent data on Yolngu mortuary rituals at the time of European colonization (from Thomson; see Warner 1958, 412ff, and Peterson 1976). However, far from seeing this data as a means of establishing a baseline from which to measure subsequent changes, we see it as itself evidence of a continuing process of change. At the time of European colonization and of the first ethnographers, Yolngu mortuary rituals were best seen as the outcome of a diverse body of practice that varied across the region and according to individual circumstances, the place and context of death, and the social status, age, and gender of the deceased. Certainly European colonization has been the catalyst for significant change. But Yolngu mortuary rituals have probably always been in a state of change and have always responded to external factors. For some three hundred years before European colonization, trepang harvesters from Indonesia (*manggatharra*, or the Macassans) visited the Yolngu coast annually. Evidence of Macassan influence can be seen in many aspects of Yolngu mortuary rituals.

While acknowledging that external influences have always been a factor in Yolngu mortuary practices (which are, if anything, characterized by their diversity), we nonetheless approach them as a body of practice with a trajectory that is relatively autonomous and that must be understood only partly in terms of adaptive responses to new circumstances. Yolngu mortuary rituals are not hybrid creations made up through combining elements that history has brought into contact. Rather they are the product of a regional ecumene, which has at its center distinctive value creation processes, beliefs about the nature of being, and ways of structuring action to express these beliefs and values. This is why, in hindsight, it is possible to see in Yolngu mortuary rituals many features that display continuity over time.

Yolngu mortuary rituals have always been an extended body of practice or performance, comprising the disposal of the body and purificatory and commemorative rituals. In Warner's and Thomson's time a person was in effect "buried" several times. Ceremony began while the person was dying and when possible always involved them as an actor (Warner 1958, 413). In certain (perhaps ideal) circumstances, the dying persons initiated ceremonial activity themselves. This initial stage has changed little and involves the performance of songs and dances prefiguring those that will be performed after death. In the past, the initial disposal of the body, after it had been painted with clan designs, was through burial or by exposure on a platform, and it was then left until only the bones and hair remained. These were subsequently collected and re-"buried" in a bark container that was carried about by close relatives for a number of years. Parts of the skeleton were given to male relatives (Morphy 1997), the hair was made into string, and the skull may have been painted and on occasion worn suspended around the neck of a female relative (Thomson 1939). In the final stage of the mortuary rituals, a hollow-log coffin would be constructed and painted, and the bones placed inside. The main theme of the mortuary ritual, according to Thomson and Warner, was to guide the person's *birrimbirr* (soul) back to the *wangarr* (ancestral dimension), where it would be reincorporated in a *mangutji* (spiritual reservoir; lit. eye, waterhole) in the person's own clan country. Each stage of the process, each reburial, was directed toward the same objective. The spirit's journey was accompanied by the performance of songs and dances and the production of paintings celebrating *wangarr* beings who connected the place of death with the spirit's destination. A detailed analysis of Yolngu mortuary ritual reveals many other themes (Morphy 1984, 2008), but we will focus on this one.

Over time the events of Yolngu mortuary rituals have changed, but they have always remained an extended performance. During the period of missionization the main changes that occurred were the gradual disappearance or removal of the actual body from the commemorative process and its replacement by representations. Although secondary and tertiary reburial was still being practiced on the boundaries of Yolngu country at the time of our initial fieldwork (Clunies, Ross, and Hiatt 1977), they had long ceased to be practiced in mission settlements such as Yirrkala. When we first arrived at Yirrkala in the early 1970s, funerals comprised burial in a coffin in a grave. The body of the deceased was no longer painted with clan designs; instead the same designs were placed on the coffin lid. The bones were no longer dug up to be eventually placed in a hollow-log coffin. Instead, possessions of the dead person, in particular items of clothing and objects of "contagion" such as mattresses, bedding, and personal effects, were placed in a suitcase or an unused room and kept for a subsequent occasion. That occasion might be a circumcision ceremony or a special memorial event. The "remain(der)s" were then treated as if they were the bones of the deceased and buried in a special coffin or burned in a hollow inside a sand sculpture. The ritual performance associated with these events drew from *mada-yin* ceremonial law exactly as if it were the bones that were being placed in a hollow-log coffin. This appeared to us to be a relatively simple process of substitution in which analogues for the body and body parts were acted upon. The substitutions could be explained in part as a response to missionary sensitivities and concepts of hygiene (though rules of hygiene were in fact always integral to Yolngu ritual practice). The painting of the coffin lid as a replacement for the painting of the body was a logical substitution; the coffin became an outer skin for the body. Since it was no longer possible to disinter the bones, objects closely associated with the dead person served as substitutes.

Another change that had occurred was that ceremonial performance had been organized to fit in with the timetable of the mission work routine. While some ritual activity occurred in its own time—all day and night beside the body of the dying person, with the necessary rites performed at the moment of death—the main ceremonial events had to be coordinated with the mission's timetable. The final days of the funeral, when ritual activity was at its height, usually took place at weekends. Weekends were also the major days for other ceremonial performances such as circumcisions and the major episodes of regional fertility ceremonies. The relationship with the mission and the missionaries was negotiated, and was viewed by Yolngu in a largely positive way. Missionaries participated if they wished in Yolngu performances; and the timetable of mission working life, while acting as a regulatory mechanism, did not intrude greatly on the structure of ceremonial performance. Yolngu elders carried on aspects of their law outside the mission timetable. The church had acquired a delimited role in funeral ceremonies; after the Yolngu performance ended with the body in the grave, the Methodist minister stepped up to perform the Christian burial rites. While the youthful agnostic anthropologists found this somewhat intrusive, Yolngu did not.

IN RETROSPECT: A SYNCHRONIC AND PARTIAL VIEW

Yolngu mortuary practices in 1976, forty years after the establishment of Yirrkala mission station, appeared to us a successful adaptation in response to the colonial context. The painting of the coffin lid seemed to be an established practice; it was a central component of every burial ceremony we attended over a two-year period across the Yolngu region between 1974 and 1976. The song series were the same as those that had been recorded and transcribed by earlier anthropologists, and the paintings produced in ceremonial contexts showed great continuity with the past. Yolngu participation in mortuary rituals seemed to be total and involving, with great energy directed toward the fate of the soul but equally toward the recovery and support of the living and bereaved. We had a sense of a new stability that depended on creative substitutive processes.[1]

Subsequent developments, which we would not have observed had we not returned intermittently to the field, revealed a more complex set of relationships between the relatively autonomous parts of the whole than were discernible to us in the mid-1970s. In that first period of fieldwork we were both focused on the art and material culture of the Yolngu. The painting of coffin lids and the substitution of material culture for bodies caught and held our attention.

Yet in retrospect it appears that the ancestral identity of the body could be designated without an accompanying painting, simply by dancing and singing it into existence. The act of painting in the end was not a necessary component of the event, for the painting of the coffin lid that seemed to be one of the defining elements of mortuary ritual in the mid-1970s was in fact a recent innovation going back a few years, and soon after our first period of fieldwork ended it was no longer routinely practiced. Since the 1980s it has not been practiced at all. Had we happened to undertake our first fieldwork ten years earlier or five years later, we would never have witnessed it as a component of funeral ceremonies.

There were things in our field notebooks that did not make it into our published analyses of the time (H. Morphy 1977, 1984). Our fieldwork coincided with the establishment of the local mining town and with the end of "mission time" and the transfer of local administration to the Yolngu-controlled Yirrkala Dhanbul Association. We witnessed at first hand, since we were living "in the camp," the ensuing disruption to everyday life and the violence fueled by the ready availability of alcohol. We wrote publicly of the beauty, complexity, resilience, and adaptability of Yolngu society and culture, while wondering privately whether, in fact, we were witnessing the beginning of the end of a coherently Yolngu sociality.

THE BEGINNINGS OF A MORE COMPLEX UNDERSTANDING

In the 1980s Yolngu women began to produce batik textiles at the local Women's Center. From that time, in funeral ceremonies, clan designs in the form of textiles were wrapped around the body; and later bark paintings would occasionally be hung on the interior or exterior walls of the shade where the body lay. These innovations carried with them memories from the past just as the coffin-lid paintings had done—memories not only of the person who died and their relationships to others, but of past practices. The shrouds printed with the clan designs of the deceased could be connected to the cloths that were such an important part of exchanges with the Macassan visitors. But they also made new connections by reminding people of the shroud wrapped around the body of Christ (see Magowan 2007 for the articulation of Christianity with Yolngu religious practices). Thus in the 1980s we began to learn that the values and practices underlying the form of Yolngu mortuary rituals are fundamentally both recursive and incorporative, and indeed these are precisely among the reasons why these systems of value and practice are able to adapt to new contexts and seize opportunities while appearing to carry the past with them.

Yolngu mortuary practices have certainly been adaptive, and substitution has been part of how they are in continuity with the past. But in the 1980s we were now learning that an understanding of the trajectory of Yolngu mortuary rituals required a perspective that sees Yolngu agency behind a series of innovations that take the performances in new directions. The nature of these innovations can only be understood if they are seen as the outcome of continuing value creation processes that in turn influence the way in which radical social change has its impact on Yolngu society. We were fortunate to conduct our fieldwork at the beginning of some of the most significant changes and to subsequently see some further evidence of recursion. We will focus on two interrelated but relatively autonomous value trajectories; the politics of the body and the movement of the spirit of the deceased to its ancestral home.

TECHNOLOGICAL INNOVATION AND ITS CONSEQUENCES

In the mid-1970s newly available technology began to be exploited in significant ways. A body could now be preserved in the morgue of the local mining town's hospital and transported by plane to the clan homeland. Negotiations on a death could therefore be prolonged by extending the "life" of the body, and introduced transport could be used to move the body close to the spirit's final destination. These possibilities entered the Yolngu world at a time when, in reaction to the alcohol-fueled violence of settlement life at Yirrkala, the "homelands movement" began to gather strength, initially with the support of some of the local missionaries (see F. Morphy 2008). When the mission ceded control to the Dhanbul Association, the mission work pattern no longer had to be followed so rigorously either at the homelands or at the main settlement. This set of factors moved the trajectory of Yolngu primary mortuary rituals toward larger events of longer duration held at one or another of the clan homelands.

We witnessed the very beginning of this change in trajectory. In 1976 a sixteen-year-old boy was killed in a car accident. He was one of the first to die as a result of the introduction of alcohol to the region. His body was placed in the newly opened Nhulunbuy hospital morgue while arrangements for his funeral were made. It was a tense period. His father lived at his clan homeland fourteen hour's drive away down rough bush tracks. People were angry and divided, and rumors of an avenging expedition were rife. The body remained in the morgue while negotiations took place, mediated by Narritjin Maymuru, the senior member of the Manggalili clan, who was then living at Yirrkala. In the end it was decided to fly the body to the homeland and have the funeral there. It was the first occasion on which a body had been flown for burial, and the first time that the mortuary had held the body until funeral arrangements could be agreed. The funeral was a big occasion, and a cavalcade of vehicles transported over one hundred participants down the track to take part. Yolngu had no difficulty in adapting ritual performances to the new context—in dancing the body from the morgue, in escorting it into the plane, and devising ways of ensuring the plane could be "freed" to allow passengers to travel in it afterward. The event was successful and a successful mediation had taken place. But, perspicaciously, Narritjin said to us after the event that he was worried by the use of the mortuary. He said that knowing Yolngu, if they were not careful, they would find their whole lives taken up by funerals.[2] He was more prescient than we were in predicting the direction of the trajectory; for the next two decades it did seem that funerals were gradually getting out of hand.

FUNERALS TAKE CENTER STAGE

There was a gap of nearly fifteen years in our fieldwork with Yolngu between 1982 and 1997, except for a short field trip in 1988. However, since 1997 we have been back each year. When we returned in 1997 we found that funerals had followed the trajectory that Narritjin had predicted. Bodies were held as a matter of course in the hospital morgue until people were ready to perform the burial.

Community resources had been increasing as the region became more integrated within the wider Australian economy and as mining royalties and welfare payments were introduced. And Yolngu invested much of those additional resources in increasingly expensive and prolonged funeral practices. Even once the body was collected time could be controlled, because Yolngu used their increasing resources initially to build their own mortuary in the mission settlement of Yirrkala and subsequently invested in transportable morgues— large purpose-built refrigeration units that could hold the body until the final day of the ceremony.

By the late 1990s one of the main sources of income was the Community Development Employment Program (CDEP), inaugurated in 1977 and introduced into the area in the early 1980s. This scheme was designed to provide a subsidized wage to people working in remote areas with limited employment opportunities. It had a number of different aims, from job generation to income support for community workers. The scheme was initially implemented with a degree of flexibility, and it was applied in different ways in different parts of Australia (see Morphy and Sanders 2001). In the Gumurr Miwatj region, people living at the Laynahpuy homelands could effectively take their CDEP with them when they moved temporarily to another community to take part in a ceremony or for some other legitimate "cultural" purpose. Given that the scheme was designed to support work programs that were otherwise unfunded, and given the importance of ceremonial performance in Yolngu life, such a use of resources was a perfectly reasonable interpretation of the scope of the scheme, as it was conceived of at that time.

In addition to the deployment of CDEP income, Yolngu had also gained some additional support from local organizations, government, and the local mining industry to add to the available resources, beginning in the late 1970s when the local mining company started to provide financial and logistic assistance for the funerals of significant local leaders.

In the subsequent period the resources available for funerals became institutionalized. Community organizations quite appropriately acknowledged that people should be allowed time off for cultural practices, of which participation in mortuary rituals was a major component, and they too began to subsidize funeral expenses. The local community-owned art center set up a fund to be used to help cover funeral costs, and people supported by welfare payments or CDEP wages were free to spend the time participating in funerals. The availability of vehicles increased, and a successful local airline developed to provide transport to homeland centers. All these factors worked together to create the possibility for extending the duration of funerals. And the use of the hospital mortuary and the availability of portable morgues meant that the funerals could be scheduled to maximize participation.

Scheduling became increasingly necessary. One consequence of the advent of the mine has been to greatly increase the Yolngu death rate as a result of injury, accident, suicide, and illness associated with alcohol and substance abuse. The nature of many of the deaths increased the tensions associated with funeral arrangements and prolonged them, but at the same time made a display of unity associated with a grand funeral all the more necessary. By taking advantage of the potential of new technology, Yolngu were able to manage the politics and trauma of death and burial, and to schedule the events to achieve maximum participation.

By the late 1990s a regional economy of consumption and redistribution had developed that was centered in large part on Yolngu mortuary practices. This development was perfectly logical, in harmony with Yolngu values, sustained by moral imperatives and obligations to others, and directed in part toward mitigating the trauma felt by the community as a consequence of the increasing death rate among younger people that had followed the development of the mining town. And indeed, as Donald Thomson had intuited, mortuary rituals are the context in which the politics of Yolngu society are played out and during which core values and attachments associated with kinship are reinforced.

Whereas in the past Yolngu ritual had moved in synchrony with the seasonal cycle of a hunter-gatherer economy, by the 1980s and

1990s it had become increasingly disconnected from any such constraining economic cycle. The costs became benefits for the local businesses in the mining town, whose stocks reflected the greatly increased demand for rolls of cloth, artificial flowers, tents, blankets, and other essential items for Yolngu funeral encampments.

By early 2000, Narritjin's prediction had come to fruition. Many Yolngu spent much of their lives participating in funerals. Not only was this traumatic for individuals, placing a huge responsibility on the shoulders of ritual experts, but it disrupted normal life to the extent that it had *become* normal life. And this was recognized by some Yolngu perhaps earlier than it was by outsiders. It was the elders and in some cases the dying themselves who took the initiative to change the trajectory once again.

HINTS OF RECURSION

Between 2000 and 2005 we spent several weeks or months each year based at Yilpara, a Yolngu community of about 150 people on the north of Blue Mud Bay. We were working as consultants to the Northern Land Council, assisting the Blue Mud Bay Yolngu to prepare a native title claim to the waters of the bay. During that time the community leader Djambawa Marawili and others expressed to us on many occasions their thoughts that funerals went on for too long and that they had never lasted so long in the past. People would refer both to pre-European times and to mission times and would seek confirmation from us that this indeed had been the case. In such discussions the boundaries between us as observers and Yolngu as observed became increasingly blurred. After all, we and our interlocutors had known each other all our adult lives, and we were drawn into their discourse on the basis of our shared history and our shared understandings of that history.

One reason for concern was the interruption of work schedules; another was the expense occasioned by funerals. However, people also recognized that outstations such as Yilpara bore a disproportionate responsibility for the organization of funerals. One of the reasons for holding funerals away from the main settlement was so that people could be buried close to their clan homelands. Moreover, homeland settlements were largely free of the alcohol and substance abuse that sometimes disrupted funerals at the settlements near the mining town, and homelands people had strongly maintained their ritual law. While there was a degree of prestige associated with these factors, they also imposed a considerable burden.

We ourselves felt that burden. In contrast to our extended fieldwork in the 1970s when, in typical "participant observation" mode, our lives flowed to the pace and the rhythm of the Yolngu lives around us, this time we were undertaking fieldwork in what might be called "native title" mode. This meant short concentrated periods of fieldwork with particular, narrowly defined objectives. Funerals kept getting in the way, competing for the attention of the people who were the most knowledgeable native title "applicants." It proved almost impossible, for example, to arrange general meetings of the applicants at which all the relevant people could be present.

Djambawa's father was still alive. He was in his mid-eighties and had been raised to young adulthood in the precolonial period. He strongly supported his son's view. He spoke to the community about the need to return to short funerals and insisted that when he and his wife passed away they should be buried quickly. And indeed, when they died their funerals were relatively short—though nonetheless spectacular. Many reasons contributed to the fact that he was granted his wish. One was his own authority and that of his son. Another was that his death was anticipated; it fit the Yolngu conception of a normal or "good" death (Barber 2008). Another was that he died in his own country. Finally, his distinction meant that a large attendance could be guaranteed, irrespective of competing events. All such factors are likely to reduce the tensions and the politics surrounding a funeral and enable it to start soon after the death. However, Djambawa was able to point to it as a precedent in his conversations with others, and his views began to prevail in the organization of subsequent funerals where he was a major actor.

Between 2006 and 2008 we were back in the area again for several short field trips. Frances was undertaking research as part of a comparative project on the governance of indigenous community organizations. Her case study was of the Laynhapuy Homelands Association, the resource agency and CDEP organization for Yilpara and the other Laynhapuy homelands (Morphy 2008). On one occasion when she was at Yilpara, the community got news of a death at Yirrkala. It was one of several deaths that had occurred in the region in quick succession. Before it was formally announced to the women by the men so that they could mourn, Djambawa addressed the assembled community. He asked the women to mourn briefly, as was appropriate, but then to go back about their daily activities. He said that Yolngu life had become just one long funeral, and that his father, before he died, had been worried about this. His father had told him, and he remembered himself, that when somebody died in the past the primary disposal was a quick affair, maybe one or two days, "because in those days we had to move around and hunt to eat, we would have starved if we had sat at funerals the whole time." He drew an explicit analogy between work and hunting. Working for the community, to keep it in order and to develop new enterprises and jobs, was hunting in a new form, and just as vital as the old kind of work. His father had had a short funeral, according to his wishes, and it had been a good funeral, with no arguments. He expressed the wish that people pay attention to the wise words of the old man.

However, it is hard for an individual or a small number of like-minded people, no matter how locally influential, to effect more widespread changes in a major social institution simply through force of argument. Many funerals in the region continued to be both prolonged and contentious affairs. The imperative for more widespread change came from a different quarter. In 2005 the Commonwealth government initiated a radical reform of the CDEP program on which so many depended for their income. The "old" CDEP was deemed to have led to an undesirable form of welfare dependency, and the objectives of the scheme were recalibrated away from "community development" toward a focus on the individual, and on moving people off CDEP into so-called "real" work. As part of the process of making people "work ready," the conditions under which people received their CDEP wages were tightened. CDEP participants were now to have a written description of their duties, and they were obliged to fill out time sheets at the community where they were deemed to be resident. Unexplained and undocumented absences would result in the docking of people's wages, and ultimately, for persistent offenders, to expulsion from the scheme. The organizations that administered the CDEP program, such as the Laynhapuy Homelands Association, came under more rigorous scrutiny. Failure to "deliver" CDEP in the manner prescribed by the government would lead to loss of the CDEP contract, which was one of the organization's major sources of funding. Quite clearly, these new restrictions would place limits on people's mobility, and therefore on their ability to attend prolonged funerals in communities other than those in which they were deemed to be resident.

As part of her research during this period, Frances attended several Laynhapuy Board meetings at which the Yolngu Board members and the staff of their organization grappled with the implications of these changes. The ideologies of the government and local indigenous organizations such as Laynhapuy differed widely (F. Morphy 2008), but they coincided in the aim of developing a more self-sustaining regional economy, which generated employment for Yolngu. The local organization with its Yolngu Board was more sensitive to the complexities of the local situation and the need to take account of cultural and economic realities in planning regional development. However, the new constraints on movement provided a context in which those who favored shorter funerals could advance their case. As board members of the organization charged with implementing the changes to CDEP, they could advocate measures that would both shorten funerals and help the organization to fulfill the terms of its CDEP contract.

The majority of Yolngu Laynhapuy Board members began to support policy changes that would encourage shorter funerals. In 2005 we were present at a meeting called to discuss future policy and directions for Laynhapuy. There was a general consensus that funerals needed to be managed better to enable other people to perform other duties. Over the next months the board began to put in place measures to achieve this, not all of which were mandated by government regulation. They endorsed the new time-sheets regime and the abolition of special cultural leave, so that people had to use their normal vacation time to participate in funerals. They reduced (and later abolished) subsidies for funerals, and in 2007 stopped subsidizing the use of portable mortuaries. In effect there was a transfer of expenses from the state-subsidized community chest to the funeral participants as a means of encouraging funeral practice to integrate with the evolving contemporary economy.

"TRADITION" AND "CHANGE"

It would not be correct to suggest that funerals are returning to some original, earlier form, although this is sometimes advanced as a proposition by Yolngu who favor shorter funerals. Yolngu funeral practices have to be seen as part of a complex body of practice that is connected to mortuary rituals as a whole and to all other aspects of the society. All this, not just funeral practice itself, is continually changing, always responding to contingent circumstances. Indeed, the changes we have documented are testimony to the complex nature of the interrelationships and the multiple factors determining the form of each event.

Yet at the same time each Yolngu funeral appears, at the time of its occurrence, as a set of recognizable and ordered events in which people know their roles (although these may be the subject of discussion and negotiation—that is part of normal process). Yolngu funerals are the product of a cultural trajectory that at any point in time has a known history and a set of structural properties that Yolngu utilize in the organization of particular instances of ceremony.

Narritjin Maymuru did predict that the use of the morgue would prolong funerals, and Djambawa Marawili and his father certainly did refer to the precedent of tradition in justifying a return to shorter funerals. It would be neat to see them as providing solutions to problems predicted by Narritjin in his perceptive analysis of social processes.

If only anthropology (and anthropologists) could be so predictive. Narritjin, and Djambawa and his father, were speaking from knowledge accrued through their role as agents in social processes.

Narritjin sensed the importance that funeral rituals had in Yolngu life; he was aware that mortuary rituals as a whole were a vehicle for resolving conflict and ameliorating the pain and the sense of loss felt on death. His prediction also showed an awareness of the transforming nature of Yolngu mortuary rituals as directed by a trajectory of value and a history of practice that responded to new situations and accommodated to change. It was because he recognized the important role that mortuary rituals had in value creation and in social relationships that he saw what the consequences might be of opportunities to extend the duration of funerals. His analysis acknowledged that Yolngu were agents of change, but also that they might not be able to control the consequences of change.

Djambawa and his father were equally aware that although rituals for the primary disposal of the dead had been shorter in the past, mortuary rituals as a whole had been, if anything, more extended. They were positioned as agents aware of the consequences of the changes in their own society—changes that may have been predictable because they were in accordance with Yolngu values, but which nonetheless were imposing an increasing burden. Known history— known in part through their awareness of the anthropological record to which we provided access—contained the possibility of other trajectories and alternative ways of acting on death. Interestingly, Djambawa and his father were arguing from "tradition" to pull back from a recent development that had in turn been motivated by "traditional" Yolngu values. Thus a precedent from the past is not to be seen simply as a return to the "authentic" way of doing things but as adding recursively to the ongoing trajectory. It is only through understanding the complexity of social processes and the multilayered nature of determinacy that one can escape from the simple dualism of "tradition" versus "change" (H. Morphy 2007).

AND WHAT OF THE FUTURE?

It could be argued that in "Thomson time" ceremony was one of the productive engines of the hunter-gatherer economic cycle. It is pos-

sible that the emphasis on primary burial that evolved during the mission period and intensified during the last quarter of the twentieth century will be replaced in the future by a reworking of extended mortuary processes that will fit with the new economic regime that is emerging. Yolngu have many rituals of commemoration, and there is some evidence that such changes are already taking place. There are signs of an increase in larger and more encompassing regional ceremonies in which the commemoration of the recently dead is a component. These regional ceremonies are not dependent on the contingency of death. They can be pre-planned and integrated within the developing contemporary economy with its time-management requirements. And Yolngu have recently embraced the memorial service as a cultural form, particularly for senior and prominent people. Interestingly, this is the forum for invited non-Yolngu to memorialize the deceased—non-Yolngu are often among the invited speakers at such events. Such memorial services are consciously constructed as intercultural or "hybrid" moments.

While it is unlikely that Yolngu will ever revive exhumation and reburial as part of mortuary practice, it is interesting that one of the main advocates of shorter funerals, Djambawa Marawili, has also at times advocated reintroducing reburial in hollow-log coffins. Again this illustrates the extent to which Yolngu mortuary practices are, and continue to be conceived of as, a complex, interconnected whole. Our prediction rests on the difficulties of persuading Euro-Australian society of its desirability, and on the fact that several Yolngu generations have grown up to experience bodies being buried only once. But we certainly predict that Yolngu mortuary rituals will remain

Facing top. Frances Morphy with Nyuga Dhamarrandji at Dhuruputjpi, 2010.
PHOTOGRAPH BY HOWARD MORPHY.
Facing bottom. Howard Morphy with Marrnyula Mununggurr at Yilpara, Blue Mud Bay, 2009.
PHOTOGRAPH BY JUDY WATSON.

extended affairs, and that they will remain a focal point of value creation and a generator of social and economic activity.

REFLECTIONS ON MULTITEMPORAL FIELDWORK— AND ON RESILIENCE

Paraphrasing Bruce Knauft (2002, 23) we can safely say that we could not have "extrapolated the extent and character of change" in Yolngu mortuary rituals based on the understandings we arrived at in the 1970s. Indeed, as we have shown, it was Narritjin Maymuru, a perspicacious and wise local actor, who largely succeeded in this enterprise. He could not have predicted the external factors that would interact with the Yolngu trajectory, but he had a profound understanding of the internal dynamics of the Yolngu system. Over the years we have learned that certain Yolngu intellectuals have acute insights, and these have immeasurably enriched our own.

Multitemporal fieldwork confers two unique benefits for the anthropological enterprise. First, it allows the anthropologist to be present, fortuitously, at certain moments when changes in a trajectory occur. The more times one returns to the field, the more chances there are to observe such moments directly. Second, it confers the benefits of hindsight, allowing recursive interpretation of earlier events and observations, which in turn feeds into an ever richer analysis. Theorizing relative autonomy would be difficult if not impossible without such a base of accumulated knowledge and experience of one society.

As anthropologists, we have come to both temporal and intellectual maturity with and within our experiences of Yolngu society. Our contact with it has enriched our own existence, even as we have learned to value and understand (to some degree) its complexity and its resilience in the face of its encapsulation by the Australian settler state. Aboriginal Australia is currently experiencing a second wave of assimilationist pressure, and we occasionally wonder, as we did back in the 1970s, whether Yolngu will, inexorably, be leveled to a condition of undifferentiated "Aboriginality," where all that remains of their distinctiveness is their genetic inheritance. But with the benefit of hindsight we think we know better.

NOTES

The epigraph for the chapter is from Jean Rouche, writing of the Sigui ritual of the Dogon, cited in Collette Piault (2007), Speech Dominated or Dominating: An Interview with Jean Rouche, *Visual Anthropology Review* 23 (1): 43–53.

1. Ian Dunlop's film *Madarrpa Funeral at Gurka'wuy* and the accompanying monograph by Howard Morphy (1984) document a funeral that took place in 1976.

2. For a full account of the context of this comment by Narritjin Maymuru, which also serves as the title of this chapter, see H. Morphy (1977).

REFERENCES

Barber, Marcus. 2008. A Place to Rest: Dying, Residence, and Community Stability in Remote Arnhem Land. In K. Glaskin, M. Tonkinson, Y. Musharbash, and V. Burbank, eds., *Mortality, Mourning and Mortuary Practices in Indigenous Australia*. Aldershot: Ashgate.

Clunies Ross, Margaret, and Lester R. Hiatt. 1977. Sand Sculptures at a Gidjingali Burial Rite. In P. J. Ucko, ed., *Form in Indigenous Art: Schematisation in the Art of Aboriginal Australia and Prehistoric Europe*. Canberra: Australian Institute of Aboriginal Studies Press.

Cowlishaw, Gillian. 1988. *Black, White or Brindle*. Melbourne: Cambridge University Press.

Dunlop, Ian, director. 1979. *Madarrpa Funeral at Gurka'wuy*. Sydney: Film Australia.

Hinkson, Melinda and Benjamin Smith, eds. 2005. "Figuring the Intercultural in Aboriginal Australia." *Oceania* (Special issue) 75(3).

Knauft, Bruce. 2002. *Exchanging the Past: A Rainforest World Before and After*. Chicago: Chicago University Press.

Magowan, Fiona. 2007. *Melodies of Mourning: Music and Emotion in Northern Australia*. Oxford: James Curry.

Merlan, Francesca. 1998. *Caging the Rainbow: Places, Politics, and Aborigines in a North Australian Town*. Honolulu: University of Hawai'i Press.

Morphy, Frances. 2008. Whose Governance, for Whose Good? The Laynahpuy Homelands Association and the Neo-Assimilationist Turn in Indigenous Policy. In J. Hunt, D. Smith, S. Garling, and W. Sanders, eds., *Contested Governance: Culture, Power and Institutions in Indigenous Australia*. Canberra: ANU E Press.

Morphy, Frances, and Will Sanders. 2001. *The Indigenous Welfare Economy and the CDEP Scheme*. Canberra: ANU E Press.

Morphy, Howard. 1977. "Yingapungapu: Ground Painting as Sand Sculpture." In *Form in Indigenous Art: Schematisation in the Art of Aboriginal Australia and Prehistoric Europe*, ed. P. J. Ucko. Canberra: Australian Institute of Aboriginal Studies Press.

———. 1984. *Journey to the Crocodile's Nest*. Canberra: Australian Institute of Aboriginal Studies Press.

———. 1997. Death, Exchange and the Reproduction of Yolngu Society. In F. Merlan, J. Morton, and A. Rumsey, eds., *Scholar and Sceptic: Essays in Honour of L. R. Hiatt*. Canberra: Australian Institute of Aboriginal Studies Press.

———. 2007. Anthropological Theory and the Multiple Determinacy of the Present. In D. Parkin and S. Ulijaszek, eds., *Holistic Anthropology: Emergence and Convergence*. Oxford: Berghahn.

———. 2008. "Joyous Maggots": The Symbolism of Yolngu Mortuary Rituals. In M. Hinkson and J. Beckett, eds., *Appreciation of Difference: W. E. H. Stanner and Aboriginal Australia*. Canberra: Aboriginal Studies Press.

———. 2011. "Not Just Pretty Pictures": Relative Autonomy and the Articulations of Yolngu Art in Its Contexts. In V. Strang and M. Busse, eds., *Ownership and Appropriation*. Oxford: Berg.

Peterson, Nicolas. 1972. Totemism Yesterday: Sentiment and Local Organization among the Australian Aborigines. *Man* (n.s.) 7 (1): 120–132.

———. 1976. Mortuary Customs of North East Arnhem Land: An Account Compiled from Donald Thomson's Fieldnotes. *Memoirs of the National Museum of Victoria* 37:97–108.

Piault, Collette. 2007. Speech Dominated or Dominating: An Interview with Jean Rouche. *Visual Anthropology Review* 23 (1): 43–53.

Thomson, Donald. 1939. Two Painted Skulls from Arnhem Land, with Notes on the Totemic Significance of the Designs. *Man* 39:1–3.

Warner, W. Lloyd. 1958. *A Black Civilization*. Chicago: Harper and Row.

Williams, Nancy. 1985. On Aboriginal Decision-Making. In D. Barwick, J. Beckett, and M. Reay, eds., *Metaphors of Interpretation: Essays in Honour of W. E. H. Stanner*. Canberra: Australian National University Press.

3| Returns to the Maasai

*Multitemporal Fieldwork and the Production
of Anthropological Knowledge*

AUD TALLE

Anthropologists have many reasons or motives for returning to the field, and returns can, for practical or professional reasons, take many temporal shapes: they can be for proper revisits after a long absence, regular follow-up visits of samples over several consecutive years, or a mixture of planned and more haphazard returns, as opportunities are made available. My pattern of returns to the pastoral Maasai of Kenya over more than three decades belongs to the last category; whenever the chance to return arose, I took it. This means that my returns have varied in duration as well as in intention. At times I have returned in order to pursue specific research issues, follow certain lines of inquiry, or fill gaps in my understanding of Maasai ways— to accumulate knowledge, as it were. Other times I have gone back with no other apparent motive than to greet friends, see how they are faring, and in general keep in contact. In other words, returns have also been a constitutive part of forging a relationship.

Irrespective of motives for returning, "returns" in anthropological practice can never be a purely descriptive term. They are not just a matter of going and coming; returns have implications for the interpretations that we make. We go back to look for "something," and this something is not always clear to us beforehand. It is rather after the event, as time passes, that we begin to ponder and realize its analytical value. The story in this chapter, which centers on a traumatic event revisited after a long absence, demonstrates how returns shape our understanding in profound and subtle ways.

My returning to the Maasai over the years has certainly meant intensified knowledge and a heightened consciousness of observations made in the past as well as in the present. Returns also, however, generate open endings and pose more questions, always encouraging us to go back and look for new answers. In this sense multitemporal fieldwork should not be thought of as straightforwardly cumulative in a linear sense, but rather as a movement where past, present, and future overlap in inconclusive circles.

MAASAILAND ON THE MARGINS

The Maasai—a minority group within the context of the modern nation-state—inhabit large tracts of grasslands on both sides of the border between Kenya and Tanzania, but constitute just a small fraction of the population in the two countries. Their exact numbers are uncertain, but qualified estimates suggest some half a million people, or more, live in this borderland area (Coast 2000).

My first contact with the Kenya Maasai was in 1975 when I did three months of fieldwork in one Maasai community, located some fifty kilometers southwest of the capital Nairobi, along the road to Tanzania. The fieldwork among the Maasai followed previous field research (1971, 1972) among another pastoral group, the Barabaig (or Tatoga) in northern Tanzania. The Barabaig, like the Maasai, are of Nilotic descent. Their languages are linguistically related, but unintelligible to each other. The Barabaig count less than a tenth of the number of the Maasai, and as citizens of the Tanzanian state they are utterly marginalized (Lane 1996; Talle 1974). On the whole, pastoralists as a category, whether of Nilotic or Cushitic origin as opposed to Bantu majority groups, constitute disadvantaged peoples within the contemporary East African state structures and their institutions of

Author pregnant in the field, 1975.

governance and finance (see, for example, Anderson and Broch-Due 1999, 106–124; IWGIA 2008).

Within the ethnic configuration of East Africa, Maasai reputation is unique. The image, particularly of the male Maasai "warrior" in advertisements and tourist brochures, emblematizes a "timeless" Africa in the modern era. The Maasai in his cultural outfit, including nowadays mobile phones or other modern items, collapses vast time and space distances into one imaginable trope (Bruner 2004; May and McCabe 2004; Talle 1999). The successful branding of the Maasai ethnic name by commercial interests in Kenya and Tanzania has been less lucrative for the Maasai themselves.

At the time of our first contact, ethnic Maasai dominated the field-work locality; however, today, three decades later, it is an ethnically mixed area. Pastoralists, small-holders, and large-scale, commercial farmers of different ethnicities (some are Kenyan Asians and Europeans) live side by side. These changes in ethnic composition and source of livelihoods indicate the shrinking possibilities for the Maasai to hold onto their land in this area. Their geopolitical position of occupying large tracts of common pasturelands within easy access to the capital, coupled with adjudication of land into private owner-ship, expose the Maasai to severe losses of territory by land sales and purchases (Galaty 2008; Hughes 2006; Monbiot 1994).

Since the mid-1970s I have returned for shorter and longer periods to the first Maasai community. Fieldwork has also been extended, for comparative reasons, to more research sites both in Kenya and also in Tanzania.[1] In retrospect, the repeated visits to Maasai com-munities, in Kenya particularly, during the 1980s have been more of an exercise in gaining "depth, quality and variety" (Foster 1979) than consciously employing a longitudinal perspective on the ma-terial. One reason for this is the diachronic pattern of the returns—after the first, long spell of fieldwork in 1979–1981 I returned almost every year for the next five to six years, for purposeful collection of field material. One visit more or less hooked into the other and, in the written text, this time span was reduced to one "ethnographic present."

Since a few years back, I have been involved in a follow-up study in two of the Kenyan communities researched during the 1980s. One is the very first fieldsite community in 1975; the other is located in what the Maasai themselves, as well as other Kenyans, refer to as the interior. This expression hints at a more traditional way of life—ex-isting in the present, but nevertheless living in the "past." The lat-est longer visit to Kenya (2007–2008) was explicitly formulated as a restudy, with all possible implications of that term, of earlier find-ings and interpretations. The restudy project was called Women at a Loss—25 years later, referring to the title of a book written in the mid-1980s (Talle 1988). As the word implies, a restudy refers to a re-encounter with the field after a certain period of time, where the ab-sence between visits takes on a special methodological, comparative significance for understanding change and continuity. The definition of the latest fieldwork period as a restudy and not just another return made it possible to draw a temporal boundary and make a new be-ginning, which I found both liberating and productive at the time.

My first ethnography on the Maasai was built around changes in pastoral relations of production and reproduction as a consequence of the privatization of land and livestock. The research focused on how women, as mothers and wives, perceived and negotiated these changes in their personal lives: how did Maasai women, in spite of institutional structures and government policies privileging male ownership of land and livestock, struggle to carve out spaces of autonomy and influence? The domestic realm, in particular the matrifilial house (*enkaji*) of the agnatic family, constituted a material and ceremonial focus of production and reproduction and afforded women, as house-managers, a certain degree of decision-making power (Talle 1988).

Recently, substantial changes rooted in historical process have been intensified in Maasai areas in Kenya, notably the extensive sub-division of land into private plots, intensified marketing of labor and products, a high level of school enrollment, and, last but not least, increased conversion to Christianity, particularly among the women. The speed of these changes forming a "temporal geography" in the minds of many Maasai, along a scale of development and modernization versus backwardness and tradition, however, has varied considerably from locality to locality. I will not elaborate here on the dynamics of change and the spatial/temporal conceptualization of modernization processes; instead I will focus on a more general methodological issue relating to the intersection between temporality, observational relevance (what we "see" or do not "see"), and production of anthropological knowledge.

AN ENLIGHTENED MOMENT

Early on in the research of the Maasai, in 1978, I witnessed the circumcision of a young woman. It was an operation that took a somewhat unexpected turn, as the fourteen-year-old girl who was cut refused to tolerate the overwhelming pain to which she was subjected. This episode became a formative moment for my understanding of genital cutting as a social practice, but more importantly, it demonstrated the challenges of a field-oriented methodology where participatory observation and intersubjective relations are important research tools.

In 2006, twenty-eight years later, and then completely by chance, I met with the "girl" again. She was then a middle-aged woman and the third wife of a man with four wives, and was mother to six grown children—one daughter and five sons. For me the time span of almost three decades seemed surprisingly short once the meeting had taken place. The woman, however, felt it differently; the long absence in itself gave a particular meaning to the reencounter, which I shall examine below.

The girl who was to be circumcised that day in May 1978 was an athletic and well-shaped young woman; I noted that she was tall with a strikingly composed physical bearing. As soon as the circumciser began cutting her body and she felt the pain, she began to fight back. The elderly women who performed the operation did not manage to hold her down, in spite of the fact that there were several of them thronging around her.

The girl's elder brother and guardian (her father had passed away) watched the scene from a distance, together with other men. One was her prospective husband. The brother approached the house where the operation was being performed with long and resolute paces (he was tall, like his sister) and shouted at her to stop crying for "nothing." Pain is something the Maasai must learn to tolerate and be proud to endure from an early age (see Pierre Clastres 1982 on cultural valorization of pain). The brother reasoned with the women, telling them that if they could not hold the girl using their own strength, they would have to bind her.

One of the elderly women assisting with the operation ran over to another house and came back with a bundle of leather ropes under the beaded leather gown she was wearing in honor of the day. The women made a loop at the end of each rope and tried to lock these around the ankles of the girl while she, with great force, did her best to kick them off. The struggle continued for a while until the girl got tired and the rope loops were securely fastened around her ankles and her legs were spread out. At last, the circumciser could proceed with her work: with tiny movements she carved away the clitoris and the labia minora.

When the operation finally came to an end, the girl was helped up. The blood still oozed from the cut and trickled down her legs. While standing, she bowed her head and looked down on her naked body with an apprehensive, almost curious look and was obviously relieved that the intervention was over. She said nothing, however.

The family of the girl lived in an area that I did not visit regularly during the field research at that time, and thus I never saw the girl again. She fell out of my research design, since circumcision was not a prime issue of interest in my early research on the Maasai. Hence I made no particular effort to find out what she thought or felt during her ordeal.

Many men and women had gathered in the homestead to celebrate the event. A young boy of appropriate age had also been circumcised that morning in the homestead. From speaking with the visitors it transpired that among the Maasai, circumcision (*emurata*, same term for girl's and boy's circumcision) is a necessary cut in order for a girl or a boy to make the transition from childhood to adulthood (*botor*, growing [socially]), to become gendered beings and thus productive persons in the Maasai community. In the ethno-political context of contemporary East Africa, circumcision continues to be a forceful inscription of community and ethnic belonging, of being a Maasai— body and soul (Talle 2007). Within the context of the Kenyan state, however, female genital cutting, which has been outlawed since 2001, is, in the case of the Maasai, defined as a sign of backwardness. The widespread adherence to such cultural practices, conceptualized as traditional by outsiders, reinforces their position as a marginal group within the modern nation-state.

WRITING AND REFLECTION

A few months after this incident, I wrote a short piece in a Swedish monthly journal targeted at development workers. The title of the article, "We Maasai Have Always Circumcised Our Children," was a quote from a woman from that same homestead where the operation had taken place. Her statement pointed to the significance of keeping up with tradition for Maasai cultural identity. As I was a much younger anthropologist at that time, the topic of female circumcision was relatively new to me as a researcher, and the global debate was still wanting in culturally sensitive information. The year 1978 was a time when female genital cutting (or female genital mutilation, FGM) had just entered the global international discourse as a serious infringement of women's and children's rights and bodily integrity (Boyle 2002). Activists and politicians deemed it vital to contextualize such controversial social practices for noninformed audiences in order to see them successfully abandoned.

Twenty-five years later, in 2003, I revisited the field diaries and my own memory of this incident for an article in the Norwegian anthropological journal (Talle 2003; see also Talle 2007). During that stretch of time I had done field research among Somalis, both in Somalia and in exile settings, and had begun to think more consciously about female genital cutting, not only as a cultural marker and gendering device, but also as a complex bodily and personal experience. Through fieldwork among Somali refugees in London and in Norway, I had learned that experiences of severe physical pain, which Somali women, in general, suffer during the intervention (and after), could be a powerful source of resistance under certain circumstances. While writing this article, which was called "But It *Is* Mutilation": Anthropology and Difficult Issues,[2] for the Norwegian journal, I tried hard to recall the episode of the Maasai girl in order to include it in the text. It was amazing how, two and a half decades later, the event was so vivid in my memory, even the words that had been spoken, the sight of the performance, the sound, not least the girl's heavy breathing (she did not cry, however), and the smell of blood and sweat. I clearly remembered my feelings of despair and anguish; I witnessed "torture," but could do nothing. While writing the article, I experienced the shift between what Geertz calls "experience-near" (insider) and "experience-distant" (outsider) positions (Geertz 1974) as particularly intense and challenging. In my analytical endeavors I had to remember the episode, and subsequent returns to the field were evoked from that memory.

Returns, by way of memory and fieldnotes, are an integral part of the interpretation that we make. The shift in experiential focus—writing versus fieldwork memory, in this case—was likewise a shift in time between now and then, present and past. The ethnographic present in the analysis is necessarily, as Wendy James has aptly formulated "imaginative presence," a reconstruction of passing time with the view from the present (James 2000). The fact that I had done the observations at a much younger age than the analysis adds complexity to the interpretative endeavor. The process of bringing the story into a new (con)text, by evoking memory and reading notes, highlighted the questions that could not be answered.

Writing about an event that occurred twenty-five years earlier necessarily raises new scholarly questions and concerns. One such question was the girl's own version of what she had endured. What did she remember? Why did she fight so desperately? I imagined that her personal account would bring the analysis to a new level of understanding. The reinternalization of the event during this later process of writing and reflection was, in a way, "out of rhythm with time" (Lund 2002) but was nevertheless an "imaginative presence" that, as it turned out, would bring significance to future events.

A LATER MOMENT

The second meeting with the "girl" was in January 2006. Over the years, I had revisited the community several times, but as noted above, the event, although formative for my take on female genital cutting as a social practice, had not been in the forefront of my research questions. On visiting a homestead not very far from where the girl had been operated upon, my field assistant, Simil, and I happened upon another visitor, whose appearance was familiar. He asked Simil whether this was the woman who had attended the circumcision ceremony with the elderly Norwegian professor he had known?[3] Yes, I heard myself quickly reply, now suddenly eager to learn about the whereabouts of the girl. I had narrated the story earlier to my field assistant as an example of fieldwork strains, but without being able to identify the girl or the husband. He himself had not been present at the circumcision. While talking to this other visitor, however, Simil could immediately locate the family of the girl. We were told that the girl's husband was at that very moment watering his animals at the wells of the river, not very far away. Without further delay we hurried to the watering place.

The husband turned out to be a very charming and welcoming man, although later I learned that he severely disciplined his wives and children. We told him our errand and probed details of the incident with him. He agreed that he himself had been present at his wife's circumcision and remembered everything very well when I reminded him. He said that her name was Nankei. That same day, we went home with him. The family lived twelve kilometers away from the wells on very rough roads, a part of which were only just accessible by my small Suzuki.

When I met Nankei I recognized her right away; she still possessed the same bodily poise and composure. I introduced myself and told her why I had come. She herself had no memory of my presence during her ordeal—I had deliberately placed myself in the background of the performance—nor did she question my coming, but laughed instead,[4] and immediately invited us into her house. While writing anthropological texts over the years, it had been difficult to interpret her courage to fight the women who had performed the operation. Was it only an intolerance of pain that had made her struggle so vehemently when she was cut, or did she have other motives for protesting? However, no answer was forthcoming. Her evasive answers indicated that circumcision was not worth remembering, or commenting upon. It was simply an act that had to be done—a doxic matter devoid of discourse, to speak in Pierre Bourdieu's jargon.

This first encounter confirmed for me that it was the excruciating pain that had made her protest against the cutting of her flesh—an impulsive reaction of the body and in no way a conscious resistance against a cultural practice. However, her physical struggling to escape the grip of the women did occur there and then, an effect of bodily agency and intentionality. In order to demonstrate her intolerance of pain, and thereby reducing it to a personality trait, she explained that even when her own daughter was circumcised, many years later, she was lying close by, hiding her face. She said her daughter had been much "braver" than she, which was seconded by her husband sitting next to us. Nankei also explained that of course she had cried when she was cut, because Maasai girls must show that they do not exceed men in bravery (boys are not allowed to flicker an eyelid at their circumcision or they are beaten and labeled cowards, which is a great disgrace for a Maasai). Her daughter, however, had not protested the way she had done, by trying to interfere with the operation itself.[5]

On leaving the homestead I felt that there was not much more to add. At the same time, however, the encounter had developed the relationship between me, the anthropologist, and Nankei into one of friendship and intimacy. In order to seal the friendship, Nankei untied one of the beaded string bracelets she was wearing and gave it to me. Beaded ornaments are cherished gifts (*en-kishoroto*) between female friends, between women and men, and between children on many different occasions.

On parting, Nankei made me feel welcome to come again, but took care to emphasize that next time I had to announce my arrival as she intended to prepare meat for me, the sharing of meat being a prime token of friendship in Maasai traditions. At this first meeting Nankei had efficiently cut the line of communication on the circumcision topic. At the same time, however, she had begun to forge another relationship according to her interpretation of the situation. The act of handing over the bracelet was like a turning point, or "punctuation" (Rudie 1994) in time, closing the past by opening up a new beginning, as I interpreted it. This act may be likened to the "cutting-the-network-argument" of Marilyn Strathern (1996). The gift of the bracelet brought the conversation about the circumcision to a halt, both by summing up the "past"—sharing something of value—and shaping a "future"—a potential friendship.

FURTHER EXPLORATIONS

Between October 2007 and April 2008 I visited Nankei for a second, third, fourth, and fifth time. Remembering that her homestead was located some distance away, I met her regularly on Saturdays at the local market, which she and another of her husband's four wives always visited. When I arrived at her homestead the second time, almost two years after the first reencounter, she was happily surprised to see me. No communication had occurred in the meantime, and there had been no forewarning of the visit. During this second encounter a more relaxed conversation began. With the memory of the last meeting, less than two years earlier, still fresh, this reencounter was part of the new beginning. The first meeting had been rather abrupt and sudden, and I felt it would have been inappropriate to press the point on her circumcision further. Besides, the presence of her husband at that time had made Nankei slightly tongue-tied.

At these later meetings, it was possible to revisit the episode of her circumcision in a new vein. In my view, it was important to try to arrive at some common understanding of her ordeal before the relationship could advance. Furthermore, during other conversations, her memory of the incident was activated and her account became more nuanced and detailed. For instance, one explanation she gave for the long struggle with the women who circumcised her was that she was young and strong compared to them; "They could not overcome me," she said, and smiled triumphantly. I asked what she had felt like when they had bound her. She had realized that they could not overcome her without using the rope, as she had seen happen to other girls, but they took my "strength" (agol), she added. "I was pacified and had to let go." Part of the story was that a man had entered the scene, assisting the women to hold one of the ropes that were locked around her ankles (Talle 2007).[6] When the operation was over, and she stood up, she was relieved, but she also felt proud of having come of age. The women around her declared: "Stand up! You are one of us now!" The "opening up" of her body by paring away obtrusive/"dirty" body parts transformed her into a grown-up and gendered person, who thereafter could act in that capacity (Talle 2007). Roughly three months afterward she would be a married woman and ready to give birth to children. In an age-based, hierarchical social structure such as that of the Maasai, social maturity is highly valued and yearned for by juniors within the system (Spencer 1988).

At one instance I asked Nankei how painful the operation had been, whereupon her face tightened and she responded "very" (*oleng*). On probing further about whether circumcision or delivery was most painful, she hesitated a tiny moment and replied *emurata*—circumcision. Nankei's admission that circumcision pain was a matter to contemplate could permit questions and reflection to arise. During our conversations, she seemed to show an ambivalent attitude toward the benefits of circumcision, but it is hard to say whether this was related to her own painful experiences and her feeling of triumph at nearly overcoming the women, or whether it had come from the information and knowledge she was exposed to by participating in wider fields of interaction, such as the church or the marketplace, or from the fact that I was present. My internalization of Nankei as a "fighting woman" while reflecting and writing was very much the lens through which I had seen her initially and may have affected how I interpreted her words at our first reencounter.

A MOMENTOUS AWAKENING

Shortly before my second reencounter with Nankei in October 2007, she had become a devoted churchgoer. She belongs to a branch of the African Inland Church (a Protestant church), one of the first missionary churches among the Maasai in this part of Kenya. As the family lives too far away to regularly attend the centrally located churches, they have built their own "church" underneath a shady acacia tree next to their family homestead. The homestead consists of the husband, his four wives, and six married sons and their wives and children. There are seventeen adults and fifty-five children residing together in one extended family homestead (*enkang*). All the ten married women have become churchgoers, just like many other Maasai women in the same locality and in other areas of Maasailand (for Tanzania, see Hodgson 2005). Nankei's eldest son, Silas, who is a class eight leaver, functions as the church evangelist. Sometimes he is assisted by his half-brother, a secondary school student, when he is home on leave.

Why this sudden conversion? Two years earlier there were few signs of Christian identity in the homestead. Nankei explained that the women and the adult sons, some of whom converted to Christianity while in school, and the family had come together to discuss how they should handle the problems they faced due to the husband's excessive drinking and squandering of livestock property on alcohol and other women. They had decided to make a concerted effort, to pray to *Enkai* (God) together, as Maasai women always did when things went wrong. According to Nankei, the praying had worked; her husband's misbehavior had improved. In their view, the conversion to Christianity helped them solve a problem within the family. The alliance between adolescent sons and mothers against the father/husband is a potent source of power, and even more so when performed through spiritual sayings and praying.

Among the Maasai, women pray daily as well as at larger ceremonies, and the living proof of the efficacy of their prayers are the children they give birth to—their most valuable treasure. A woman who has recently given birth is in fact referred to as *entomononi* (literally, the one who has prayed, from *omon*, to pray). Women have great confidence in the transformative power (Arens and Karp 1989) of their collective praying; it stops misbehavior and redirects actions. When fertility in people and livestock was intermittently claimed to recede, women staged fertility-blessing ceremonies (*olamal*), which toured their communities for days and gathered hundreds of women and sacrificial animals in an enormous collective effort (Llewellyn-Davis 1985; Talle 1988, 1998; Wagner-Glenn 1994).

Christianity had begun to influence Nankei's life in many ways. During the conversation it also appeared that her position on female circumcision was wavering. She thought it sinful to cut into human flesh and vaguely expressed a wish that the practice would stop. However, she also admitted that she had little say in these matters within the family—her husband was the one to decide about their children. He would not allow a daughter of his to remain uncircumcised. (Her Christian son saw no wrong in the circumcision of girls, when I asked him.) When listening to the ambivalence Nankei expressed toward this practice, I could discern her earlier resistance. By opposing the pain of circumcision thirty years earlier, when she was still very young, she demanded attention in an indirect protest against cultural (patriarchal) hegemony. Certainly she had little tolerance toward physical pain, but nonetheless, her struggle had had an impact beyond her physical self. Among other things, her protests had delayed the livestock from leaving the homestead so they missed grazing time in the pastures; her brother had been forced to intervene in the event; it had also disturbed the women in their work. She had probably also shamed her family a little by her unruly behavior. Her reaction to the pain had created "chaos," which did not pass unnoticed by her and others present. One very peculiar effect of her active protests that day had been that the visitor from far away had come back to look for her. The reencounter with me made Nankei reflect on the original event in light of her status as a Christian.

At the initial contact with Nankei, I made an effort to be honest and openly declare my motives for coming. There was no other way. As far as I was concerned, I had plausible reasons for getting into contact. I was initially driven by professional motivations, but also by a strong desire to somehow make up for my withdrawn position and for not offering any support during the circumcision. Immediately after the operation I had been thinking of her and wanted to go back to offer my sympathy.[7] The return after many years had been to rectify a fieldwork "failure," yet Nankei herself, I learned later, saw things in another way.

At one of the later meetings, I asked Nankei what she thought about the anthropologist, who, from her perspective, was a person who had suddenly appeared in her home without forewarning with a rather unusual kind of mission that awakened painful memories in her. For Nankei, however, that was completely in order and indeed highly comprehensible. Not only did she elaborate, to my surprise, on the beauty and goodness of the friendship across racial boundaries, and how she found this relationship both natural and mutually beneficial, but she also offered a very specific reason for the return visit for which I was quite unprepared. She said, "I prayed and prayed to God, and I prayed for help, and then you came along to become my 'helper' . . . you are my angel [*olmalaika*] now." Her prayer had been answered. My return to seek her out was not interpreted primarily as an effect of an earlier encounter, but rather of the fact that she now was a practicing Christian woman.

Nankei's understanding of our relationship and of my return was dramatically different from my own understanding. The search for Nankei had first been part of pursuing a more specific goal, through that of documenting her story of a past event in order to rethink connections and widen the analytical context for representing this difficult cultural reality. The scholarly interest in female circumcision had brought Nankei and her experience into focus in a more conscious way than before (Lund 2002). My first reencounter with her, however, was not something I had planned; it evolved more or less haphazardly from the fieldwork setting. Neither was I anticipating a relationship with her beyond this first reencounter. For Nankei, however, my return was part of something much larger: she was "just sitting like that" and I appeared. She said the sudden return was like a "blessing" (*amuyak*). Maasai say things that come abruptly, as an unexpected shock, and that can help, are a blessing; but misfortune and afflictions—the opposite of a blessing—may also materialize suddenly, without forewarning. Nankei interpreted the relationship as something very "big" (*sapuk, kitok*), as if the visitor's return was a gift (*enkishoroto*, from *aisho*, to give) from the Lord—a wonder (*a-ing'asia*). She interpreted the return visit in order to find her as a kind of divine manifestation. Of importance here is the fact that I am a white woman—a wealthy woman, in her eyes—who can actually help her situation. Nankei and her family would probably not read a penniless Maasai woman returning after a long period of time as a blessing in the same way. The fact that I potentially could help is of significance.

On the point of leaving the field in Kenya for the last time, I asked my field assistant whether it was appropriate to give Nankei the gift of corrugated iron sheets for her new house for which she had asked. They were moving to a homestead some hundred meters farther away. I thought it was a relatively big gift and sought his advice. The assistant explained that Nankei had asked for this gift because she saw me as a great friend (*ol-core*). He explained his point by referring to the greatness (*en-kitoo*) of a reunion after a long absence and emphasized that her request must be appreciated in that larger cultural context of sudden interconnections and friendship formation. Even though Nankei and I did not know each other in person when we first met face to face, our paths had nevertheless crossed earlier, at important events in our lives. Our commonality was founded on a shared past. My unexpected reappearance after a long period of time seemed to add, in Nankei's view, a particular value to our friendship. Her faith had materialized, and the absence in itself, the time distance between the two encounters, provoked a particular significance to the return, for which I myself had not been prepared. For while I was preoccupied with the "past"—to recreate a series of events through memory—in our first reencounters Nankei seemed to be more concerned about the present and the time coming. She was, as I perceived it, forging and anticipating a new friendship relation. This is also how I in fact have gradually come to look upon our relationship.

Last time I met Nankei was in March 2009. It was on a Sunday, and as Simil and I arrived at the homestead, the women were just about to leave for church. Without further ado and with great confidence, Nankei took my hand and said, "Let us go." She showed the way by walking in front while seven of us trod through the scrub for about a mile before reaching the fenced-in space under the tree, which served as the church. Her eldest son conducted the service for a congregation that included only people from their homestead.

Author with Agnes, her informant over many years, 2007.

During our latest few encounters we did not discuss the circumcision event, chiefly because I have not raised it. Nankei herself would not dwell upon past events in conversation.

* * *

One particular merit of long-term fieldwork is that it enables the researcher to follow the parallel passing of time in the lives of others and her own. What becomes clear in this case study is what Wendy James and David Mills (2005) refer to as significant timing; how a time frame gives social worth and meaning to actions and events. In other words, the way we define and experience time is not value-free; time is concretely constituted. My search for Nankei's memory of a traumatic event in her past life, buried in layers of cultural oblivion, coincided in time with her newfound status as a Christian convert. The memory of the original event many years later was also for

Nankei be interpreted in a new frame of a Christian consciousness. The master narrative of the revival church to which she belongs is one of sudden change and rupture, with a better life—socially and materially—in sight. If people adamantly pray hard and praise God, as the stories of the priests and evangelists tell, they will be heard— and answered. The charismatic churches in Kenya, as elsewhere in the region, are centers not only of spirituality but also of material promises. The unexpected appearance of a potential friend of European origin made great sense to Nankei not least within her life trajectory as a newly converted Christian. My (re)appearance just as she had become a Christian was indeed a fortunate coincidence.

While multiple returns to the field allow the anthropologist to gain valuable insight into cultural processes over time, it is also a risky project that poses specific challenges and carries considerable responsibility. I could not have foreseen Nankei's reactions to my search for a difficult moment in her life at the time of searching. In hindsight, however, I understand that my venture was more risky than I first realized. The scholarly project of the anthropologist, of which "returns" make a sensible part, and the life project of informants, which entails other concerns, are closely entangled and intertwined— they impact each other deeply and unpredictably. As others are drawn into our projects, we also inevitably become part of their lives. This interface between their concerns and ours opens up a fertile space for the production of anthropological knowledge, and over time, through repeated returns, in my experience, this space is likely to widen.

NOTES

1. The longest fieldwork in Kenya was a two-year period from 1979 to 1981 when I was involved with a Swedish-funded vaccination program against foot-and-mouth disease in Maasai herds. During the early 1990s (1991–1994) AIDS research was done in several Maasai communities in northern Tanzania.

2. The quote is from a Somali female informant in London, who had become a strong opponent of the practice after she fled Somalia. She wanted to emphasize that the cut is indeed mutilation.

3. My teacher and professor at the University of Oslo did field research in this community at the time, and I had been visiting him for a few days. We had both been invited to the circumcision ceremony.

4. This was a typical reaction from Maasais when they learned about my motive for finding the woman. I also met the elder brother and her mother again, who, likewise, found the purpose of my visit rather peculiar. The brother remembered my presence, but had not given it any thought till I reminded him. Although I had experienced him as a very harsh person at the critical moment when the decision to bind the girl had been made, he now showed an openness and understanding to the recent banning of circumcision of girls by the Kenyan government. If the government said so, he would be ready to reconsider the practice. His mother and his wife, on the other hand, would under no circumstances abandon the practice. If they had to, they would continue to do it clandestinely. Without circumcision, they claimed, Maasai would lose their cultural distinction.

5. There are stories of Maasai girls who are so scared that they run away when they realize that their time to be cut has come (some manage also to free themselves from the grip of the women and flee). Individual parents may leave their daughters uncut in anticipation of a later chance. When these uncircumcised women (I learned of four, in one community) give birth, those helping with the delivery, get angry when they see the uncut vulva and circumcise them on the spot.

6. From conversations with other informants, I learned that in the case of recalcitrant girls, it is not uncommon that men help the women to hold the ropes. In one case a girl broke her leg during this ordeal.

7. The circumcision of Nankei occurred early in my fieldwork with the Maasai. Since that incident, however, I have tried to avoid direct contact with these operations by participation. I have, however, listened to numerous circumcision stories.

REFERENCES

Anderson, David M., and Vigdis Broch-Due. 1999. *The Poor Are Not Us: Poverty and Pastoralism in Eastern Africa*. London: James Currey.

Arens, William, and Ivan Karp, eds. 1989. Introduction. In *The Creativity of Power: Cosmology and Action in African Society*, xi–xxix. Washingon, D.C.: Smithsonian Institution Press.

Boyle, Elizabeth Heger. 2002. *Female Genital Cutting: Cultural Conflict in the Global Community*. Baltimore: The Johns Hopkins University Press.

Bruner, Edward M. 2004. *Culture on Tour: Ethnographies of Travel.* Chicago: University of Chicago Press.

Clastres, Pierre. 1982. *Samfunnet mot staten (La Société contre l'État)* [Society Against the State]. Oslo: Dreyers Forlag, Perspektivprosjektet.

Coast, Ernestine. 2000. *Maasai Demography.* PhD diss., University College of London.

Foster, George M., Thayer Scudder, Elizabeth Colson, and Robert V. Kempert, eds. 1979. Introduction. In *Long-term Field Research in Social Anthropology,* 1–13. New York: Academic Press.

Galaty, John. 2008. Revisiting Pastoralism and Marketing in East Africa. *African Studies Review* 51 (1): 131–134.

Geertz, Clifford. 1974. "From the Native's Point of View": On the Nature of Anthropological Understanding. In Richard A. Shweder and Robert A. Levine, eds. Culture Theory: Essays on Mind, Self, and Emotion, 123–136. Cambridge: Cambridge University Press.

Hodgson, Dorothy L. 2005. *The Church of Women: Gendered Encounters between Maasai and Missionaries.* Bloomington: Indiana University Press.

Hughes, Lotte. 2006. *Moving the Maasai: A Colonial Misadventure.* Basingstoke: Palgrave Macmillan.

International Work Group for Indigenous Affairs. 2008. *IWGIA Yearbook 2008.* www.iwgia.dk.

James, Wendy. 2000. Beyond the First Encounter: Transformations of "the Field" in North East Africa. In Paul Dresch, Wendy James, and David Parkin, eds., *Anthropologists in a Wider World,* 69–90. New York and Oxford: Berghahn Books.

James, Wendy, and David Mills. 2005. Introduction. In Wendy James and David Mills, eds., *The Qualities of Time,* 1–15. Oxford: Berg.

Lane, Charles. 1996. *Pastures Lost.* London: International Institute for Environment and Development.

Llewellyn-Davies, Melissa, director. 1985. The Women's Olamal—The Origin of Masai Fertility Ceremony (1985). Films Incorporated.

Lund, Sarah. 2002. Å Bestige Andesfjellene: fem og tjue års klatring mot en "opplyst" utsikt [Ascending the Andes: Twenty-five years of climbing toward an "enlightened" viewpoint]. *Norsk Antropologisk Tidsskrift* 13 (4): 228–234.

May, Ann, and Terence McCabe. 2004. City Work in a Time of AIDS: Maasai Labor Migration in Tanzania. *Africa Today* 51 (2): 3–32.

Monbiot, George. 1994. *No Man's Land: An Investigative Journey through Kenya and Tanzania.* London: Macmillan.

Rudie, Ingrid. 1994. *Visible Women in East Coast Malay Society: On the Reproduction of Gender in Ceremonial, School and Market.* Oslo: Universitetesforlaget.

Spear, Thomas. 1993. Introduction. In Thomas Spear and Richard Waller, eds., *Being Maasai: Ethnicity and Identity in East Africa*. London: James Currey.

Spencer, Paul. 1988. *The Maasai of Matapato: a Study of Rituals of Rebellion*. London: Manchester University Press for the International African Institute.

Strathern, Marilyn. 1996. Cutting the Network. *Journal of the Royal Anthropological Institute* 2 (3): 517–535.

Talle, Aud. 1974. *Barabaig: økonomiske dilemmaer i kombinasjon av budskapshald og jordbruk*. MPhil thesis, Hovedoppgave, University of Oslo.

———. 1988. *Women at a Loss: Changes in Maasai Pastoralism and Their Effects on Gender Relations*. Stockholm Studies in Social Anthropology 19, University of Stockholm.

———. 1998. Sex for Leisure: Modernity among Female Bar Workers in Tanzania. In Simone Abram and Jackie Waldren, eds., *Anthropological Perspectives on Development: Interests, Identities and Sentiments in Conflict*. London: Routledge.

———. 1999. Pastoralists at the Border: Maasai Poverty and the Development Discourse in Tanzania. In Anderson and Broch-Due, eds., *The Poor Are Not Us*, 106–124.

———. 2001. "But It *Is* Mutilation…": Antropologi og vanskelig temaer. *Norsk Antropologisk Tidsskrift* (1–2): 25–43.

———. 2007. Female Circumcision in Africa and Beyond: The Anthropology of a Difficult Issue. In Ylva Hernlund and Bettina Shell-Duncan, eds., *Transcultural Bodies: Female Genital Cutting in Global Context*, 91–106. New Brunswick: Rutgers University Press.

Wagner-Glenn, Doris. 1994. *Searching for a Baby's Calabash: A Study of Arusha Maasai Fertility Songs as Crystallized Expression of Central Cultural Values*. Frankfurt: Philipp Verlag.

4 | Contingency, Collaboration, and the Unimagined over Thirty-five Years of Ethnography

DAVID HOLMBERG

Social anthropology has become more and more decentered as practitioners create specialized networks focused on distinct problems in different "fields" working from diverse theoretical and antitheoretical vantages in differing national and institutional contexts.[1] In this inchoate world of knowledge production, I regularly hear or read "ethnography" invoked as an integrative theme for the discipline. This return of attention to "ethnography" is striking if for no other reason than much of the 1980s and 1990s were framed in a critique of ethnographic practice and production as inherently literary, residually colonial, naively authoritative, and potentially exploitative, a kind of bad, unreflexive literature. These critiques figured ethnography less as method than as *writing*, whether it be fieldnotes (Sanjek 1990) or monographs—as a literature to be deconstructed (Geertz 1988).

Much of the critique of ethnography that emerged in the 1980s both within the discipline and without—salutatory though it may have been in accentuating a reflexivity that has always been with the discipline—put anthropologists on the defensive (Comaroff and Comaroff 1991, 15–16; Ortner 1995) and by definition, as a kind of deconstruction, put to the side the question of whether ethnography produced anything positive even when it made reflexivity part of the project. Indeed, the focus in much of the critique was oriented toward ethnographic practice and representations that were in many quarters passé, if they existed at all in quite the form they were critically reconstructed, at the time the critiques were being written. If anthropology had ever been as naïve as it was made out to be, it no longer was.

What was and is overwhelmed in privileging this particular form of a reflexive critique of ethnography, especially by those outside the discipline but also by some within, is that ethnography remains, at least among the human sciences, a distinctive form of knowledge production irreducible to the characterizations embedded in classificatory schemes that distinguish "soft" from "hard" social science and, as others in this volume have noted, "qualitative" from "quantitative" methods or, in the critiques alluded to above, "literary" over "empirical."

CONTINGENCY

The distinctiveness of ethnography as method relates at least in part to the conscious allowance of the unimagined and the unanticipated to become primary data in the process of knowledge production. The ethnographic research process is by definition open to things that are unknown. The prestructuring constraints inherent to nonobservational social scientific methodologies tend to preclude discovery, except as an artifact of data already prestructured in its production. Of course, ethnography too has its multiple forms of prestructurings. Nevertheless, one could argue that ethnographic research—in its very prestructuring to allow for the unexpected and unimagined—is more radically empirical than other approaches. By the time I began my ethnographic work in the mid-1970s, it was—if it had not been already at the beginnings of systematic field research—a truism in anthropology that you did not study so much what you proposed as what you found. The lore of the discipline is rife with tales of the abandonment of research proposals for the engagement with what was "happening" at a particular time and place. Openness produces results that are unimagined whether ethnography is conducted at the margins or in the metropole, but one hardly needs to make this point to anthropologists. These discoveries unfold in the everyday flow of life as well as in its effervescent moments. Thus ethnography is *contingent* on what is happening, the human events that present themselves to us as we, in the classic rendition of ethnography, observe and participate.

Here are a few examples of how the unimagined and unexpected played a role in my initial research. I remember my surprise and my frustration, when falling asleep on one of my early months of residing in a small Tamang village in the mid-hills of Nepal, to hear the beats of shamans' drums at the start of an all-night shamanic sounding. My original research proposal did not directly include shamans. I subsequently dragged myself out of slumber to attend, fixated like other villagers, on the performance as it continued all the way through the night. It was here that I first heard the myth of a spirit being called *tsen* as the shaman sang it to the drum's cadence while dancing in full regalia on one foot. The same myth became focal in my later analyses of Tamang social organization, gender relations, and ritual (Holmberg 1983, 1989). I also remember the slow movement of a man's lover, down from herding shed to herding shed to the upper part of the village, and finally into his house to become a second wife, when the man's family opposed the union and had gone to great lengths, including getting his sister to become a ritual sister with the woman in question to make the union technically incestuous. It was in such contexts that my understanding of how affect played along with the formal exchanges of bilateral cross-cousin marriage became enriched. In other contexts, I would be hauled along with the headman hither and yon to resolve disputes, to administer punishments, or to drink copious amounts of local spirits, eat spicy meat, and converse and laugh into the night, learning all sorts of things about local history and politics. I went on forays with young men (who were then more or less young like me) to dance and sing into the night at revelries on promontories high in the moonlit Himalayas. It is these contexts, as well as more focused conversations, directed interviews, recordings, transcriptions, translations, life histories, participations, observations, and sufferings, that are the classic stuff of extended fieldwork. My investigations, like most ethnography, are contingent on witnessing the reality of Tamang social and ritual life in practice.

Two other senses of the term *contingent* were fundamental in my ethnographic research. My field research was elementally contingent on the social relations I developed over the three decades of my research. In social relations and the interactions that ensue, ethnographers, as often as not, are *not* the ones who control interactions. The knowledge we get is contingent and coproduced. Ethnographers are not just in a dialogical or discursive engagement with interlocutors (Dwyer 1982; Tedlock 1983) but also and always embedded in both macro and micro social relations, which defy a reduction to a simple equation of a powerful ethnographer operationalizing a research project focused on research subjects. In other words, the critical fiction that ethnographers control the interactive research situation does not do justice to the multiple factors at play in the outcome of ethnographic research where "the observed" are as much in control as the "observer." In the ethnographic situations in which I have found myself, I have rarely felt in control of the encounters; in most instances my interlocutors have had as much control as I, and in light of the ethos of Tamang social life, they were if anything framed in an ideal of reciprocity. I was also regularly caught in situations where I found myself powerless.[2]

As I will relate below, I was brought into relations with particular people in particular social positions in a very particular place, a fact that not only shaped both my access to the world of the Tamang and thus my research, but enhanced it in ways that became more prominent decade by decade during my research. As we will see below, the very particular relations I made at the outset of my research were *contingent* in yet another sense: they were serendipitous or fortuitous; I happened to be in a particular place at a particular time. Fortuitous encounters and events continue to unfold for me as a researcher and began from the moment when I went to work in a Tamang community. If I had not met Suryaman Tamang, my long-

Author with Iron Lama, 1976.

term research associate, in a chance meeting on a bus, I would have ended up in a different place, probably witnessing many different things. I have maintained close relations with Suryaman from that chance meeting in 1975 to the present, a relation that extends out to all his kin (including his daughter who, as I write this chapter, is living with us in the United States, helping to organize three decades of research materials and make them more accessible to the village and to the greater Tamang community).

CONTINGENCIES OVER TIME

In this review of my own research with western Tamang over the last thirty-five years, I will highlight all three of these senses of contingency: 1) the contingency of being present as life unfolds and coming to know the unexpected and unanticipated; 2) the contingency of specific social relations with particular people over time; and 3) the contingencies of chance. I will try to show how these contingencies developed into particular collaborations at a set of inter-graded levels in both academic and other domains, which opened up new vistas both for my ethnographic research and for the Tamang themselves.

The key values of multitemporal field research reside in the fact that it is an amplification and expansion on the same values of ethnography conducted over a year or two, opening up wider and deeper understandings; moreover, the multitemporal, as I will note in conclusion, often leads to the "multisited," invoked now as a standard mode of research. If I had returned from Nepal to my university in 1977, written my dissertation, published articles and a monograph, and turned attention in other directions of professional development (perhaps reflecting on ethnographic fieldwork!), and had suspended research contacts with my friends/relations in the village and elsewhere, my knowledge of the Tamang and their history in Nepal would have been limited absolutely by that time frame. My initial research on ritual and social organization among Tamang took place from 1975 to 1977 in the canonical frame of anthropological practice: extended residence in a comparatively remote village among a population that had not had much anthropological attention. Communications out while I was resident and back when I had left were limited to short letters, usually hand carried back to the United States by friends or colleagues. I returned for a few months in 1982 and then for seven months in 1986–1987. Beginning in 1990, I made almost annual trips to Nepal for at least a few weeks usually spending many days or weeks in the villages I knew best. In 1993–1994 I resided in Nepal for the year, undertaking a new ethnohistorical project on forced labor that took me and Kathryn March around to multiple villages in the region surrounding the community in which I had lived longest, a project that continued for another five months in 1997–1998. Annual short trips of a month or so continued through until 2005, when I spent eight months in Nepal.

By 2001 a Maoist (Communist Party of Nepal—Maoist) insurgency had expanded to most districts in Nepal, and it was not until 2006 that a Comprehensive Peace Agreement was signed, ending a very difficult period for villagers in the mountains. During the most intense periods of the insurgency, my closest associates in the villages were terrorized by both the Royal Nepal Army and the Maoists, between whom they were caught. I worked on chronicling the effect of state violence and Maoist violence on villagers. I was able to make annual trips to Nepal, but for only one day at a time in the village; sustained stays would put friends in jeopardy for associating with an American. Nevertheless the burgeoning community of migrants to Kathmandu meant in social terms that the villages were very much in the city. I returned in the spring of 2008 to witness elections for a Constituent Assembly that was being formed to write a new constitution. I was back to Nepal briefly in the fall of 2008 and again to conduct research on the rise of a new political ritual called *Lhochhar* in the spring of 2009. I was in the village community most recently in December and January of 2009–2010. My involvements over thirty-five years include eleven or twelve dedicated research trips in both village and city, ranging in length from a month or two to a year or two, and many other shorter trips that kept me in contact with my Tamang associates in both city and village. Village friends over the last few years have acquired wireless phones, and we keep up with each other through regular calls. The old closures of departure from the field have been overtaken in the potential of regular but incomplete communication.

If long-term field research accomplishes nothing else, it enforces a transformational perspective on ethnographic reconstruction, a kind of historical perspective, if you will, not of the *longue durée* but of the short. The histories at play in my case are at a minimum the changes in the lives of the Tamang people whom I know best, changes in my relationship with the people, modifications in my own anthropological perspectives, transformations in the discipline in the United States and in Nepal, and finally changes in communication and transportation. I am able to engage only a few of these dimensions here.

I will frame these changes in the context of political and cultural transformations that have brought the Tamang, formerly enclosed and isolated in a feudal state, to a dynamic presence in what is now called the "new" Nepal, a Nepal that has had to take the Tamang and groups like them seriously. This transformation has been accompanied by an explosion of ethnological and historical work being produced by Tamang scholars working in tandem with Tamang political activists. We have been fortunate to have been working in Nepal during this period; the collaborations and associations that we have been a part of over the last thirty-five years are intimately bound up in these evolvements. It has been through close relationships with particular people that we have been allowed access to dimensions of Tamang life that would have otherwise been unknown.

FROM THE MARGINS TO THE METROPOLE:
TWO HEADMEN THROUGH TIME

The most dramatic transformation for the Tamang over the three decades I have worked with them has been a movement from the margins and from the position of a denigrated, rustic minority to a vibrant, "indigenous" or "ethnic" presence in a polity that is haltingly becoming multicultural.[3] I will trace these changes out through my embedded relationships with two Tamang headmen whose lives mark the transformation from the feudal past to a dynamic present. The first, Iron Lama, became prominent at the demise of the old feudal regime in Nepal in 1950 and emerged as an important, if not the most important, Tamang leader in the region surrounding his home village through the 1960s and into the 1970s. He had even been designated by the ruling Congress party in the late 1950s in a brief experiment with democracy as "Block Development Officer" for a region comprising an area that encompasses three contemporary districts to the northwest of the Kathmandu valley. It was unheard of before this time for someone from the Tamang community to hold such a position. He had been to jail seven times over his political career, for terms ranging from several months to over a year, for organizing against the feudal system of forced labor and exploitation. He was removed from politics in the late 1970s in a purge of populist leaders by the royal regime and withdrew from politics. He died in early January of 2010 while I was staying with him. Since his withdrawal from active politics in the late 1970s, his nephew (younger brother's son) has emerged as a regional political leader. Bahadur Singh Lama Tamang rose to political prominence over a decade ago due in part to the fact that he was able to establish himself as a prominent construction contractor in the Kathmandu valley.

Through a series of fortuitous encounters, Iron Lama became, in the fictive kin system of village life that encompasses all outsiders, my village "father" and local patron. After a long illness in the fall of 1975, I was anxious to locate a place for research. I jumped on a bus up to the Tamang region to the northwest of the Kathmandu valley to explore possible fieldsites. While on the bus I struck up a conversation with a young man, Suryaman Tamang, who turned out to be one of the most educated young men in that region, having attended high school in the district center through the eighth of the ten years of secondary school in Nepal. He turned out to be the most educated Tamang in a large array of villages in the northern part of his district. He invited me to his village, where he introduced me to his father, Iron Lama. Suryaman Tamang became my research assistant (and "younger brother"), and he and I have worked together ever since. I lived first in their house and then in their compound, and when we return to the village we always stay there. For better or for worse, they both gave me entrée into the Tamang village world. Our close personal relations with this family and their most immediate kin mediated most relations I had in the village and region and my knowledge of the community and of Tamang culture, especially in my early research. Tamang village society and Tamang kinship were largely coextensive, and the fact that I was figured as a "son" and an "older brother" of these two, with Iron Lama being a powerful man, constrained all social relations I had.[4] In certain respects, they provided the lens through which I was introduced to the cultural and political realities of Tamang life in greater Nepal.

My departure at the end of my first extended research from 1975 to 1977 captures the climate that prevailed in Nepal and demonstrates, moreover, the impact of particular relations I had with Iron Lama and his son Suryaman Tamang, a major contingency, if you will, in my research. I was on my final return to their village of Mhanegang from Kathmandu, where I had gone to renew my visa and permits for the final weeks of a twenty-month residence. I was walking up to the village for the last time, with washes of premonitory nostalgia as I looked over the countryside, remembering the brilliant starlit walks through the high Himalayas with friends as we trooped from village to village for various social rites. On my way up the last steep four-hundred-meter incline to the village proper, I encountered my partner, Kathryn March—who had joined me to conduct research for the preceding nine months—descending along with two state policemen, policemen rarely encountered in villages. The new Chief District Officer (CDO) had sent the policemen to escort us down to be questioned at headquarters, even though one or both of us had been living in the village for over the previous nineteen months and we were the guests of the most influential political leader among the Tamang in that region. They asked what we had been doing in the village, about our reasons for being in the village, and a host of questions, which we tried our best to answer not knowing the motivation for this new surveillance. A day or so after that two secret policemen from what was then called the Home and Panchayat Ministry (which oversaw internal security and civil administration) arrived in the village and subjected us politely to similar queries and interviewed prominent villagers.

The following day a low-level policeman arrived bearing a letter from the CDO. The messenger said the letter he brought instructed us to vacate the village and the district within twenty-four hours. We asked if we could read the letter, and he said that we could not because it was "top secret." We then asked if he would read it to us; he replied that he could not read. After tea and polite chitchat we persisted and cajoled him into handing us the letter, which indeed had TOP SECRET stamped on the top and was an order for us to be removed from the village and the district. We then made our way to the District Center, a five-hour walk, to speak to the CDO, who after hearing our pleas extended our deadline for departure to three days. The only explanation he offered was that he was under instruction from the ministry and our removal was "for our own safety," which struck us as odd because we had lived comfortably and without any threat for the entire time we had been there. We had been planning to depart in a few weeks, and although we had loose ends to tie up, this sudden turn of events was not the calamity for our research that it would have been if the order had come several months earlier. We hurriedly packed up, distributed gifts, accepted invitation after invitation, received unsolicited mantras—powerful and secret—from shamans to attack our enemies from across the oceans, made a last few interviews, and left for a little-used access road to a dam where a Nepali friend of ours from Kathmandu met us with a Land Rover. We were accompanied by dozens of villagers beating drums and forming a procession which, after we rode away, marched to the District Center for a demonstration denouncing our removal and the representation of the village as a "village of thieves." We were told several people were beaten for their involvement in accusations against us. We returned to Kathmandu and left Nepal several weeks later. According to acquaintances in the US Embassy, the Home and Panchayat Ministry kept making inquiries about our whereabouts for months after our departure.

We came to know from headmen in the village that the Home and Panchayat Ministry and the CDO removed us because political enemies of our patron in the village, Iron Lama, had submitted formal complaints charging Iron Lama with "stabling foreigners, slaughtering a cow, and feasting them." Apparently, due to the fact that translators/missionaries from the Summer Institute of Linguistics had resided a few years before in a not-too-distant village, the accusations, formal or informal, hinted vaguely that we might be involved in Christian proselytizing at a time just after SIL (which among other things worked on translating the Bible into indigenous languages) had been expelled from Nepal in 1976. The accusation of cow slaughter was especially inflammatory, because to kill a cow at that time in the Hindu state of Nepal was a capital crime and aroused intense ire among Nepal's dominant Hindu populations. Cow slaughter had been banned since the formation of Nepal in the late eighteenth century CE, but Tamang continued to eat the meat of deceased cattle. Iron Lama's enemies in the district had lodged the complaints in a campaign to destroy his political credibility. Ironically, Iron Lama was one of the only people in the village at the time who would not eat beef from naturally deceased cows and who carefully performed rituals for the well-being of cattle, due to his extensive political interactions with high caste Hindu Brahmans and Chhetris, who monopolized the administration and politics in both the district and the center. He had been jailed earlier in his life on false charges for crimes against cows and anti-monarchical speeches.

Tamang, as an ethnic group, had been stigmatized as carrion-eating Buddhists who did not respect Brahmans from the moment the Nepali state consolidated under an essentializing Hindu ideology that incorporated the Tamang as a lower form of humanity, marking them as alcohol drinkers, beef eaters, and potential slaves. Protection of cows remains a rallying cry for Hindus, and violence against cows inspires angst and rage among devout Hindus in Nepal and elsewhere. The symbology of cows in the state of Nepal still plays strongly in the formation of identities (Holmberg 2006). Iron Lama's high-caste rivals in the district had successfully removed him from eligibility in local elections, and they were attempting to destroy him finally through formal charges and inflammatory rumors. Even though Iron Lama had sworn off beef decades before, his wife, my village "mother," had no such qualms. During the *lham chhang* (trail beer)—the departure food and drink offered to those who are leaving for an extended period—she asked us if we would like *lakshmi sag* (Nepali; the greens of the Hindu goddess Lakshmi, closely associated with cows), an ironic Tamang euphemism for beef. She then proceeded to feed us smoked beef and local spirits for our farewell.

If Iron Lama's life reflects the old order and a symbolic violence that kept him and his fellow Tamang at the margins, his younger brother's son (and by extension "my younger brother") Bahadur Lama Tamang represents a new and dynamic era. A decade after Iron Lama retired from politics, the first Nepali People's Movement introduced a new democratic system under a constitutional monarch, and the first national-level elections in over thirty years were held in 1991.[5] I first came to know Bahadur when he was a boy. At the request of villagers, I would regularly hold English classes for the children in the neighborhood where I lived during my first fieldstay, and Bahadur would always come to class. Bahadur's family—closely related to Iron Lama—lived in a house right next door, in a neighborhood composed of members of the economically dominant clan in the village, and was one of those students. As a young man, after completing his studies Bahadur Lama Tamang had gone into the contracting business and lived in Kathmandu. He began as a labor contractor for large construction companies in Kathmandu, locating and hiring "coolie" labor for various projects, mostly roads. While he was a labor contractor, he was occasionally given small subcontracts to build side roads or access roads, and from there he broke his way into the construction business in Kathmandu and beyond. His company holds one of the highest classifications among all contractors in Nepal and is eligible to work on the largest projects. He has a reputation of being able to complete projects that other contractors do not dare touch due to their difficulty and complexity. He has risen to become the treasurer of the national association of contractors in Nepal. Beginning in the late 1990s he increased his political activity, becoming the elected representative of the village and active in one of the major Nepali political parties.

Bahadur's rise to prominence has paralleled the rise of a cultural consciousness among Tamang and the role of ethnic identity in the politics of Nepal. It was not until 1990 and the first people's movement in Nepal that indigenous peoples were allowed to organize into associations. Prior to that time the royal regime had outlawed almost all such organizations. Since 1990, however, these associations have grown in number and prominence in Nepal, focusing their agendas on recognition and representation in an administration that had denied most of these groups cultural, economic, or political rights in the state.[6] Several Tamang cultural organizations now call for an autonomous territory and state: Tamsaling. In tandem with these developments the Maoist insurgency, beginning in 1996 and culminating in the collapse of the monarchy with the peace agreement of 2006 and the succeeding elections that swept the Maoists into a majority, incorporated the inclusion of indigenous minorities and *dalit* (untouchables) as part of their agenda. They have made recognition of indigenous minorities a central demand in the creation of a "new" Nepal by backing the formation of a federal system based in part on territorial units defined in the hill areas as autonomous regions named after major indigenous groups residing in them.

The effects of indigenous activism, Maoist advocacy, the demographic reality of minority ethnic/indigenous populations (who number, according to the census, almost 40 percent of the population), and subsequent formal rules of proportionality in representative institutions that have taken form since the peace agreement (e.g., the Constituent Assembly) have completely altered the field for political agency. Where Iron Lama was marginalized through identity politics and downplayed his identity, his nephew, Bahadur Tamang, has acquired a more central position, as yet not fully empowered but no longer pushed to the side. Bahadur did not downplay his Tamang identity; instead he emphasized it and used it as the basis of organizing support.

Bahadur Tamang has become a regional political figure on a new foundation and with a new orientation, including the positive assertion of his Tamang identity in an area of Nepal where indigenous Tamang are, if not the majority, at least the overwhelming plurality. Although careful to cement alliances through party affiliations to high-caste Hindus in his home district, he works out from a distinctively Tamang base. He has in particular used "cultural" events to organize Tamang in the region. Thirty years ago, western Tamang did not observe *lhochhar,* or what is now being forwarded as the Tamang new year (to be distinguished from Tibetan New Year, *lhosar*), a ritual that leaders in Kathmandu are designing as a direct counter to the national rites of Nepal, the Hindu Dasain. Beginning roughly a decade ago Tamang activists organized large-scale Lhochhar events in the capital, claiming that the Hindu state had repressed performances beginning in the distant past. By 2009 Tamang performed one mass celebration in Kathmandu attended by tens of thousands on the central parade grounds there. Leaders in villages and districts went on to organize many regional and village celebrations, something that is possible now that the Maoist insurgency has come to an end. The major national association of Tamang held programs in all seventy-five districts of Nepal, furthering their demand for national recognition of this holiday. Bahadur has been instrumental in organizing two performances in the region of his home village, the first in January of 2008, in the run-up to national elections in April, and another in January of 2009.

Lhochhar grounds consist of some sort of substantial open space decorated with colorful prayer flags for gathering of a crowd of people, a stage fully equipped with loudspeakers and draped with banners proclaiming the event, and seats for dignitaries. The performance itself always includes speeches, usually focused on the event and the importance of Tamang autonomy and self-determination, unique cultural heritage, and rights to dominion over specific territory. Important big men from the Tamang community are introduced, their scholars recognized, and when possible ministers of state are honored. Buddhist lamas produce power blessings, as do shamanic *bombo,* who make propitiations and empower the ritual field. Dignitaries, including a "chief guest" (the more prestigious the better), always grace the event and are asked to say a few words. In local celebrations this is a role I am often invited to assume, an invitation that cannot be refused. My long association with the Tamang has led to numerous invitations over the years, most recently in the winter of 2009 when I was a guest in three separate celebrations of Lhochhar.

Tamang singing and dancing troupes perform throughout the event, and usually these new Lhochhar festivities terminate with young people dancing through the night.

In light of his profitable construction business and his political acumen, Bahadur has been able to muster the labor to provide the infrastructure, cajoled famous singers, enlisted groups of dancers, and brought together influential leaders in the Tamang community, ostensibly around a celebration of a distinctively Tamang New Year. During the 2009 Lhocchar celebrations in the Kishpang region, his speech went on at length invoking Tamang dominion over local territory. He cited example after example of official Nepali place names that were corrupted and Nepalized versions of indigenous appellations; he called for all names in their territory to be returned to the Tibeto-Burman Tamang from the Indo-European Nepali. His demand, as those in the center and in other districts, was for the establishment of Tamsaling, or an autonomous Tamang federal unit with Tamang self-determination in the very geopolitical center of the Nepali state. Although the practicalities of establishing Tamsaling and other autonomous units face perhaps insurmountable hurdles, this public bid would have been unheard of a generation ago and has moved from the margins in the early years of democracy to the center of political discourse in Nepal.

Through embedded relations with two big men, from two different generations, that developed from a chance encounter on a bus almost thirty-five years ago, we have been fortunate not only to witness key developments, but to have been witnesses from a position that it would have been impossible to have obtained otherwise. Relations with these two big men are but one slice of a dense set of relations that have unfolded through time. As these relations have unfolded, their character has also transformed. We have been brought into Tamang history in a way that moved beyond simply one of what used to be called "rapport" to a more complex collaboration / mutual appreciation / appropriation—collaboration that has extended to our academic identity. These evolving relationships go beyond narrow relations of the researcher and the researched.

SONGS REMIXED

As an anthropologist who had written a systematic overview of western Tamang ritual and social life as I came to know it, I was brought into Tamang cultural and political revival in unintended ways. In the early days of activism by Tamang associations, I would find portions of my monograph reproduced verbatim in pamphlets and on early web sites of Tamang ethnic associations as they provided information on their ritual, social, and cultural life. Photos I had shared with leaders of the ethnic movement cropped up on the covers of their magazines. Beginning in 1994, I was interviewed for Tamang publications and for Nepali magazines, for one of which the editors provided the headline: "There Is No Reason for Tamang to Be Embarrassed [about their culture]" (Holmberg 1994b). I also provided a short descriptive article for a Tamang cultural publication on an important ritual celebration known as Chhechu. We were interviewed in the Tamang language for new Tamang radio programs for the first time in 1998, and subsequently, with the further liberalization of Nepali media, we were interviewed on three new FM stations with Tamang-language programs in one year, as well as on a nationally broadcast television program produced by an indigenous journalist. I was regularly invited to sit on the platform at various Tamang cultural and celebratory events as a dignitary and was usually asked to offer a few words. Bahadur even organized a celebration of my contributions to the ethnology of his region, which I unfortunately missed due to three days of canceled flights out of a remote region. This event, about which I knew nothing, was a vehicle for Bahadur to organize politically and enhance his position, inviting as he had party and government dignitaries. Young Tamang activists asked us to sit on their advisory boards for new media ventures. We went to observe two international conferences of the Tamang people organized by the oldest and largest Tamang association, Tamang Ghedung, one in Kathmandu in 2002 and the second in Darjeeling, India, in 2005, and we were asked to sit on the stage and to speak briefly at both events.[7] To the extent that a public reaction to foreign research has emerged, it has come from a few high-caste academics, who have asserted that by focusing attention on indigenous culture and society, foreign anthropologists were fueling a divisive and disruptive force in Nepali society.

Tamang villagers were more intrigued by what brought foreign academics to study a dialect of Tamang, and to learn about cultural practices that had been denigrated by the politically dominant and ignored in the academic histories as well as nationalist histories of Nepal. From Tamang perspective, we added a modicum of external legitimacy to their efforts at cultural assertion and revitalization. Tamang, of course, had their own specialists and lay experts, whose knowledge far surpassed ours and we were deeply indebted to them for their generosity in teaching us what they could. What we brought was a recognition that sidestepped the mediations of the dominant society within Nepal at a time when there were few nationally recognized academics in Nepal who came from the Tamang community. This situation has transformed dramatically over the last two decades, with a number of Tamang scholars gaining recognition within the Tamang community and beyond, including the first PhD in anthropology (Mukta Singh Tamang 2008). Although I can hardly name all these scholars and activists, Parshuram Tamang (1992, 2051 vs[8]) and Sita Ram Tamang (1991, 2001), longtime leaders of the Nepal Tamang Ghedung, were early in deploying Tamang ethnology and history both nationally and internationally for the recognition of Tamang. Tamang scholars such as Amrit Yonjan-Tamang (2054 vs, 2063 vs), Ajitman Tamang (2002), and Manchhiring Tamang (Mamba) (2060 vs) as well as many others have actively taken the forefront in documenting and studying Tamang language and cultural formations in both print and video and have made major contributions to Tamang ethnology.[9]

Many Tamang in the immediate area where I do research now lament the "loss" of their old songs and the demise or truncation of some of their key rituals. Villagers now joke that we are the ones that know the old songs and that most of the elders who could sing are now gone. Our tape recordings of songs, photographs, notes on ritual practice, and the documentation of forced labor began to be viewed a decade or so ago as a resource, and we have worked to make sure that copies of all our materials are in the community. The first hint of the documentary potential of my research actually occurred during my first fieldstay, when my fieldnotes took on an unantici- pated value. The political rivalry between Iron Lama and a collat- eral relative was coming to a head in the period immediately before the accusations of cow killing had been leveled at Iron Lama and we had been removed from the district. Iron Lama's rival in the village was activating alliances with the very high-caste political enemies in the greater district who were attempting to defeat Iron Lama. A loud argument broke out during the initial evening of Chhechu, the most socially encompassing ritual in the set of villages in which I was working. One group of specialists sponsored by Iron Lama and another group sponsored by his rival began to argue over ritual pro- cedure in a proxy clash. The ritual was held in suspension as I was asked to bring my written fieldnotes from the previous year's per- formance to provide precedent. Fortunately my notes provided no authoritative resolution.

In the last decade, our photos, recordings, and notes have been incorporated in various ways into Tamang campaigns of ethnic as- sertion and revitalization, a process that thankfully is superseded by the efforts of Tamang scholars and activists to produce their own archive. The Nepal Tamang Ghedung and the Tamang Language, Literature, and Cultural Research Association, to name just two or- ganizations, foster documentation and research, as do many inde- pendent scholars. Numerous youth associations have formed under the patronage of prominent Tamang in Kathmandu, where Tamang constitute some 10 percent of the urban population and where many young Tamang go to study and pursue employment. For instance, Bahadur Tamang, among others, sponsored a youth association for the Tamang in his home region. Working from tapes we recorded in the mid-1970s, the youth group resuscitated several songs, some se- rious and some playful, that were current in the 1970s, remixed them with instrumentation, and distributed them on a CD. These same songs now blast over loudspeakers at large Tamang gatherings, including the national Lhochhar performances, especially in the celebratory dancing and singing that always break out in concluding moments of these events. These songs are also played at urban weddings and other social gatherings where young people dance while singing along with the words on CD. The revival of songs is paralleled by a revival of dress, especially when Tamang sing these songs at public events. When they "dress up" for political or cultural events, many Tamang women and men wear a revitalized Tamang dress modeled on western Tamang traditions. Where some old-timers see loss of Tamang culture, one can detect a vibrant transforming culture skillfully recreated through new media, not only taking the old and remixing it but coming up with new distinctively Tamang cultural productions.

On another front, Tamang scholars are taking new interest in researching a ritual dance drama that was ubiquitously performed in villages in the western area of Tamang residence. Until the late 1970s, Tamang in the main village of my residence over my years of research performed, according to them, the largest and most famous Chhechu in the region, a dramatic ritual spectacle featuring historic, mythic, comedic, and exorcistic dances (Holmberg 1994a, 2000). This performance went into demise very shortly after Iron Lama, the key organizer of the event, retreated from active politics. Over the past decade, there has been more and more talk of reviving the event. As a matter of fact, where the ritual had died out in many villages, in the spring of 2009 it had been revived in at least two neighboring villages where it had not been performed regularly for decades. In one village I visited it was being performed at the same time as the new ritual Lhochhar.

FROM ELICITATION AND TRANSLATION TO COLLABORATION

Our research with Tamang has been intimately connected to our relations with Suryaman Tamang, relations that have evolved substantially. From the time I first met him on that bus ride to his district that brought me to his village, his home, and his kin, he has worked directly with us on all aspects of our research projects. Not only did Suryaman teach us the Tamang language and work as an intermediary in the local Tamang community; we lived in his compound and became close to him and his family in ways that extended far beyond the professional roles we played. Suryaman was initially "the assistant" in a typical researcher/assistant relation, translating and transcribing in all kinds of situations, but by the end of our initial research, he had gained both extensive knowledge of his own community and an independent ethnological and ethnohistorical interest in the kind of things in which we ourselves were interested. In 1988 we invited Suryaman and a companion to visit the United States for several months. We felt deeply obliged to Suryaman both during and after the time of our original research. We had endlessly answered questions about this mythic place called America with its tall buildings and huge roads. We always would tell him "You have to visit," but it would have to be when we were not struggling graduate students. It was not until the mid-1980s that we found ourselves in a position to bring Suryaman for a visit. During his entire time in the United States Suryaman flipped roles with us. He became the researcher and we became the intermediaries and translators in his understandings of US society.

He kept a careful written log of his visit, which a Nepali friend of ours had the occasion to read over Suryaman's shoulder. This friend told us that we had to read the very fine writing and observations of this man with little formal education from deep in the Himalayas, a man who had never ventured beyond the borders with India, had never traveled internationally, and was observing America for the first time. After reading his journal, Kathryn March—as lead editor and translator—and I invited Suryaman and his companion back to write a jointly authored book/pamphlet that was then published in Kathmandu, the proceeds of which went to the local schools (Tamang et al. 1995). The book unfolds with facing pages, one with the Nepali version and the other with the English, and was made up of two parts, the first being Suryaman's journal and the second being some of our journals from our first encounters in his village. Suryaman's text is superior by far to ours.[10]

Although, as I noted above, we made a few research trips in the 1980s, professional demands and our family situation precluded extended research stays. For a year in 1993–1994 followed by another six months in 1997–1998, however, we opened a second major front of research focused on the ethnohistory of forced labor regimes that had been imposed in the region following the conquest of Nepal by high-caste Hindus in the early nineteenth century. We also pursued information about rebellions active around 1960. Suryaman was again integral to our research; he accompanied us from village to village in the region helping to locate old-timers and record their recollections of life under the old regime and the details of a system where each roof had to contribute something on the order of 70–100 person-days of labor per year to state operations such as herding / butter production, paper production, fruit production, porterage, and the like. We also pursued every scrap of paper we could find locally related to this regime. This research led to a major co-authored publication (Holmberg, March, and Tamang 1999). Suryaman has continued to be the key field researcher in a major project on migration pursued by Kathryn March. In the community Suryaman has become the local receptacle of all the photographs and tapes from our research over the years and is recognized locally as one of the most knowledgeable people in the region. In turn he has worked with other researchers, including Mukta Singh Tamang, the first Tamang to receive a PhD in anthropology in 2008. Beyond the village, we have combined with other Tamang scholars in establishing a fledgling organization called the Tamang Studies Center (Tamang Dupkhang), which is devoted to producing an archive of ethnographic and historical documentation accessible to all Tamang and other researchers, an association that is for scholarly advancement only and is complementary to similar efforts initiated by specific Tamang political organizations.

These collaborations—not all of which I can recount here—began with a chance meeting on a bus from Kathmandu to Trisuli Bazaar and expanded out into the greater Tamang community especially as it is now centered on Kathmandu. Parallel to these specific associations and collaborations with Tamang—in a spirit of reciprocity familiar to the Tamang—we have worked over the years to foster relations on an institutional level with anthropological colleagues in Nepal, relations that worked against the grain of an extractive history of anthropological engagement in Nepal.[11] We had long felt that non-Nepali anthropologists who conducted research in Nepal were obliged to support the development of anthropology there.

We were fortunate to find ourselves in an institutional context in which we could try to fulfill that obligation. We began in the 1980s to find ways for faculty and students at Tribhuvan University to come to Cornell University for doctoral training, at that time unavailable in Nepal, and now four Nepali graduate students have received PhDs and a fifth is currently studying for the degree. Three of these students were from indigenous communities in Nepal. In 1992 we initiated a formal exchange between Cornell University and Tribhuvan University in Kathmandu. Led by Kathryn March, in collaboration with myself and colleagues in Nepal, we established a program for both Nepali postgraduate students and US students to study jointly under the tutelage of faculty at the Tribhuvan University, including many master's students in sociology-anthropology. This project, which began as a student program, led to very close ties with faculty in anthropology and sociology with regular faculty exchanges. We presented lectures on occasion in classes at TU and provided guidance to master's students; for eight months in 2005 we were in residence at the University, where Kathryn March taught the gender curriculum jointly with colleagues in the department. From this moderate exchange relation, we recently became the collaborating institution with the Department of Sociology/Anthropology at Tribhuvan University in a five-year project to enhance anthropological training in Nepal, the Dor Bahadur Bista Project for Advanced Training in Anthropology.[12] Under this program, one PhD student enrolled in the program at Tribhuvan University will study for a semester at Cornell University to enhance international exposure. Faculty at both

Author with Suryaman, 2005.

institutions will work jointly to create a new graduate curriculum and enhance "pure" research opportunities for faculty and PhD students in Nepal.

* * *

Multitemporal research, then, has been in our case both a deepening and a broadening of social relations. When I used to arrive in the village children would call out, "Older brother has come," "Sister's husband has come," "Younger/older father has come," or "Mother's brother has come." Now when I arrive they call out simply, "Grandfather has come." When I was first in the village, I ran with the young men; now I am seated with the established men of the community. All the positions in which I have found myself have allowed me shifting vantages on the same society and their changing circumstances through time. Our relations became thicker and thicker through time, but they also spread out socially and spatially to other communities of Tamang in the mountains and in the city, to other ethnic communities, to the academic community. The multitemporal morphed into the multisited. In fact, the best multisited research is a function not just of place but of time.

Finally, if the genius of ethnography lies in the inter-nested contingencies I outlined at the outset, it only realizes its full potential when, as Lévi-Strauss noted many years ago, "the observer himself is part of his observation" (Lévi-Strauss 1987 [1950]). Reflexivity does not necessarily mean, then, the end of ethnography as positive knowledge production; rather, it shifts it to a more complex level. In other words, as long as the social and cultural mediations at play in the production of ethnography are integral in analysis, ethnography produces empirical knowledge produced nowhere else. I hope this bit of reflection on relations of the observer and the observed through time contributes to an eventual analysis at that level.

NOTES

1. Although I have authored this chapter, the research and collaborations are as much Kathryn March's as mine (March 2002). Moreover, as I relate below, Suryaman Tamang is inextricably bound up in the experiences I recount. That said, I am responsible for any representations found herein.

2. This absence of control defies the simplistic representation of anthropology as necessarily the handmaiden of colonialism or neocolonialism, even though the history of anthropology can provide egregious examples of such relations.

3. Tamang, a Tibeto-Burman–speaking minority in Nepal residing in the districts that surround the Kathmandu valley, were conquered in the eighteenth century by the high-caste Hindus who consolidated the state of Nepal. As a defeated population who had fought the advances of this "Gorkha" re-

gime, Tamang were subject to various forms of domination, including, in most villages in the western region, forced labor, a system that continued until the 1960s. This shift has been accompanied by a radical transformation of the economic life of the Tamang. The community, historically enclosed upon itself, subsisting mostly on maize and millet, where all surplus labor was extracted in state enterprises, has opened to the world in a host of ways, the most obvious being that at least one member of every household if not more (most often young men but also young women) was working outside the community either in places like the Gulf states, Malaysia, India, Kathmandu, Iraq, Afghanistan, and beyond to Europe, Israel, and the Americas.

4. Use of fictive kin terms is common throughout Nepal and a principal way of articulating relations across ethnic groups. One of the consequences of long-term research is that use of fictive kin terms begins to elide—in my case early on—into real obligations and expectations. I happened to be in the village when Iron Lama died in January 2010, and villagers viewed my relation to Iron Lama to be so long and deep that I too, as a son, had to shave my head, something I did out of both affection and respect for a great man.

5. Tamang villagers, who constituted a significant plurality and possibly the majority in the official census, expected Iron Lama and other Tamang freedom fighters to get tickets (endorsements) from key parties to run for national office from the district. There was deep disappointment, however, because the party structures were dominated by high-caste Hindus, and no Tamang even made it on the ballot until seventeen years later, after the Maoist Insurgency and the second People's Movement, which abolished the monarchy in 2006. Bahadur Singh (Lama) Tamang gained a place on the ballot for a constituent assembly to write a new constitution in the spring of 2008.

6. It would be fair to say that in the 1970s there was almost no active organization around "Tamang" identity in the western region where I worked, and there was little sense of unity of Tamang nationally. Although a kind of ethnic politics in the form of an anti-Brahman movement had flared around 1960, advocacy for language and cultural rights was not part of the local agenda. Accommodation through "Nepalization" and Hinduization were more common modes of assimilation cum adaptation.

7. See Middleton (2010) for observations of our participation in the Darjeeling Conference.

8. *Vikram samvat* (vs) is the official calendar of Nepal, which is 56–57 years ahead of the Gregorian or Common Era (CE) calendar.

9. Yonjan-Tamang has comprehensively documented all contributions to Tamang studies and Tamang media in Nepal and India (2063 vs).

10. Suryaman's two trips have been succeeded by yet two more. Bahadur Tamang has come to our house in the United States twice, once with a cousin-brother. Suryaman's daughter will be coming in the spring of 2010 to work with us on processing field materials.

11. I first heard the phrase "extractive anthropology" from my colleague Mark Turin, Director, World Oral Literature Project Museum of Archaeology and Anthropology, Cambridge University.

12. This project is being funded by the Wenner-Gren Foundation under an Institutional Development Grant.

REFERENCES

Bateson, Gregory. 1958 [1936]. *Naven: A Survey of the Problems Suggested by a Composite Picture of the Culture of a New Guinea Tribe Drawn from Three Points of View.* Stanford: Stanford University Press.

Comaroff, Jean, and John Comaroff. 1991. *Of Revelation and Revolution: Christianity, Colonialism, and Consciousness in South Africa,* vol. 1. Chicago: University of Chicago Press.

Dwyer, Kevin. 1982. *Moroccan Dialogues: Anthropology in Question.* Baltimore: John Hopkins University Press.

Geertz, Clifford. 1988. *Works and Lives.* Stanford: Stanford University Press.

Holmberg, David. 1983. Shamanic Soundings: Femaleness in the Tamang Ritual Structure. *Signs: Journal of Women in Culture and Society* 9 (1): 40–58: Chicago.

———. 1989. *Order in Paradox: Myth, Ritual, and Exchange among Nepal's Tamang.* Ithaca, N.Y.: Cornell University Press.

———. 1994a. The Dance Drama of Chhechu among Western Tamang. *Syo-Mhendo* 16: 14–18.

———. 1994b. *Tamangharule laj mannu parne kunai karun chaina* [There Is No Reason for Tamang to Be Embarrassed]. *Syo-Mhendo* 164–165.

———. 2000. Derision, Exorcism, and the Ritual Generation of the Power. *American Ethnologist* 27 (4): 227–249.

———. 2006. Violence, Nonviolence, Sacrifice, Rebellion, and the State. *Studies in Nepali History and Society* 11 (1): 31–64.

Holmberg, David, Kathryn March, and Suryaman Tamang. 1999. Local Production/ Local Knowledge: Forced Labour from Below. *Studies in Nepali History and Society* 4 (1): 5–64.

Lévi-Strauss, Claude. 1987 [1950]. *Introduction to the Work of Marcel Mauss.* F. Baker, trans. London: Routledge and Kegan Paul.

March, Kathryn S. 2002. *"If Each Comes Halfway": Meeting Tamang Women in Nepal*. Ithaca, N.Y.: Cornell University Press.

Middleton, Townsend. 2010. Beyond Recognition: Anthropological Knowledge and Belonging in Darjeeling. PhD diss., Cornell University.

Ortner, Sherry B. 1995. Resistance and the Problem of Ethnographic Refusal. *Comparative Studies in Society and History* 37 (1): 173–193.

Sanjek, Roger, ed. 1990. *Fieldnotes: The Making of Anthropology*. Ithaca, N.Y.: Cornell University Press.

Tamang, Ajitman. 2002. *Tamang jatiko maukhik itihaska awasheshharu* [The Remnant Oral History of Tamang]. Kathmandu: Nepal Tamang Ghedung.

Tamang, Manchhiring (Mamba). 2060 VS [2003 CE]. Ankhu kshetraka tamang jati [Tamangs of the Ankhu Valley]. Kathmandu: Ganesh himal samaj samitiko kendriya karyalaya.

Tamang, Mukta Singh. 2008. Himalayan Indigeneity: Histories, Memory, and Identity among Tamang in Nepal. PhD diss., Cornell University.

Tamang, Parshuram. 1992. Tamangs Under The Shadow. Himal 5 (3): 25–27.

———. 2051 VS [1994 CE]. Tamang Jati [Tamang Caste-Ethnic Group]. Kathmandu: Nepal rajkiya prajya-pratishthan.

Tamang, Suryaman, Bhim Bahadur Tamang, Kathryn March, and David Holmberg 1995. Dohori Namaste/Mutual Regards: America and Nepal Seen through Each Other's Eyes. Kathmandu: Jivan Support Press.

Tamang, Sita Ram. 2001. Vishwa adivasi andolan [On the Indigenous Movement]. Kathmandu: Nirantar Prakshan.

Tedlock, Dennis. 1983. The Spoken Word and the Work of Interpretation. Philadelphia: University of Pennsylvania Press.

Yonjan-Tamang, Amrit. 2054 VS [1997 CE]. Tamang—vyakaran [Tamang Grammar]. Kathmandu: Nepal rajkiya prajya pratishtan.

———. 2063 VS [2006 CE]. Tamang pahicanka sandarbhaharu [The Context of Tamang Identity]. Kathmandu: Amrit Yonjan-Tamang.

5| Nostalgia and
Neocolonialism

PETER METCALF

Nostalgia, we are told, is a characteristic of anthropology. How then
are we to render the nostalgia of others?

When I began research in central Borneo in the 1970s, the people
I worked with expressed a profoundly nostalgic view of a previous regime. Old people in particular spoke of a Golden Age that had lasted
roughly from the end of the nineteenth century to the Japanese invasion in 1941. They reminisced about the splendor of festivals in their
longhouse communities, when hundreds of guests, assembled from
far and wide, had feasted for weeks at a time. Traditional wealth in
the form of woven cloth, glass beads, and brassware changed hands
as part of elite marriages, and the prowess of dancers and musicians
exceeded anything now to be seen—a veritable cultural florescence.

NOSTALGIA

Their Nostalgia

It so happens that this was a period when the region was ruled by whitemen (Malay *orang puteh*; the terms "whitemen" or "white people" are
commonly used in Malaysia to designate white Westerners). It was a
distinctly eccentric polity, founded in the middle of the nineteenth-
century by an Englishman who perfectly filled the role of adventurer

in the romantic ideology of his time. James Brooke had invested his family's modest wealth in buying a schooner—little more than a yacht—and arming it with cannon. Then he set out to seek fame and fortune in the pirate-infested waters of Southeast Asia. He found his opportunity in the service of the Sultan of Brunei, who was hard pressed to contain rebels in Sarawak, the southernmost province of his realm. Brunei had been a major trading center for centuries, giving its name to the whole island, but its influence was waning. As his reward for suppressing the rebellion, Brooke was made Rajah of Sarawak. Having no legitimate children, in 1861 Brooke named as his successor his sister's son, Charles Anthoni Johnson Brooke. Charles Brooke extended the borders of the Raj a step at a time, to the point where his territory surrounded that of his nominal overlord. He did this by establishing a minimal administration—a Pax Brookinensis—in the interior, in regions that had previously known nothing of the kind. Lacking any significant armed forces of his own, he brought about "pacification" by playing one "tribe" off against another. For the most part this was accomplished without much bloodshed, apart from the odd "punitive expedition" that got murderously out of control. The process was largely completed by the beginning of the twentieth century, and the third Rajah, Vyner, was content to enjoy the fruits of his forebears' labor. In the 1920s and '30s the Raj slipped into a kind of torpor (Runciman 1960; Pringle 1970).

This was the regime that spurred such fond memories among old people in the 1970s, but no great skepticism is required to point out that they were being recounted to a whiteman, indeed an Englishman. Surely, my informants were simply flattering me, someone they took to be associated with the former ruling elite. In the process they no doubt reproduced colonial attitudes that they had acquired as children.

Even if that is true, however, their statements cannot be dismissed as mere lies, since they showed evidence of being part of a cultural system that existed whether or not there was an Englishman present to hear them. My model here is Ira Bashkow's *The Meaning of White-*

men (2006), which describes the reactions of Orakaiva people in New Guinea to their experience of colonialism. In some ways, the Orakaiva view of whites is surprisingly positive: whites, they say, have the power to get things done in an orderly way, where blacks fall into fighting among themselves and cheating each other. What convinces me that Bashkow is describing an indigenous moral system is that the qualities of whiteness are not restricted to whites. In fact, almost all the Australian administrators, teachers, and missionaries are gone. Nowadays it is Orakaiva themselves who must struggle to achieve a balance between the competing values of whiteness and blackness. Whites were "light" because they were apparently able to shrug off the heavy obligations of kinship. They took their pay and spent it as they liked. They went here and there as they pleased. For Orakaiva people, this is extremely difficult. Even if a man moves to one of the coastal cities, kinsmen will turn up at his doorstep and feel entitled to eat his food and share his possessions. Young men with access to government funds are under the same pressure to share as a farmer who has had the good fortune to pull off a bumper crop. To refuse is social death, and perhaps physical death as well.

At this point, I must emphasize that this dyadic logic of black and white, "heaviness" and "lightness," "progress" and "tradition," is not found in central Borneo. The historical experience of Borneans is more complex, since they have been in contact with the ancient civilizations of India and China for two millennia. Rare and valuable jungle products, such as bezoar stones and hornbill casques, were exported from Brunei, and in return came high-prestige manufactured goods, especially glass beads, brassware, and glazed ceramics. Heirloom property was individually owned, and no one felt obliged to share food. Poor people were simply *jat,* "bad"—just as in the West. I cite Bashkow's study to make a different point: the positive evaluation that people in interior Borneo placed on a previous regime run by whites was part of an overall assessment of their historical experience, and especially of their encounter with modernity. By the mid-1970s it was apparent to many of them that their world was changing rapidly, and not for the better. They were shocked by what had happened to them since the passing of the Brooke Raj, and worried about the future. They had good reason to be.

Our Nostalgia

I am still, however, skating on thin ice. Even if the attitudes of interior people to the Raj were not to be dismissed as simply a response to my presence, I still have to deal with the nostalgia, or nostalgias, that haunt my account of their world. The authors of this volume came together to reflect on the challenges of long-term fieldwork. All of us have been returning to the same places for decades, watching lives unfold and circumstances change, and gradually coming to a deeper understanding of what we saw—or so we hope. Looking back on the process as we were asked to do, it is hard to escape a very personal nostalgia. When we began our fieldwork we were young— now we are old. Whether we are wiser is an open question, but we certainly have a lot of questions to ask ourselves about our experiences: what was gained, and lost, and at what cost. There is no possibility of objectivity in such reflections. When I read the fieldnotes from my first period of fieldwork, lasting just over two years, I am taken back immediately to the strange little person I then was. As with all old men, I reflect on my own innocence and inadequacies with a poignant mixture of affection and disappointment. But how am I to sort out my nostalgias from those of my informants, who were even then old men and women?

Anthropology's Nostalgia

Moreover, there is a nostalgia that comes to me professionally. At least until recently, ethnography was a nostalgic discipline. In the late nineteenth century, the first generation of anthropologists treated "primitive" people as relics of prehistoric epochs, without of course having actually met any of them. In the twentieth century, fieldworkers fiercely rejected such naked chauvinism, instead defending the uniqueness and worth of each culture, however alien to Europeans. There was a trap waiting for them: in the process of defending the

Nostalgia in paternalism.

values and lifeways of "their" people, ethnographers often set themselves up as unappointed spokespersons—a move now heavily criticized. But we should not lose sight of the generosity of their intentions. When my teachers talked about the moral superiority of gift economies over the ruthless commodification of the current world, there was nothing condescending in their rhetoric. I was convinced by it then, and I still am. It will be a great mistake if the self-criticism that anthropology has subjected itself to in the last couple of decades causes us to reject the very real achievements of the discipline in the previous epoch.

Nevertheless, the implicit nostalgia of classical ethnography—if I may use that phrase—complicates the job of describing other peoples' attitudes to the past. If I assert, following Bashkow, that the nostalgia of at least some people in central Borneo for a previous colonial regime was a social fact, I still have to describe the nature and origins of that nostalgia without getting it tangled up with the admiration that I have for a culture and society that has now largely disappeared. I know first-hand that what has happened to the communities I knew in the 1970s is a disaster, and if that sounds like the reactionary sentimentalism of an aging ethnographer toward "his" people, then I cannot help that.

As I understand it, contemporary anthropology has struggled mightily to eliminate the last vestiges of nineteenth-century evolutionism, including the kind of nostalgia to which I just confessed. That is to say, would-be ethnographers no longer seek out people who could in any conceivable way be seen as representing something ancient, premodern, or "primitive." That my generation continued to do so is evident in the number of them who chose fieldsites in New Guinea—that last refuge of Stone-Age technology.

At the beginning of the twentieth century it had been Borneo, filled with headhunters, that had provided the archetype of barbarity. The inferior state of Borneo ethnography is a result of the discovery of dense populations in the unexplored interior of New Guinea, just at the moment when first-hand fieldwork was becoming standard in the discipline. Borneo was promptly abandoned by ethnographers who saw richer hunting grounds elsewhere.

My teachers were ethnographers in the classic mode, and my admiration for them and what they accomplished puts me in the position of expressing nostalgia for a former nostalgia. What could possibly be more postmodern than that?

Imperial Nostalgia

This rapidly conducted tour of alternative nostalgias brings me back to my original doubts about reporting the warm memories that the people of interior Borneo had for a former colonial order. Given who I am, I shall be suspected of secretly nursing an affection for the former British Empire, and how can I deny that? It is like announcing earnestly that I am not a racist: I hope it's true, but is it for me to say? Racists constantly announce that they are not racists, and they probably believe it. When teaching US undergraduates about the British Empire, I never fail to point out that it was the greatest empire ever to exist, in terms of both population and land area. I grew up in a part of London whose poverty had made it a recruiting ground for the Army of India. Almost every house had dusty souvenirs of Cairo or Colombo. No doubt I have unremembered ancestors who fought at Delhi Ridge and Chillianwala.

What I must point out, however, is that none of these putative ancestors did very well out of the empire. No doubt their hearts swelled with pride when they thought of serving Queen Victoria, but their service did nothing to lift them or their families off of the bottom rung of society. On the contrary, during the colonial period the British class system hardened, its hierarchy and values ever more rigidified. This was the legacy of the empire that I knew: half patriotism, half class warfare. Such ambivalence almost matches that of the Orakaiva: admiration of the "lightness" of white men, balanced by the shock of encountering people who have things but will not give them away, who do not understand the things in life that are "heavy." What I need to do in my reportage of the memories of people in central

Borneo is restore the balance between the positive and negative aspects of their historical experiences, in order to see what lay behind their nostalgia.

NEOCOLONIALISM

The Colonial Double Cross

Japanese forces occupied Vyner Brooke's Sarawak in 1941, and they were still there when Japan surrendered in 1945. There was almost no fighting. Having seized the oil wells on the coast, the Japanese seldom ventured up the great rivers that lead to the interior. Consequently, the people who lived there experienced the occupation simply as a vacuum, and absence of something rather than something new. In the previous half century—the reputed Golden Age—the Raj had become an integral part of their worldview, and its sudden unaccountable disappearance came as a profound shock. By their own account of it, the assumption of direct British rule after the war came as a relief. Once again, there were sunburned Englishmen arriving at their longhouses, usually ready to get drunk, and to get up and make fools of themselves when invited to dance in the indigenous manner.

They took no part in the political process, however. There was a visiting mission of British MPs, but no adequate transport arrangements were made for people from upriver to get down in time to meet with them. Some leaders signed documents that they could not read, only to find out later that they had agreed to the abolition of the Raj. There was some resistance in the cities on the coast, rallies and marches protesting that Sarawak had not endured a world war just to become a British colony. The argument was entirely reasonable, but it was squashed by Vyner Brooke, who coolly announced that it was his Raj and he would do what he liked with it (Reece 1982, 207–240).

Amazingly, the scenario was repeated a mere eighteen years later, when Sarawak found itself parceled out to the new nation of Malaysia, comprising the former British possessions in the Malay Peninsula, plus North Borneo and Sarawak. In the 1960s, as Britain sought to divest itself of its expensive colonial commitments, federation was all the rage in Whitehall. In the modern world, it was argued, small nations could neither defend themselves nor find the resources for development. Some truly bizarre schemes were floated, and almost all of them foundered. The grandest was the Central African Federation, consisting of what were then Northern and Southern Rhodesia, plus Nyasaland. It was immediately denounced by African leaders as a plot by white settlers to retain power, and it died a natural death (James 1994, 611). In the Caribbean, all manner of combinations were tried, none of which survived. The logical conclusion came when tiny Anguilla, population 7,019, refused to be ruled from nearby St. Kitts-Nevis, population 45,000. Despite the arrival of London bobbies, who organized a cricket match, the Anguillans stubbornly insisted on "independence."

Malaysia, however, is still there. The British-supervised elections in June 1963 resulted in the appointment of a chief minister, Stephen Kalong Ningkan, who had reservations about the Malaysian federation. In particular, he opposed the introduction of Malay as the medium of instruction in schools, arguing that English would give better access to education overseas. In making his case, Ningkan im-plied that Sarawak had the right to quit the federation. Others agreed with him, but the prime minister of Malaysia, Tunku Abdul Rahman, dismissed such ideas as "a dream," saying flatly that Sarawak would remain in Malaysia "until doomsday" (Porritt 2004, 132). Three years later, Kuala Lumpur engineered a political crisis as a pretext for removing Ningkan from office. Refusing to resign, Ningkan made this challenge: "If the Prime Minister thinks he will, with the help of his puppets, succeed in making Sarawak a colony of Malaya, the Tunku is suffering from a terrible illusion" (Leigh 1974, 105). But that is exactly what happened.

A few statistics will demonstrate the neocolonial situation. Sarawak is by far the largest state in the federation. Indeed, at 48,235 square miles, it is almost as big as all the other states of the Malay Peninsula put together (50,790 square miles). Its population, however, is only about a tenth of the peninsula's (1,233,000 compared to 11,427, 000, using data from the 1980 census). Meanwhile, the state is rich in natural resources, notably oil and timber. The profits from the extensive offshore oil fields go directly to Kuala Lumpur, and very little find their way back (Leigh 1974, 135). At the same time, images of the primordial rainforest stretching across mountains and valleys, seemingly endlessly, convinced everyone in West Malaysia that Sarawak was virgin territory, ripe for exploitation, and inhabited by only a few scattered natives in dire need of civilization. This mind-set is evident in newspaper reports and even scholarly writing from West Malaysia. "Malaysia" almost invariably turns out to be just West Malaysia, and the existence of the colonies in East Borneo is ignored. Sarawak is Malaysia's Wild West.

"Malays" vs. "Chinese"

Something else was imported along with rule from Kuala Lumpur: an ethnic struggle that has riven the Malay Peninsula for decades. As independence for Malaya drew near in the 1950s, the British administration looked for ways to safeguard the rights of indigenous Malay people against the overwhelming Chinese control of the economy. The solution they arrived at was to enshrine special political and educational privileges for Malays, perhaps with the belief that this balance would encourage a slow integration. But neither party trusted the other, and each guarded its powers jealously (Comber 1983). In this way, the politics of the peninsula became rigidly dualistic. Other minorities, notably people of Indian descent, had no place in the equation.

The ethnic equation in Sarawak is completely different. The Sarawak people who call themselves "Malay" are for the most part indigenous people who adopted Islam, or whose ancestors adopted Islam. For centuries, Malay city-states such as Jahore provided the maritime infrastructure among the islands of Southeast Asia. Malay traders brought with them not just commodities, but an entire culture, to which many of their trading partners were attracted. As they in turn began to take on Malay lifestyles, they were said to *masok Melayu*, or become Malay, and an important part of that process was conversion to Islam. Even the Sultans of Brunei are, by their own dynastic history, descendants of local people who became Muslims. Consequently, being Malay is not a matter of ethnicity, but of lifestyle and religion. Many Sarawak Malays in their own homes do not speak Malay, and are no more comfortable than other Sarawakians in what Tunku Abdul Rahman insisted was Behasa Kebangsa'an—the National Language.

Meanwhile, Chinese traders have been visiting the shores of Borneo for at least two millennia. Some waited out the unfavorable monsoons in sheltered spots, and there is archaeological evidence of settlements producing iron and ceramics. It was not until the nineteenth century, however, that large numbers of Chinese immigrated to Sarawak, fleeing warfare and poverty in China. They spoke a range of languages, including Hokkien, Cantonese, Hakka, and Henghua, and they found niches in fishing and growing pepper, and—crucially—in running shops. The Chinese in Sarawak are hardly a uniform or unified bloc, but it was easy for Malay politicians in the 1960s to see the same pattern of economic dominance that so haunted them in Malaya, and to impose the same simplistic ethnic dualism (Chew 1990).

From the Third World to the Fourth

The irony of this is that it leaves out of consideration almost half the population of Sarawak. Using figures from the 1980 census, Evelyn Hong (1987) finds that some 44 percent are Dayak, meaning neither Malay nor Chinese. This is probably an underestimate, since the census counts whole ethnic groups, such as the Melanau, as Malay when not all of them are Muslims. Those counted as Malay comprised 26 percent of the population, while the Chinese were 29 percent. Just who are the Dayak people is a complicated story involving migrations and linguistic variations among Austronesian-speaking peoples who have inhabited the island of Borneo for at least three thousand years. Suffice it to say that there are many ways to be non-Chinese and non-Muslim. The largest single Dayak population are the Iban, who share a single language and are relatively culturally homogeneous. They alone outnumber the Malays and are about as numerous as the Chinese. Following the strident rhetoric of Malaysian politicians in favor of independence for indigenous peoples, Sarawak should be run by Iban, but it is not. Since the overthrow of Stephen Kalong Ningkan (an Iban), it has been run by "Malays."

The forced entry into Malaysia effectively disenfranchised Dayak peoples. In the politics of the nation-state they are simply swamped by numbers. Dayaks make up only 3.8 percent of the population of Malaysia, too few to have any impact in Kuala Lumpur. The concept of the Third World is losing currency, because of the emergence of such new economic powers as China and India. But I still find useful the idea of a Fourth World, that is, ethnic minorities so small that they can never expect to gain representation through the ballot box. In Sarawak, the Dayak population moved from being residents of the Third World in the 1960s to being stuck in the Fourth World by the 1970s. As for the people among whom I worked, the Upriver People, they comprise less than 4 percent of the population of Sarawak, and about 0.35 percent of all of Malaysia.

When the British arrived in Sarawak, they found an independent nation. When they left, they handed it over as a colony to another nation, chosen to suit their own convenience. That is the legacy of the British Empire in Sarawak.

Orphans of the Soil

The legal privileges accorded to Malays are considerable, including not only preferential access to education, but also priority in hiring to government positions, gaining contracts for government work, and obtaining all manner of government-issued licenses. Malays are said to enjoy these privileges because they are *bumiputera,* an expression that is invariably translated into English as "sons of the soil." But this status is a product of the Malay/Chinese duality. In Sarawak, Dayak people are denied the privileges of *bumiputera,* which are reserved for those who have *masok Melayu.* But such people are neither more nor less indigenous than their Dayak neighbors. The absurd result is that nearly half the population is treated as foreigners in the land where their ancestors lived for generations before the arrival of Islam in Southeast Asia.

Plundering the Forests

It would be wrong, however, to portray the situation in Sarawak as oppression by Muslims of non-Muslims (the majority of whom are now Christian). To give that impression would be to surrender to the obscurantist anti-Muslim rhetoric now so familiar in the West. On the contrary, there are "Malay" communities in Sarawak that are among the poorest and least empowered in the state. Their traditional land rights are as casually ignored as anyone else's. What is going on in Sarawak is a struggle between the exploiters and the exploited, and what made that plain was the haste with which the timber resources of the state were plundered in the 1980s and '90s. Nothing was allowed to stand in the way of the destruction of the rainforest, which was accomplished in record time by Chinese and Japanese corporations, working hand-in-hand with the clique of corrupt Malay politicians. Timber licenses were handed out to the families and cronies of chief ministers, who promptly auctioned them off, thus becoming fabulously rich overnight. All this money concentrated in a few hands distorted civic culture in Sarawak in the same way that profits from banana plantations created dictators in Guatemala.

The tragedy is that the profits from timber, carefully husbanded and not embezzled, could have funded economic development in the state for decades to come.

WATCHING NEOCOLONIALISM

Longhouse Communities

The process of neocolonialization provided the backdrop of my field research in Sarawak. For a long time, however, I was barely aware of it, because I was so absorbed in the life of the longhouse. Longhouses are the characteristic mode of residence of that small fraction of the Dayak population that calls itself *Orang Ulu,* or Upriver People. The one I lived in in the mid-1970s housed about 350 people, and it was not a large one. There were others twice or even three times as big. They were massive structures, their plank floors raised ten feet above ground, their shingled roofs soaring another thirty feet above that, all supported on sturdy pilings. Running the length of the side facing the river ran an open veranda, and on the landward side a line of family apartments. It was not the size of the longhouses that was most striking, however, but the fact that they were surrounded by miles of rainforest in every direction. There was no ecological reason for populations to be concentrated in this way. On the contrary, they obliged their residents to travel large distances back and forth to their farms, cut anew each year in secondary forest. Nevertheless, Upriver People insisted that there was simply no other civilized way to live. Are we animals, they would ask, that we should live in the jungle?

The social life of longhouses was intense and absorbing, especially in the period after the rice harvest, when there were festivals lasting days or weeks, including a spate of marriages. During my first two years of fieldwork, I was kept busy staying apace of events in the community. When there was a lull, I snatched the chance to travel to other longhouses in the same river system to compare my findings. Since I had my own longboat and outboard motor I could do this as I chose, but there was never any lack of companions wanting to visit relatives, or simply to see places they had not been before. I never lacked for conversation, or new topics to explore.

During this period, I shared an experience that was once familiar to ethnographers working in many parts of the globe: I fell into the life of a community in such a way that the outside world became distant, vague, and irrelevant. This experience can no longer be repeated in Sarawak because such self-contained communities no longer exist there, and I assume that the global economy is now so powerful and all-pervasive that they are rare anywhere. Certainly, very few current research projects are based on village studies or anything resembling them. Naturally, I feel nostalgic about this. I feel sure that something has been lost to anthropology, and to young ethnographers. Surely, the experience of escape from one's own culture can hardly be profound if one is never allowed to lose sight of the booms and busts of the stock market.

Logging in the 1970s

Logging was certainly in progress in the '70s. Sitting on the longhouse veranda, I often saw huge rafts of logs, hitched together with cables, slowly drifting by. Each was headed by a diesel tug, whose power was just sufficient to give the ungainly mass enough steerage way, above the flow of the current, to avoid the frequent sandbars. A swarm of speedboats buzzed about, trying to nudge logs away from obstacles. Meanwhile, other crew members ate, or hung out their washing on top of the rafts, so that there was a strange sense of alien worlds drifting past each other, with no sign of recognition from either. Meanwhile, there were always men away from the longhouse working in the logging camps. Needless to say, they did the heaviest and most dangerous jobs, and for small wages. Men who suffered injuries, sometimes crippling injuries, received negligible compensation. Living conditions in the logging camps were primitive. Amid a sea of mud churned up by the logs as they were bulldozed into the river, the workers lived in low hovels roofed in corrugated iron. Much of the men's pay went into alcohol and gambling. What made its way back to the longhouse was spent on the little luxuries that had become indispensable. No longhouse event could proceed without paraffin for the lamps, and sugar, coffee, and cookies to offer the guests, and a man returning from the camps always had sweets to hand out to the kids. In this way, the lumber industry coexisted with longhouse life throughout the 1960s and '70s.

Logging Roads

What now seems remarkable, with the wisdom of hindsight, was that very few people were detached from their communities by this form of migrant labor. Every person still belonged to a particular room in a particular community, and expected to be included in all major rituals. Beginning in the late 1970s, however, and gathering momentum through the '80s and '90s, new technologies were introduced that rapidly increased the pace of rainforest destruction. Massive bulldozers cut dirt roads across ridges and mountains, directly into the heart of the forest. Along them passed equally massive trucks, hauling out the trunks of the tallest trees, often more than a hundred feet long and weighing many tons. Going beyond the statistics—which are horrifying enough—William Bevis (1995) gives a moving account of the process as seen up close. He describes in detail a single forest tree, and the amazing variety of eco-niches it provided for different species—vines of a dozen different species, lichens, flowers, parasites and epiphytes, not to mention insects and birds. Each tree was an entire microcosm. As he wanders around the logging camps, he sees waste everywhere—logs thirty feet in length and six in diameter pushed aside to rot because bigger and more valuable ones were already piling up awaiting transportation.

Trees and People

The environment of Upriver People was destroyed, but this aspect attracted little media interest. What green organizations wanted to talk about was trees, not people. There were even those who swallowed the government line that the traditional farming methods of indigenous peoples were to blame. Some advocated the establishment of national parks from which indigenous people would be excluded. The government did not explain, nor did the environmentalists ask, how it was that after three millennia Upriver People had not already destroyed the forests. The answer is that farms were almost always made in secondary forest near the rivers, and the primary forest in the mountains had never been touched.

Nor did the international media report the resistance of local people, largely because government efforts to enforce a blackout were successful. The Malaysian press was entirely subservient, and cooperated in portraying activists, both local and foreign, as communists. By the mid-1990s paranoia ran high, and I was amazed to find Upriver

People who did not care to be seen talking to me, even though I had research clearance and no connection to green organizations. Consequently, it is unlikely that the full story of indigenous resistance will ever be told. Community leaders were bribed or intimidated into signing "agreements" with timber companies, which were then enforced by company goons assisted by police and soldiers. There were many incidents of Upriver People blocking roads, often by camping in the middle of them, but they occurred piecemeal, and there was no mechanism to organize any widespread response. Communities only understood the danger when the bulldozers were at their front door. Regarding the abuse of land rights, however, the situation has been documented in a remarkable piece of research by Evelyn Hong (1987).

Multiple Diasporas

There could be no more apt symbol of neocolonialism than the bulldozer, and it destroyed more than the forests; it destroyed the longhouse communities that I had known in the 1970s. The first noticeable effect was more men away working in the camps, especially young men. But the camps hardly provided a career. Camps opened, were beehives of activity for a couple of years, and then were abandoned when the nearby timber resources were worked out. Some parts of the lower Baram region had been worked over three times by the end of the '90s, as mounting timber prices made it worthwhile to harvest ever smaller trees. The ecological damages—loss of the thin layers of topsoil, rivers so muddy that no fish could survive— are well known, and I will not elaborate them here. The point for the present is that a generation became habituated to cash income, but could not find steady work. When there was none available, the young men sat around in their longhouses wearing their new jeans and T-shirts and drank store-bought beer. What was inconceivable was that they would return to farming. No doubt there had always been tensions between elders and youngsters in the longhouse, but there now emerged a full scale "generation gap." What old people knew, everything from choosing farm sites to the meaning of life, became irrelevant to the young. Even before the longhouses emptied out, they already had a dead feeling about them.

When young men could no longer find work in their neighborhood, they had the choice of going farther afield in search of active lumber camps, or drifting down the newly built roads to the cities on the coast, notably Miri. Needless to say, there was no housing for them in Miri, so squatter settlements sprang up. Despite houses made out of scrap materials and rusty sheet iron, some corners of the settlements managed to convey the atmosphere of Malay villages, with trees to give shade, neatly dressed children carrying their books to school, and neighbors visiting back and forth in the evenings. One in particular, at Canada Hill, was on a piece of prime real estate, a hillside within walking distance of downtown. Needless to say, it was not long before the bulldozers arrived there, to begin "development," amply funded by the profits of the timber business.

In the '80s and early '90s, I spent many evenings at Canada Hill. It was often possible to there to learn a great deal about what was going on upriver, even far upriver, without ever leaving Miri. A contact from one longhouse community would have a friend or neighbor from another, who knew someone from yet a third, and so on. Mostly, I pursued my long-standing ethnographic interests, but inevitably I heard about the changes going on upriver. One man supplied me with a map showing all the logging roads built and planned, a document that was a virtual state secret. Had he been discovered, he would certainly have been fired, or worse. The projected roads led right up to the border with Indonesian Kalimantan—no corner of the Upriver would be left undisturbed. I heard which villages were resisting and how, and which leaders had sold out, and for how much. During my last visit in the 1990s, I was interviewed by police before being allowed upriver, and I had a police tail during part of my trip. But whatever I wanted to know about the destruction of the rainforest I learned easily enough in the squatter settlements on the coast. What was happening was no secret to Upriver People.

Canada Hill was not a longhouse community, however, nor did it contain anything that might be construed as daughter communities. On the contrary, people of different backgrounds were all mixed up together there. An immediate consequence was the declining use of indigenous languages. Borneo as a whole displays great linguistic diversity, but it was greatest among Upriver People. Effectively, each longhouse community had its own dialect, or even dialects. But children growing up in the settlements had no incentive to learn these languages. Often their parents, being from different communities, had different mother tongues, neither of which was much use in school or with their friends. Language death is pervasive; Miri has become the metropolis of Upriver People and the graveyard of their languages.

Unemployment ran high in the settlements, and there was no possibility of falling back on a subsistence economy. What follows from that is familiar throughout the world: parents unable to provide for their children, teenagers being drawn into crime, old people left to fend for themselves.

THE "ROLE" OF THE ETHNOGRAPHER

Lord Jim and Bruno Manser

I might now be asked what I did about all this, apart from wringing my hands. The greatest claim I can make is that my writings were cited in a court case in which a longhouse community tried to gain recognition of their rights in a piece of real estate adjacent to a national park. But a developer, largely funded by the chief minister's wife, wanted to build a luxury hotel there to cater to high-end tourists, and after endless delays the community's claims were denied. What I found ironic in this, however, is that my information came mainly from the oral histories of Upriver People, augmented by the colonial records. Everyone in the region knew that the community had been located not so long ago near the site of the hotel. My authority as an "expert" did not in the end do the community any good, but the written word was accorded lip service, at least. I also helped young people start a business, and helped a few teenagers go to school and one to college, but my impact was negligible compared to the exploits of a young Swiss man, Bruno Manser.

Manser came to Sarawak in the late 1980s determined to share in the life of the people who lived deep in the rainforest, motivated by the familiar romance of the virtues of those living close to nature. In particular, he sought out not the swidden-farming people but the hunting and gathering Penan. The Penan are not in fact nomadic, but their houses were flimsy by comparison with the massive long-houses of their neighbors, and they did travel far and wide in what was then still extensive primary forest. He stayed on long after his visa expired and became something of a legend, the white man living just like a Penan, showing up here and there and then disappearing back into the forests with his friends.

Manser's visit coincided with the rapid expansion of logging, and the people most directly affected were the Penan. They thought of the primary forest as their home, while the swidden agriculturists preferred to cut secondary forest in the valleys. Longhouse dwellers insist that they live *beside* the forest, not in it. When vast tracts of primary forest were cut for the first time ever, the Penan put up a stronger resistance than anyone had imagined them capable of. In some cases, they maintained roadblocks for weeks or even months at a time. Penan regularly arrived to bring food to the blockaders, and to take their place sitting in front of the huge earthmoving equipment. The legend of Bruno Manser fit neatly with this surprising response; clearly he was the one behind the Penan resistance.

Curiously enough, there was in this a bizarre echo from the nineteenth century. In Joseph Conrad's novel *Lord Jim,* a displaced Englishman finds himself in a corner of Asia where the apathetic local people are appallingly exploited by piratical overlords. He inspires them to stand up for themselves, and leads them in a successful rebellion. The model for Conrad's hero was none other than the first White Rajah, James Brooke. I have no idea if Manser had ever read Conrad, or knew much about the Brooke Raj, but consciously or unconsciously he reproduced an imperial stereotype characteristic of boys comic books in the early twentieth century: the mission to free "native" peoples from their oppressors (Orwell 1946). What part Manser actually played in organizing the Penan resistance to logging I do not know, but it is surely condescending to imagine that they could not have done it by themselves. Longhouse-dwelling people generally look down on the Penan as simple folk, if indeed they do not treat them as slaves. What we should be asking now is how everyone—ethnographers included—could have so underestimated them.

Ethnographers and the Media

All of this is going to sound like sour grapes, however, when I concede that no one has ever been so successful as Bruno Manser in drawing worldwide attention to the plight of the people caught up in the destruction of the rainforest. When he finally arrived back in Europe he became a media celebrity, appearing on television and being interviewed for journals like *Paris Match.* I do not imply that his goal was from the start personal publicity. On the contrary, he struck everyone as shy and sincere. He went to Oxford to visit Rodney Needham, the best-known ethnographer of the Penan, and made a good impression. Manser did, however, play into the same European romantic ideas that had taken him to Sarawak in the first place. What followed was an avalanche of coffee-table books, with glossy pictures of a lost Eden. The longhouse-dwelling neighbors of the Penan were conspicuously absent from these books. As Tim Ingold (1994) remarks, in Western mythology hunters and gatherers are animal-like themselves, as innocent and vulnerable as other "wildlife."

Meanwhile, my attempts to convince journalists that I have an interesting or timely story to tell have met with little success. At one time the editor of a major British newspaper showed interest. It was at the time when huge forest fires were sweeping through central Borneo, feeding on the detritus of the forest floor that had never previously been exposed to the sun. Palls of smoke drifted downwind, making it hard to land aircraft as far away as Kuala Lumpur, and pumping vast amounts of carbon dioxide into the atmosphere. This story got back-page coverage in the international press for about two weeks. I wrote my piece for the newspaper with unaccustomed speed, but even so I was told that the story had gone cold by the time I finished it. It had been a green issue, and the mere exploitation of indigenous people in some remote corner of the globe was hardly news. Finally, I was branded as an academic, and everyone knows academics cannot write. My only successes have been radio interviews, which I have done in Britain, the United States, and New Zealand. I make no claims as to their impact. This is just one small case of a larger phenomenon: the failure of anthropologists in the last half century to communicate to a broader audience.

As for activism in the Manser mode, I certainly did not try to stir up resistance to the lumber companies or the Sarawak government. That would have been irresponsible, in my view, because the Upriver People would have been the ones to pay the price, not me. As for armed resistance, no one who knew about the wars in Central and South America could wish such horrors on anyone. In fact, I am gloomy about the chances of Upriver People ever getting a better deal. What Sarawak needs is independence, and I cannot even imagine a scenario by which that might come about. There have been organized attempts by academics to come to the aid of Fourth World peoples. The one I know best is Cultural Survival, which was founded in Cambridge, Massachusetts, while I was a graduate student there. The goal of its founder, David Maybury, was to provide sophisticated legal council to people in remote corners of Brazil so that they could defend themselves against illegal land grabs. This strategy had some successes, but I cannot believe that the most polished lawyers in the world would have stemmed the tide of forest destruction in Sarawak.

Finally, we are left with the time-honored function of the ethnographer as witness to things that are past, or passing. I count myself lucky to have had the chance to experience longhouse culture in a way that will never again be possible. I can add a little to that invaluable archive that is the principal achievement of twentieth-century anthropology. Perhaps, in the long run, this will even be of value

Our nostalgia.

to the descendants of longhouse peoples. In the 1990s I met several times with young men who had profited from educational opportunities, found jobs in the city, and lived thoroughly suburban lifestyles. These men, to their credit, had not forgotten their origins, and were anxious to find ways to help former members of their communities now living in the town. On one occasion I met with a group of them for Sunday brunch in a swanky hotel in Miri. What they wanted from me, they explained, was a list of all the important things in their cultures that needed to be preserved. I was, of course, dumbfounded, and scrambled to make some useful response. The first thing I seized on was longhouse residence, but that was the one thing that was no longer thinkable. These young men in fact knew little of longhouse life, having gone away to boarding schools as children. My next response was to talk about the Maori of New Zealand, who are now largely urban but who gain considerable strength from their *marae* or ritual centers, whether in the home community or in the city. I never did, however, provide the list they wanted, and I was clearly a disappointment to them. Just what strands of the old life can be reworked to provide resources for the next generation I cannot predict. We shall have to wait and see.

Nostalgia and Paternalism

Having reviewed the legacy of the British Empire in Sarawak and the current neocolonial situation, the nostalgia of Upriver People for the Raj seems reasonable enough. During that epoch, the hand of colonial rule rested very lightly on them. It lacked the financial resources to do much more than impose "pacification," which Upriver People took to readily. The more numerous Iban to the south remained restless throughout the Raj, with constant raids, and even full-scale rebellions, but Upriver life was mostly peaceful. Other than the occasional murder, British district officers only rarely visited the longhouses. Remote ones might not see a whiteman for years at a time. There was a handful of "native officers," and headmen were appointed in each longhouse, but to a very large extent communities were left to take care of their own affairs. All but the most serious

legal matters were settled in traditional ways, and there was no inter-
ference in economic or religious affairs. Meanwhile, trade in jungle
produce flourished as never before, providing all that was necessary
for the rich cultural life that was associated with the Golden Age.

For Upriver People in the 1970s, the Raj had been unmistakably a
good thing. As an ethnographer, I fully share their nostalgia. Had I
arrived a half century earlier I would have found indigenous religions
in full swing in every longhouse, uncorrupted by Christian missionaries. But I cannot let things rest there, because what followed the
Golden Age showed clearly that it was in its very nature a trap. The
Raj was guilty of all the crimes of paternalism.

As Robert Pringle describes it, Charles Brooke thoroughly dis-
trusted nineteenth-century dogmas of Progress and thought his Dayak
subjects materially and spiritually better off than the working classes
of industrial Europe:

> Charles Brooke appreciated Sarawak as he found it, and for that reason neither
> education nor economic development came high on his list of priorities. He of-
> fered only limited inducements to European planters, tending to regard them
> as a class of unscrupulous speculators who deprived gullible stockholders in
> England of their savings and natives in Asia of their lands. (Pringle 1970, 138)

Even after all that followed, it is hard not to admire Charles Brooke's
cultural relativism, which was even rarer in his day than in ours.
Nevertheless, his hands-off approach left Upriver People without
resources to respond to historical events over which they had no
control.

What Upriver People most conspicuously lacked in their confrontation with the British Empire and Malaysia was any kind of economic
infrastructure, which in turn denied them any political clout. But
there had been sources of wealth upriver, notably rubber plantations.
Being opposed to foreign-owned plantations, Brooke established agricultural stations, at government expense, from which seedlings could
be bought at subsidized prices. He also protected small holders by
prohibiting the sale of their land to non-natives, because he foresaw
that Chinese traders would encourage indebtedness among Upriver
People and then take over their plantations. The strategy worked

well, and during the rubber boom of the 1910s several longhouse communities became so rich that they could afford to hire Chinese laborers newly arrived from China to harvest the sap for them.

What never happened, however, was that Upriver People learned to save and invest. What was needed was the establishment of some kind of banking arrangements, however simple. Had Upriver People absorbed as part of the colonial order of the Raj the idea that adults each had a well-thumbed savings book tucked away in their trunks along with valuables such as beads and jewelry, they might very well have found the means to gain some control of their own futures. All that was required was that a corner of the district office be set aside for financial records, and that officers traveling on business would carry a money box. But it was part of the colonial ethic, even for Charles Brooke, that gentlemen were above mere "trade." That was a matter for "box-wallahs." The window of opportunity closed when the Great Depression caused the market for rubber to collapse, along with everything else. Upriver People fell back into a virtually cash free subsistence economy.

Meanwhile, no efforts were made to teach Upriver People, even a tiny elite, about the world outside the rivers they knew. Charles Brooke was content that they remain undisturbed by such unwelcome things, and so it was that the arrival of the Japanese in 1941 came as a total surprise, a shock from which longhouse communities never entirely recovered. From then on they were to gradually awake to their own powerlessness and irrelevance, and that was the ultimate legacy of their three colonialisms.

REFERENCES

Bashkow, Ira. 2006. *The Meaning of Whitemen: Race and Modernity in the Orakaiva Cultural World*. Chicago: University of Chicago Press.

Bevis, William. 1995. *Borneo Log: The Struggle for Sarawak's Forests*. Seattle: University of Washington Press.

Chew, Daniel. 1990. *Chinese Pioneers on the Sarawak Frontier 1841–1941*. Singapore: Oxford University Press.

Comber, Leon. 1983. *13 May 1969: A Survey of Sino-Malay Relations*. Singapore: Brash.

Hong, Evelyn. 1987. *Natives of Sarawak: Survival in Borneo's Vanishing Forests*. Pinang: Institut Masyarakat Malaysia.

Ingold, Tim. 1994. From Trust to Domination. In A. Manning and J. Serpell, eds., *Animals and Human Society*, 1–22. London: Routledge.

James, Lawrence. 1994. *The Rise and Fall of the British Empire*. New York: St. Martins.

Leigh, Michael. 1974. *The Rising Moon: Political Change in Sarawak*. Sydney: Sydney University Press.

Orwell, George. 1946. Boys Weeklies. In *A Collection of Essays by George Orwell*, 279–308. New York: Harcourt Brace.

Porritt, Vernon L. 2004. *The Rise and Fall of Communism in Sarawak 1940–1990*. Victoria: Monash University Press.

Pringle, Robert. 1970. *Rajahs and Rebels: The Ibans of Sarawak under Brooke Rule, 1841–1941*. Ithaca, N.Y.: Cornell University Press.

Reece, Robert. 1982. *The Name of Brooke: The End of White Rajah Rule in Sarawak*. Kuching: Sarawak Literary Society.

Runciman, Steven. 1960. *The White Rajahs: A History of Sarawak from 1841 to 1946*. Cambridge: Cambridge University Press.

PART 2

EXPANSION IN TIME,

EXPANSION IN SPACE

6 | Cumulative Understandings

Experiences from the Study of
Two Southeast Asian Societies

SIGNE HOWELL

I have returned to my fieldwork sites in Malaysia and Indonesia[1] many times during the past three decades. In conformity with the overall argument of this book, I shall seek to demonstrate that the cumulative understanding of the premises for social and cultural organization of a particular society that springs out of multitemporal fieldwork is, necessarily, qualitatively different from knowledge gained by doing just one repeat study some twenty to twenty-five years after the initial fieldwork. In what follows, I explore some theoretical, methodological and interpretative challenges that have arisen from my two experiences of multitemporal fieldwork in what are two highly differing societies, and compare the kind of knowledge generated through each series of fieldwork. The differences—and similarities—will be accounted for in terms of each society's cosmology and social organization and the history of their interaction with the outside world. I will also examine how changes in my own personal circumstances and motivations affected my interpretations over time.

Multitemporal ethnographic research is likely to influence one's perception about social change more generally. Apart from anything else, what has emerged from my many visits over many years is a dawning comprehension of change as a process that is zigzag rather than linear; and that some external factors result in rapid change, whereas others seem to have little or no impact—and that it not easy to predict which may be which.

Because the impact from recent relations with the external world has been particularly dramatic in the case of the Chewong, a hunting-gathering-shifting cultivating group of aboriginal people who live in the rainforest of Peninsular Malaysia, most of this chapter will be devoted to a discussion of my observations of the resultant changes that have taken place in their circumstances. At the time of my first fieldwork, the Chewong lived relatively isolated inside the rainforest and their interaction with the outside world was minimal. This situation was very different from that of my second fieldwork site with the Lio, settled agriculturalists in the highlands of the island of Flores, Eastern Indonesia, whose interaction with the outside world had developed much more gradually before my arrival and who, therefore, had developed ways of handling the pressure of outside influences. They also lived according to clear structures that, it seems to me, made them more resilient in the encounter with the new, and this enabled them to maintain the relevance of traditional central values and practices. My discussion about the Lio, in contrast to that of the Chewong, will, therefore, concentrate more on continuity than on change.

The many ethnographic presences I have experienced in both my ethnographic settings have made it possible to witness events that have turned out to have important consequences. Had I not been present at the appropriate time, the sequence of events would have remained obscure. An example of this took place in 1981, during my second period of fieldwork with the Chewong. A local Chinese buyer offered an exceptionally high price for a special kind of rattan, which, according to Chewong ontological understanding, was a "person" and therefore might not be "killed" by cutting it down. However, an encounter in a shamanic dream revealed the plant to be not a person but the food for a different species of nonhuman person. By offering that person some alternative food, the Chewong enabled themselves to cut and sell the rattan (Howell 1983). Today, this sequence is forgotten by most, and certainly never referred to. When asked today if the species of rattan is a person, people reply in the negative. Had I not happened to be present at the time, and had I not already known much about their animistic universe, I would not have discerned this cultural compromise. The event alerted me to the likelihood that similar choices are routinely performed more generally in the face of new demands and changing circumstances. Conversely, events that seemed very important at the time may turn out not be so. An example of this is when, in 2003 and 2004, several Chewong converted to Islam and seemed set on that path, only to leave little trace of it a year later. To be present at decisive moments that produce long-term effects, as well as at other short-lived or abortive events, undoubtedly contributes to making one's interpretations diachronically "thick." Minimally, such events teach one to be extremely careful in the way one predicts the future, and in how one interprets new or altered practices that one encounters after an absence.

On my first visit to the Lio in 1984 I encountered a very different situation. Most people under the age of fifty identified themselves as Catholic, were literate, and spoke Indonesian. The Catholic Church began to establish itself among them approximately fifty years prior to my arrival, but the pre-Catholic religion continued to be of relevance.[2] My unannounced arrival was viewed with suspicion and it was difficult to walk freely about. During my second visit two years later, I was allowed to take part in the protracted and expensive rebuilding of an ancestral temple. The local Catholic priests told me that this would be the last occasion for rebuilding, as, according to them, the temple's ontological and moral significance had lost its force. Although I was not convinced of the demise of local religious traditions, I nevertheless counted myself extremely lucky to be able to witness this event—only to be present at a similar rebuilding in another village domain eight years later. On that occasion, the Catholic priest insisted on performing mass in front of the temple after its completion—an act that I interpreted as deliberately confrontational. Certainly many Lio expressed dismay at this act, but

Author participating in a Chewong wedding ceremony inside the forest, 1978. PHOTOGRAPH BY KWE.

they felt powerless to prevent it. Since then, several other temples in the vicinity have been rebuilt. Had my only fieldwork been the second one, I might have observed the first rebuilding, but had I not returned I would have believed that I was indeed lucky to have been present at what I took to be the last performance of a dying belief system. What many return visits have taught me is that Catholicism and the original religion live side by side, occupying themselves with different aspects of social and religious life—although the church tries to prevent this from continuing (I return to this below)—but, more importantly, I learned that the original ontology maintains an existential and moral hold on people's imaginings.

TO CAST ONE'S FISHING-NET

Ethnography has been characterized as a dipping of different nets in a teeming ocean, each time producing a different catch (Clifford 1983, 130).[3] Despite its somewhat essentializing attitude to ethnographic research and the kind of knowledge to be generated, I nevertheless find this an evocative image. From such a perspective, anthropology may be thought of as the task of making sense of each catch, not only through relating to what is inside the net, but also through contextualizing each catch in relation to other catches—synchronically and diachronically. This necessitates intermittent fieldwork, with periods of time in between to reflect upon one's most recent catch and ponder its significance in relation to previous knowledge—ethnographic, theoretical, and personal. To cast one's metaphorical net again and again over an extended period of time allows one to refocus one's ethnographic gaze each time; to identify the new and follow the fate of the old. I must emphasize, however, that the informed ethnographer does not throw her metaphorical net blindly, but chooses her direction each time, fully informed by her previous knowledge, always on the lookout for interesting details and novel constellations. An important factor to bear in mind is that the ocean is never identical each time one throws a net into it—and yet it is the same ocean. Similarly, the anthropologist is not the same person each time she throws her net. Like the people she studies, she changes as she passes through her personal life cycles—and yet, from an existential point of view, she is, just as they are, the same.

Repeated return visits enable one, inter alia, to investigate the history of one particular practice and observe how it changes or continues over time, and to discern completely new practices and values as they appear and place them in context. This makes it possible to test the relevance and validity of previously identified core values discerned, and to pursue the depth and complexity of "total social facts"—those that encapsulate the many strands of social life that are particularly significant and that crop up in a multitude of contexts, and upon which moral social action is predicated (Mauss 1925). Hence my enthusiasm for repeated fieldwork.

MY FIELDWORKS

What has emerged from my many return visits to the Chewong and the Lio is a newfound interest in anthropological approaches to social change. Most literature on vulnerable populations, such as hunter-gatherers and remote, small-scale "traditional" societies, tends to present a scenario of an inevitable path toward acculturation, disempowerment, and poverty. There is also an assumption that individuals seek to maximize personal benefits from the new opportunities that present themselves. But my observations of Chewong as well as Lio responses to the new challenges—and opportunities—that followed in the wake of increased involvement with the outside world have demonstrated the complexity in people's understandings, motivations, priorities, and choices and have convinced me that in handling new situations people seek much more than maximizing benefits—personal or communal.

My fieldwork engagement with the Chewong began in 1977, when I spent eighteen months with them as part of my doctoral research. Having completed my dissertation, titled *Chewong Modes of Thought*, in which I explored the meaning of animism and personhood as I came to understand this through a focus upon their ontology and epistemology, I returned for three months in 1981 before completing a revised version for publication (Howell 1984/1989). During this period I became very close to the people and felt very much at home. Initially very shy and timid, they came to accept my presence with few reservations. I felt privileged to live among them and to feel how their trust in me became undisputed. I started fieldwork with the Lio in 1984 and did not visit the Chewong again until 1991, after which I made five more visits until the last one in 2010. During this period the Chewong caught the attention of the outside world, and their way of life was changed, probably irreversibly. Parts of their forest environment were logged; the authorities made serious efforts to settle them in a permanent village on the forest fringes; and an elephant reserve was established next to that village, bringing an increasing number of tourists to look at elephants and primitive people.

I have watched these changes with dismay and sadness and with a growing sense of impotence. Unlike some of the other contributors to this book, I have not found an opportunity to actively involve myself as an advocate on their behalf.[4] At the time of my first fieldwork, the Chewong conformed, broadly speaking, to Sahlins's

(1972) characterization of the original affluent society as having material plenty and needing low physical exertion in order to satisfy most needs. They also conformed, broadly speaking, to Woodburn's (1982) immediate return society, which he characterized by a number of features that include an egalitarian, non-competitive ethos and economies that discourage saving and accumulation. Equality is achieved through direct and individual access to commonly held resources, and these values and practices discourage the accumulation of wealth and property, and encourage sharing. This Woodburn contrasts to a delayed return system, which implies a settled lifestyle with rights over valued resources, including land, delayed yield on labor, and food processing and storage; which "depend for their effective operation on a set of ordered, differentiated, jurally-defined relationships through which crucial goods and services are transmitted" (1982, 433).

Woodburn's contrast between two ideal systems has been questioned as being too clear-cut, but I found it useful for ordering my thoughts when I started to think systematically about how best to approach an interpretation of the many serious challenges to Chewong way of life that I had witnessed. I had never defined myself as a "hunter-gathererist" and did not involve myself in those debates, not least because I missed in that work a serious attention paid to cosmology and religion. Today, however, with my new interest in their subsistence activities, I find much of that literature to be of relevance; an example of how refocusing one's disciplinary interest over time results in a refocus not just of the literature being read, but also of the observations being made in the field.

It was a desire for contrast that made me move from the Chewong to the Lio. As a student I was excited by Structuralism. To my disappointment, this proved to be largely irrelevant as a tool for analysis of Chewong way of life. A more phenomenological approach proved helpful in unraveling the parameters of their social and cultural life. However, I retained my desire to study a social organization constituted upon clear categories—social, political, religious—and where a complex cosmology necessitated large-scale ceremonies. With this in mind I turned to eastern Indonesia. Although dramatically different from each other, the two societies are geographically and linguistically within the same region in which Malay/Indonesian is the *lingua franca*. This made my move between them more easy to accomplish. At the same time, the fact that they could hardly be further apart, culturally and socially, demonstrates the enormous variety within a relatively small geographical area. Largely because of this, each culture area had developed its own gate-keeping concepts (Appadurai 1986). I was curious to see to what extent the experience of having worked with a loosely structured social organization influenced my approach to a highly structured one. As I moved between my two fieldsites during the 1990s and early years of the second millennium, I found that insights gained in the one sharpened my approach in the other. A sort of triangular relationship developed between myself, the Chewong, and the Lio that worked itself out under an umbrella of changing anthropological concerns more generally.

In sharp contrast to the egalitarian Chewong social organization, that of the Lio is highly stratified. Their kinship is tantalizingly complex, being an empirical example of prescriptive matrilateral cross-cousin marriage, with all that this entails in terms of formalized exchange and symbolic practices. Their cosmogony makes the ancestors, together with the Original brother-sister couple, central to their model of the world. They perform lengthy and elaborate ceremonies in connection with rites of passage and the agricultural cycle; and they live in ancient villages with temples, graves, and clan houses. Moreover, although self-contained and peripheral to the Indonesian state, the Lio—unlike the Chewong—did not live cut off from the outside world when I first encountered them. The Dutch colonial presence began to be felt at the beginning of the twentieth century, and the conversion to Catholicism among the mountain Lio took off during the 1930s. At the same time, their existential orientation was firmly predicated upon their pre-Catholic beliefs and practices—illustrated by the rebuilding of the temple described above—and they were able to handle the requirements of both traditions with apparent ease (Howell 2001). Not only had the major upheavals to their way of life been more prolonged, making it possible to deal with them more leisurely, but the very fact of being used to a clear-cut authority structure, as well as a firmly conceptualized religion manifested through a number of large-scale ceremonies, rendered them more self-assertive and resistant to being dominated. Perhaps because of this, they are today not as disoriented as the egalitarian, loosely organized Chewong, who have had to face an onslaught on their way of life during a very short period of time. Much of my research on the Lio has been concerned with unraveling how they handled a situation that at first sight appeared to me as a stressful juggling act of two world-views—those of the Catholic Church and the pre-contact religion—but which, as time went by, I began to understand as parallel discourses that were made relevant according to different contexts (Howell 2001). Having said that, the performance of Mass on the ceremonial occasion that marked the completion of the temple (discussed above) may be an indication that the church is losing patience. In fact, on my last visit, I discovered that the Catholic Church in Indonesia is actively seeking to implement "inculturation."[5]

During my repeated returns to the Lio I was continuously having to revise my understanding of the premises for their social organization. This arose from internal circumstances, not external ones as was the case with the Chewong, namely the tight control over knowledge exercised by the priest-leaders. They were in charge of what I should be allowed to learn. As I kept returning, they slowly gave me access to the more esoteric—indeed secret—details of their knowledge. I will return toward the end of the chapter to a consideration of these differences on the history of my interaction with the two groups.[6]

THE CHEWONG 1977–2010

On my many visits to the Chewong I observed how external activities and demands began to affect the Chewong way of life and attitudes. Logging, with the accompanying roads, set a series of events in motion: the government policy of settling the nomadic aboriginal populations and converting them to Islam; the introduction of cash crops and the rapid growth of a cash economy; the arrival of traders and a new proximity to shops, which led to an increased pursuit of non-timber forest products for sale rather than for indigenous consumption; and, as mentioned above, the establishment in 1986 of an elephant sanctuary, which has developed into a highly popular tourist attraction and brings tourists into the nearby Chewong village established by the authorities. Chewong reactions were, at least superficially, to acquiesce. Many moved out of the forest and started a desultory form of cash cropping, and most men took up the sale of non-forest timber products in a big way.

Although I had kept detailed notes during my early fieldwork about hunting and gathering activities and about various people's sporadic interaction with the outside world through the sale of jungle produce, economic life as such was not part of my original research interests. However, externally imposed changes during the 1980s and '90s, which led many individual Chewong to an increasing preoccupation with money—or rather with the many fascinating objects that money could buy—encouraged me to study their economic activities closely. In fact, my interest in the analytical consequences of return visits arose when I was trying to systematize some of the changes in the Chewong way of life in what was probably the most tumultuous period they will ever experience. I realized that I was no longer just an anthropologist and ethnographer of the Chewong, but had become, inadvertently, a historian of their society during this time of major upheavals.

An ever pressing question became how my persistent engagement with them during these years affects my interpretation of these changes. I do not claim that a fresh anthropologist arriving for the first time today to a previously unstudied Chewong would not be able to provide good, well-informed, and sensitive ethnography. But I think it is highly likely that such an anthropologist would miss many significant aspects of their sociocultural practices due, not least, to the fact that many are becoming muted (see below). They are not necessarily losing their importance, but they are much less in evidence. In some cases earlier values and practices may take on novel connotations as they are being challenged by opportunities for individual accumulation of wealth and property in a world that increasingly pursues this. In fact, it is likely that much of what I caught in my earlier nets is not caught in later ones; or at any rate, is less in evidence and, as such, would be less discernible as significant by a new anthropologist unfamiliar with the past. The returning anthropologist, on the other hand, continually readjusts her understanding of the premises of social reality.

CORE VALUES UNDER THREAT: FROM SHARING TO KEEPING?

In all societies there are certain values that seem more profound than others, that are constitutive of self-perception and of the moral discourse of meaning. By definition, it seems likely that these are most resistant to external influences; that they absorb or transform new incidents and values in ways that ensure their continuity. Multitemporal fieldwork provides unique opportunities to identify and pursue the fate of such values. In what follows, I isolate a couple of what I regard as Chewong core values and follow them through the period from 1977–2008. They were central to Chewong identity in 1977, and they still constitute a basis for their understanding of personhood and sociality. At the same time, they are becoming muted and are, perhaps, becoming less relevant for the new circumstances in which the Chewong find themselves.

The two Chewong values that I think qualify as core values, and on which I therefore have chosen to concentrate, are, first, the cosmologically derived ideology of equality, which gives rise to a profoundly egalitarian social organization. This is predicated upon their understanding of personhood and sociality and dictates the premises for their interaction not just with each other, but with the forest environment, which, cosmologically speaking, is animated. Second, and closely related to the first, is the moral prescription of *punén*, which asserts that "to eat alone," not sharing whatever food one has, is the greatest antisocial act imaginable. The growth of monetization and the irregular, but steady, move from subsistence activities to cash-generating activities are showing signs of affecting both these values, giving rise to new uncertainties and an ambivalence regarding the sharing ethos. So far, however, Chewong are resisting the negative impact of money on their inclusive and egalitarian sociality.

All products caught or collected in the forest must, according to punén, be displayed and shared among everyone present. If this is not done, someone not informed may feel desire that remains un-fulfilled. This emotional state renders a person vulnerable to spirit attack, which leads to illness or some accident. However, money—and things bought with money—fall outside the punén prescription to share. The implications of this are beginning to be felt. During my two first fieldwork periods, punén was constantly evoked—not least for the pedagogic effect on children. By not including money in punén, the Chewong are, in effect, establishing different spheres of exchange (Bohannan 1959), a fact I would not have discovered had I started my fieldwork today. People still invoke punén, but it has be-come muted as a practice and, in many cases, is applied selectively. Goods that are bought from shops are understood to belong to the in-dividual, and probably always were in the case of the few such goods people previously owned, such as knives, cooking pots, and cloth. Bought food occupies a more uncertain position. It is not displayed and distributed in the same public manner as is (was) the case with foraged food. This is different from the time of my early fieldwork when the few foodstuffs that people were able to buy were a matter of curiosity and were shared upon return to the settlement. This change may be accounted for by the fact that people in the new forest fringe village are more dependent upon shop food, and hence it no longer represents a luxury; in fact, bought rice has here replaced cultivated tapioca as a staple. It can also be explained by the size of the popula-tion there, which is much larger than is usual in a forest settlement. Keeping rather than freely sharing is, nevertheless, regarded with unease. Perhaps more disturbing to many of the older people is the fact that game caught in the forest is no longer displayed in the vil-lage. Close relatives who live nearby are automatically given a share, but people try to withhold information about such catches. In the forest settlements food sharing goes on much as before, but as the men are spending more time on collecting saleable forest products than on hunting, bought food items may be kept for the family.

This development toward keeping rather than sharing is further apparent in attitudes toward the exploitation of land in the newly settled areas on the fringes of the forest.[7] The notion that the forest and land belongs to everyone and that anyone may clear a swidden anywhere is losing its imperative force due to this settled life style. The establishment of small rubber plantations and the reuse of cleared plots for cultivation have meant that the early settlers in the gateway village on the forest fringe now talk in terms of "our land." Increased monetization and a settled way of life thus challenge old values of communality and sharing, and we may observe a fragmentation into self-sufficient households who live next to each other in the village—not scattered as before in the forest. As people increasingly engage in cash-generating activities, through cash crops or collecting non-timber forest products (NTFP) for sale, previous exploitation of the forest for subsistence is declining.

EMERGING INEQUALITIES?

The potential for two kinds of inequalities to emerge from these changes is real: that between men and women, and that between individuals and/or kin-based groups. Due to increased foraging for NTFP for sale, men earn more money than women, and some men earn more than other men. With the arrival of money on a large scale, men have become the principal cash earners (Howell 1983, 2002, 2011a, 2011b). It is noticeable that men are gradually taking on the role as decision-makers in money matters as well as in more general household activities, and that they spend the bulk of earned income on goods of their choice, such as motorbikes, television sets, and clothing. Those men who make more money than the rest buy more commodities, and their families eat more shop-bought food. Outsiders (traders and bureaucrats) notice this and tend to single them out for interaction, paving the way for social stratification. So far, however, despite the fact that the many cosmologically informed rules regarding sharing and general behavior in the forest are practiced less and less in the new permanent settlement (but are declining less inside the forest), the high value placed on equality is still sufficiently strong to prevent individuals from maximizing personal benefits and emerging as entrepreneurs or as "leaders." Moreover, the forest life practice of immediate consumption of all surplus food—a practice that is extended into the immediate spending of earned cash—prevents the emergence of permanent inequality of wealth. The economy is still "embedded in the social," in Polanyi's term (1944). For profound changes to take place, it seems to me that the Chewong will have to engage in "disembedding" the economy—that is, removing economic practices from the broader sociocosmological type of sociality. However, the exclusion of money from punén is one sign of such disembedding, exacerbated by bought food increasingly being excluded from punén prescriptions. At the same time, a combination of a deeply held egalitarian ideology and an ethos of immediate consumption of all surplus has meant that no Chewong individual has thought it worthwhile to engage in long-term planning in order to accumulate wealth and maximize profit.

As far as gender relations are concerned, there are clear signs of change. The easy mixing of roles and a more or less equal share in subsistence activities that were the norm at the time of my early fieldwork are being replaced by more delineated male and female spheres. Again, these trends are much more noticeable in the gateway village than in forest settlements, but signs of change are noticeable there also. In short, women living on the forest fringe have little to do beyond child care and cooking. This may be brought back to changes in work practices as discussed above. As men engage more and more in activities that will provide cash, they no longer clear swiddens for cultivation of staples for their own consumption, and they hunt less. Although there is nothing that prevents women from cultivating their own crops, from making mats and baskets, and from gathering edible forest produce, they tend not to do this. On the whole, I am increasingly struck by a new kind of passivity among women who lead more settled lives. Days are spent sitting inside their houses, visiting each other languidly, and consuming large quantities of cookies and sweetened tea and coffee. Today I observe female obesity, a totally novel phenomenon.

SOME EFFECTS OF EXTERNAL RELATIONS

Although change is always part and parcel of social life, generated from inside as well as from outside, the changes that I have observed to have occurred in Chewong life during the past thirty years are predominantly due to external factors. But I have come to realize that the process I have been observing over time is more complex than at first I realized. Not only are the effects of external factors largely unpredictable, but despite appearances to the contrary, the Chewong are not simply passive victims. They feel coerced by the authorities to settle, certainly, and they exercise little or no influence on the developments that have taken place in their neighborhood; but the intense fascination with and desire for consumer goods and shop-bought food have also meant that many individuals are collaborating in their own change, willingly giving up much of their old way of life in return for possessing the goods. Nevertheless, the main triggers for observable change among Chewong can be located in the outside world.

However, what my many return visits have demonstrated is that the nature of change is not necessarily inevitable, nor predictable. Further, change may move in a zigzag fashion. Based on what I saw during my visit in 1991, when large numbers of Chewong had moved to the newly established government village on the fringes of the logged forest, I concluded that they were set on an all-too-familiar path of acculturation, exploitation, and disintegration. Many families had moved, seemingly permanently, and men concentrated their efforts on purchasing motorbikes and TV sets. All had virtually given up foraging for food. However, when I came back a few years later, the village was all but abandoned. People had returned to the forest and taken up the forest way of life. They were explicit about the reason for doing so: they disliked being so close to *gob* (derogative term for Malays and Chinese), and they felt that they had to work too hard for too little cash and were consistently being cheated by traders and employers. Further, they missed eating forest game and food. It seemed to me that people were more content whenever they were back in the forest. Certainly, women who had been leading rather passive lives in the village became active again. They went fishing, they plaited mats and baskets, and they cleared fields and made tapioca bread. Boys who never went blowpipe hunting from the gateway village, and who claimed not to know how to do this, miraculously knew how to hunt—and derived pleasure from this (Howell 2002). At the same time, the lure of shop food and consumer goods did not diminish in any absolute sense, but people seemed to weigh up the advantages and disadvantages of spending time on foraging for cash and for consumption. At the same time, there are many families who have never lived in the gateway village and who keep their money-earning activities to a minimum. Others may move there for short periods, while others again spend most of their time in or near it.

I have observed fluctuations between living in the forest and the village; between foraging and hunting for consumption, on the one hand, and cash crop agriculture and foraging for salable forest products on the other. Some individuals seemed more fascinated by the lure of the outside world than others. Based on my knowledge of most Chewong individuals, I thought I would be able to predict who would return less to the forest and who was most likely to remain inside it. However, this has not always proved to be the case. A good example is Lamait, a young man living in my household deep inside the forest during my first fieldwork, who at the time I found to be a lazy layabout. My "mother," who was the sister of his dead mother, never complained and never failed to give him his share of all food, but he rarely lifted a finger to help with the daily chores, let alone go foraging or hunting. He occasionally sold some rattan, but invariably spent the money on purchases for himself only. This is a good example of the value the Chewong place on noninterference, even when the moral injunction to share is not observed.[8] In 1991 Lamait had left the area altogether and taken employment as guard in the police force in a nearby town. Although surprised at his courage, I was not surprised that he was the first Chewong man to venture so far into the "modern" world. I did not expect ever to see him again. However, by the late 1990s he had returned, married a girl whose parents had never left the deep forest, and settled happily with them. Today he is the father of several children; he is an accomplished hunter and hardly ever leaves the forest. This example (and there are many others) have demonstrated to me that Chewong are not without agency, but that they continually evaluate their situation and their preferences. The movement between forest and village is made possible because, by pure chance, much of their traditional habitat lies within a game reserve and is therefore protected from logging. Chewong are thus able to employ a fair amount of choice in how they move in space. This they take advantage of, and in exercising choice they demonstrate that they understand many of the ramifications of what is happening to them.

WHAT IS THE ROLE OF THE ANTHROPOLOGIST IN FIELDWORK?

In light of my discussion thus far, I want to raise some questions concerning participation and belonging—the extent to which the anthropologist is able to be included in the community and the means by which she achieves this, as well the obstacles to inclusion. To keep returning deepens one's relationship with the people and may make them willing to include one in arenas previously closed. This was more manifest in my research with the Lio—where knowledge is power, and those who hold it are not going to give it freely away to anthropologists—than with the Chewong. From my experience with Chewong and also, albeit in a somewhat different way, Lio, my many returns undoubtedly helped to deepen my relationship with the people and to make it, in some cases, ever more relaxed and profound. Anthropologists commonly develop a more personal relationship with a few individuals than they do with the majority, and these are the people that we gravitate toward upon every return visit. They are the ones who assisted us in our grappling with unfamiliar circumstances when we first arrived and who give exegesis upon events and narratives. In my experience, such relationships provide us with a kind of social alibi in the eyes of the rest of the community; we become associated with them—and vice versa. Just as we turn to them when we return, they turn up when they hear that we have arrived. Such relationships can be strong and emotionally rewarding despite seemingly irreconcilable gulfs of knowledge and experience. I made such friends in both my fieldwork sites, and the fact of our friendship is something that has become more valuable to me upon each return. However unlikely these friendships may appear whenever I think about them back home, they are real, and I cherish them. They make each return visit tinged with a special kind of anticipation.

These days when I turn up among the Chewong, parents calm their frightened children with words like, "She is no stranger. She is one of us [bi he]. She was Modn's daughter [my 'adoptive' mother during the first long field period and on all subsequent returns until she died in 2003]. She used to live deep inside the forest, and she speaks our language." Words that warm, but which nevertheless make me wonder what this really means: to what extent I am one of them? Geertz once said (1968, 154) that anthropological fieldwork creates a kind of fiction of being a member of the moral community within which one lives during one's fieldwork—a fiction, he is at pains to emphasize, not a falsehood. All concerned are to some extent aware of this, and it renders this kind of research "continuously ironic." This is not to be regarded as something negative, however. Rather, Geertz argues that it is this fiction which "lies at the very heart of successful anthropological field research" (ibid.). I think this is a very perceptive observation. As a benevolent fiction, it need not prevent anthropologists from becoming part of the moral community during those periods when they are in the field. Our repeated return visits consolidate the relationship ever more firmly in everybody's minds. It is easier each time to blend in. Nevertheless they, and we, know that our real life lies elsewhere. But, as we keep returning, however sporadically, our mutual moral engagement enables us all to transcend our cultural boundaries and experience our common humanity. When I was taken to visit Modn's grave (my "mother") by my "sister" and her children in 2006, they and I cried. When we returned to the settlement, those who had stayed behind asked, "Did she cry?" as if seeking confirmation of my (Chewong) humanity. When receiving an affirmative reply, they nodded—acknowledging to themselves my part in their sociality.

Although I never developed the same kind of emotional connectedness with any individual Lio, I nevertheless found some person(s) in each village domain who acknowledged my returns with pleasure and whose households became the obvious place to settle in each time. My first field visit to the Lio was marked by having to ingratiate myself with one particularly powerful and arrogant priest-leader. I was completely at his mercy—something he seemed to enjoy. Over time, however, we developed a kind of mutual respect and friendship, and he was pleased to see me on my subsequent returns, when he allowed me new glimpses into the world of knowledge that he so jealously guarded.

FIELDWORK WITH CHEWONG AND LIO COMPARED

The experience of having performed multitemporal fieldwork in the same locality, engaging with people as they and the anthropologist change, gives rise to a special kind of reflexivity. We return. We reflect on the experience of return. We take up old questions and look at them anew in the light of personal as well as local history—just as new events and issues are placed in the existing trajectory. But each fieldwork site and each fieldwork experience is unique. In my case, my engagement with Chewong and Lio afforded very different experiences of doing fieldwork. This may be accounted for by my personal development and changing situation as much as by the quality of the two communities. During my initial engagement with the Chewong, I was inexperienced, I was filled with romantic notions of "the noble savage" and very anxious not to offend in any way. Once I got to the

Lio I was older, I had a lot more anthropological self-confidence, and therefore I controlled our interaction more deliberately. But the two communities were dramatically different. The Chewong—timid and fearful, living in a loosely structured and egalitarian social world where knowledge was shared by all—were initially pretty much at a loss as to how to relate to me. They were fearful of possible consequences and kept their distance. Lio, stridently self-confident and socially aggressive, living in a highly stratified social world whose guardians of knowledge, the priest-leaders, were not shy about dictating the terms of our interaction (Howell 1986b).

As the Chewong and I slowly got to know and trust each other, we were able to create a fiction of belonging. I learned through doing; I participated in daily life pretty much as I had interpreted the Malinowskian ideal. I pulled my weight in household chores, I ate and slept and walked in the forest as they did. I adopted the numerous taboos as I learned them and I was held responsible for my actions in conformity with these. Slowly, the significance of the obvious boundaries between us mattered less and less. A similar fiction of belonging to the same moral community did not take place in my relationship with the Lio. Inhabiting a society where knowledge definitely means power, the priest-leaders, who compete among themselves for prestige and authority, decided what and when I should be told about local history, cosmology, and ritual. Lio priest-leaders were determined to control what knowledge they imparted, and when; and the more I returned, the more they imparted. To the Lio it became important that I proved my serious involvement by returning. Upon each return visit I sensed that another door to their sociocultural life was deliberately opened for my benefit, revealing previously hidden knowledge.

Consequently, every time I returned, I had to adjust my understanding in ways I had not suspected. For example, it was not until my fourth visit that I was introduced to the ultimate senior priest-leader of one large domain, of whose existence and symbolic significance I was completely unaware. Similarly, thinking that I understood

Author with old friends in the new gateway village, 2010.

the complexities of their kinship system, I was totally unprepared during my fourth fieldwork to realize the sociological and symbolic importance played by descent through the mother. Theirs is a kinship system that corresponds in most features to that of an elementary structure of prescriptive matrilateral cross-cousin marriage and that seemed relentlessly patrilineal. My understanding of the female structural and symbolic role had, until that time, been of wife and wife's brother, not of mother.[9] Having been alerted to the ritual significance of the latter relationship, I then concluded that the mother's line is no less important in marriage and alliance transactions than is that of the father. Although much less elaborated, together they constitute one of the most persistent Lio core values (Howell 1995, 1996a). I do not think that this feature of their kinship system was deliberately withheld from me, but it is no accident that I became aware of it only as I was allowed closer into ritual spaces—literally and figuratively. It occupied a muted position in Lio ritual activities, but, as it turned out, no less significant.

Having undertaken my initial fieldwork with the Chewong at a time when they lived relatively undisturbed and more or less as they had for generations, my ongoing relationship with them while they experienced three decades of extreme external pressure to change enabled me, I suggest, to contextualize their reactions to the novel circumstances that have affected their way of life. I am confident that this has resulted in a more profound and nuanced picture of their life today (and also of life before my arrival) than had I undertaken a restudy after a period of twenty-five or thirty years. Chewong themselves are just beginning to understand the magnitude of what is happening to them. My engagement with the Lio over a period of eighteen years has not been one of equal emotional strength. This can be attributed to the factors mentioned above concerning their attitude to me, but also because they have not undergone dramatic changes during the period of my involvement. What I have learned from my many returns to them is the relevance of their precolonial practices and values that persist despite the arrival of Catholicism and the introduction of general education to the secondary level in which only the Indonesian language is used. I have found it of great interest to observe how the priest-leaders in some village domains are extremely adept at taking advantage of economic opportunities offered by the modern state at the same time as they expertly manipulate traditional values in ways that confirm and enhance their positions as religious and political leader (Howell unpubl. ms.).

Perhaps surprisingly, despite long exposure to alien values and practices, the Lio have retained much more of their precontact ontological and moral orientation than have the Chewong. Lio core values are predicated upon a clear-cut dual classification system that links the social and the cosmological in ways that orchestrate social and ritual life. Though Chewong orientation in the world is predicated upon a number of central values deriving their pertinence from a cosmology that merges the social and the natural worlds, there is an inbuilt flexibility in their approach that is mirrored in an extremely egalitarian social organization and ethos. This, I suggest, makes them also more fragile in the encounter with stronger and more powerful neighbors. One manifestation of this difference may be discerned in the place that myths and legends occupy in their respective life-worlds. Both have a large body of cosmologically significant narratives[10] that play(ed) a significant role in their understanding of reality (Howell 1982, 1986a, 1996b). It is undoubtedly the case that narrative is a major source in the way we construct our reality, and that repetition is important for narratives to take hold. During my first two fieldwork periods with the Chewong, people were constantly recounting their myths and referred to these for guidance in daily life. Today they are hardly ever told in the gateway village and seem to have lost much of their relevance there. Lio sacred narratives, on the other hand, retain their central role in all ritual activities. In fact, knowing a large number of such stories is a significant source of a priest-leader's authority in the social domain of "tradition" that, I have argued, runs parallel to the domains of "religion" (i.e., Catholicism) and "the state" (Howell 2001).

*   *   *

The value of ethnographic research rests on its ability to reveal the premises (explicit and implicit) for the flow of routine social life. Through multitemporal fieldwork, this knowledge enables one to identify changes, alterations, and new directions and to account for the seemingly unexpected. Such work also equips one well to pursue the fate of core values and practices. In this, multitemporal fieldwork becomes a useful tool that is qualitatively different from making one return visit many years after the initial fieldwork. Multitemporal fieldwork gives rise to unique cumulative knowledge unachievable by any other means. My two ethnographic engagements over a long period of time have convinced me that repeated returns to the same community have given rise to a more sophisticated attitude to knowledge; not least, paradoxes become less of a problem and are instead accepted as part of normal life.

Furthermore, as anthropology is in its very nature a comparative discipline, maintaining engagement with two very different societies in different countries during the same period, and over a long stretch of time, is rather unusual. I am certain that the fact of my having moved between Lio and Chewong has sensitized me to the special qualities of each and made me appreciate their differences— and similarities—but has also alerted me to question the very fact of these differences and similarities. I have developed a skeptical attitude to grand theoretical claims and come to question the validity of gatekeeping concepts, except as heuristic devices to be used with extreme caution. But I am confident that my eyes and ears have been sharpened through the comparative situation that I created for myself; undoubtedly, the longer the anthropologist keeps engaging with the community through repeated fieldwork, the more nuanced and informed will her insights be.

NOTES

1. I undertook fieldwork with the Chewong in Peninsular Malaysia for eighteen months from September 1977 and for three months in 1981, and I made shorter visits in 1991, 1994, 1997, 1999, 2002, 2006, 2008 and 2010. My fieldwork with the Lio on the island of Flores, Indonesia, started with a brief reconnaissance trip in 1982 and included five months each in 1984 and 1986, and shorter visits in 1993, 1997, and 2001.

2. Dutch colonialism and the establishment of the Catholic Church in the region before World War II and the efforts to create an Indonesian nation-state after independence had meant that features of modernity had slowly entered the communities. At the same time, profound core values and practices were allowed to continue in parallel with Catholicism and state requirements (Howell 1996b, 2001).

3. Clifford attributes this metaphoric statement to Marcel Mauss.

4. The Chewong are among the last indigenous population groups anywhere to be unaware of the existence of the category Fourth World and the political battles fought for their rights to be acknowledged. I have found it extremely difficult to talk to them about this; apart from anything else, there is no common vocabulary.

5. In Vatican II in 1962, the pope instigated the ideology of inculturation, an effort to incorporate native beliefs into Catholic dogma. Inculturation was not actively pursued on Flores until the 1990s.

6. Even though both my fieldworks sites are relatively delineated, I wish to make one further point. In both cases, my repeated returns allowed me to

travel widely in the region and settle for shorter or longer periods with other communities than the main one. In the Chewong case I came to meet virtually every Chewong—those who lived in the forest area as well as several more who lived in settled villages with mixed aboriginal population some distance away. My work with the Lio involved extensive periods spent with three self-contained village domains whose practices displayed recognizable variations on what, as time went on, I isolated as dominant values. This relatively modest multisited fieldwork has proved useful not only in giving me a deeper understanding, but also through facilitating subsequent comparative studies of the wider region in each case.

7. The British colonial administration drew a circle on a map in 1926 and designated the area as a game reserve. This happened to include much of Chewong traditional territory. The first British authority to enter the area was a game warden, who did so in 1936 and made contact with the Chewong for the first time. The Malaysian government has respected the reserve until the present, but logging has been carried out right up to its boundary. An elephant reserve was established in 1986 on the forest fringe, dislocating a Chewong settlement. This has been developed into a major tourist attraction, bringing a steady stream of local and foreign tourists to the area.

8. People were fully aware of Lamait's negligence and commented on this at the time. However, no one ever confronted him and no one ever withheld his normal share from him. There are no mechanisms for sanction.

9. In my defense, I must mention that the Dutch Catholic missionary, whose knowledge of Lio culture was extensive, had also not been aware of this until I pointed it out to him, and he double-checked with some of the priest-leaders (see also Sugishima 1994).

10. I collected seventy-seven of these during my first fieldwork (Howell 1982).

REFERENCES

Appadurai, Arun. 1986. Theory in Anthropology: Center or Periphery? *Comparative Studies in Society and History* 28 (2): 356–361.

Bohannan, Paul. 1959. The Impact of Money on an African Subsistence Economy. *Journal of Economic History* 19: 491–503.

Clifford, James. 1983. Power and Dialogue in Ethnography. In G. W. Stocking, ed., *Observers Observed: Essays in Ethnographic Fieldwork*. Madison: University of Wisconsin Press.

Geertz, Clifford. 1968. Thinking as a Moral Act: Ethical Dimensions of Anthropological Fieldwork in the New States. *Antioch Review* 28: 139–158.

Howell, Signe. 1982. *Chewong Myths and Legends.* Royal Asiatic Society, Malaysian Branch, Monograph no. 11.

———. 1983. Chewong Women in Transition: The Effect of Monetisation on a Hunter-Gatherer Society in Malaysia. University of Kent Centre of South-East Asian Studies, Occasional Paper 1: *Women and Development in South-East Asia.* 1984, revised version. In Adela Baer, ed., *Orang Asli Women of Malaysia: Perceptions, Situations, and Aspirations.* Subang Jaya: Centre for Orang Asli Concerns.

———. 1984. *Society and Cosmos: Chewong of Peninsular Malaysia.* Oxford: Oxford University Press (repr. 1989, University of Chicago Press).

———. 1986a. Formal Speech Acts as One Discourse. *Man* (n.s.) 21 (1): 79–101.

———. 1986b. Of Persons and Things: Exchange and Valuables among the Lio of Eastern Indonesia. *Man* (n.s.) 24:419–438.

———. 1995. Rethinking the Mother's Brother. *Indonesia Circle* 67 (November 1995): 293–317.

———. 1996a. Many Contexts, Many Meanings? Gendered Values among the Lio of Indonesia. *Journal of the Royal Anthropological Institute* (incorporating *Man* 2 (2): 253–269).

———. 1996b. A Life for "Life": Blood and Other Life-Promoting Substances in Lio Moral System. In S. Howell, ed., *For the Sake of Our Future: Sacrificing in Eastern Indonesia.* Leiden: Research School CNWS, Leiden University.

———. 2001. Recontextualizing Traditions: "Religion," "Government," and "Tradition" as Co-existing Modes of Sociality among the Northern Lio of Indonesia. In John Liep, ed., *Locating Cultural Creativity.* London: Pluto Press.

———. 2002. Our People Know the Forest: Chewong Re-creations of Uniqueness and Separateness. In Geoffrey Benjamin and Cynthia Chou, eds., *Tribal Communities in the Malay World: Historical, Social and Cultural Perspectives:* Leiden and Singapore.

———. 2011a. The Uneasy Move from Hunting, Gathering and Shifting Cultivation to Settled Agriculture: The Case of the Chewong (Malaysia). In Monica Janowski and Graeme Barker, eds., *Why Cultivate? Anthropological and Archaeological Perspectives on Foraging-Farming Transitions in Island Southeast Asia.* Cambridge: McDonald Monograph Series.

———. 2011b. Sources of Solidarity in a Cosmological Frame: Chewong, Peninsular Malaysia. In Tom Gibson and Kenneth Sillander, eds., *Anarchic Solidarity: Autonomy, Equality and Fellowship in Southeast Asia.* New Haven: Yale University Press.

Mauss, Marcel. 1966 [1925] *The Gift.* London: Routledge and Kegan Paul.

Polanyi, Karl. 2001 [1944]. *The Great Transformation.* Boston: Beacon Press.

Sahlins, Marshall. 1972. *The Original Affluent Society*. Chicago: Aldine Atherton.

Sugishima, Tadiko. 1994. Double Descent, Alliance and Botanical Metaphors among the Lionese, Central Flores. *Bijdragen Tot de Taal-, Land, en Volkenkunde*. CL (1): 146–170.

Woodburn, James. 1982. Egalitarian Societies. *Man* (n.s.) 17 (3): 431–51.

7 |

Repeated Returns and
Special Friends

*From Mythic Encounter
to Shared History*

PIERS VITEBSKY

THE BASELINE MOMENT

What can we know about the workings of time in remote, small-scale societies? Often the only substantial source will be an ethnography written by an anthropologist. Yet ethnographies are themselves subject to time: they date quickly, and the educated grandchildren of the people featured may have difficulty understanding a thirty-year-old work, let alone believing it. How can we evaluate an anthropologist's own later account of how those people have changed? And how does this account relate to changes in the anthropologist's own self?

Though time is apparently without beginning or end, one's own insertion into it, the intersection of time and self, creates an impression of a baseline. This baseline can serve as a lifelong ethnographic present against which we measure our notions and experiences of "change." This present appears to refer to the people being described, but it is also about the anthropologist and the moment of their first encounter. For some anthropologists, including myself, the emotional intensity of first fieldwork can tinge this baseline with a magical aura. The irrevocable pastness of the experience combines with this magic to create something mythic. This makes it hard to avoid a sense of this baseline as a pivotal or axial age. If ever there was a time when personal and historical baselines coincided, this was surely (by a happy coincidence) in that moment between decolonization and mass aviation, around the time of my first youthful fieldwork in the 1970s.

But what if you have worked in two very different locations, and have two widely separated baselines? I first met the Sora of southern Orissa, one of the many so-called tribal peoples of central and eastern India, in 1975. They were a rugged people, living in the remnants of a jungle and clad only in loincloths or wrap-around skirts. In every village, almost every day, the dead would speak through shamans in trance in what was surely the most elaborate form of communication between the living and the dead ever documented anywhere in the world (Vitebsky 1993). My interest in shamanism later took me to the indigenous peoples of Arctic Siberia, where I have worked since 1988 among a group in northern Yakutia (Sakha Republic) called Eveny, who live in the coldest inhabited spot in the world and nomadize around a huge jagged mountain range, riding on the backs of their reindeer in summer and on sledges in winter. The word *shaman* originated from their Tungus-family language, and though most shamans were exterminated by the Soviet Communists, the people still live on a landscape suffused with spirits (Vitebsky 2005).

Both physically and politically, the Sora and the Eveny were among the most inaccessible people in their respective countries, and to reside among them felt like a triumph of diplomatic negotiation at the official level, as well as a quite magical experience on the ground. These two locations and their people have filled much of my life ever since. But as each of these fieldsites began with a personal magical epoch, so it has had its own potential to deflect me from understanding history by dazzling me with my memory of that mythic baseline.[1]

Just as the roots of that early ethnographic present lie in the anthropologist's experience of that first encounter, so evidence for later change lies in the experience of our return, and in how this con-

Author harvesting sorghum above Ladde village, 1976.

firms, reinforces, develops, refines, or refutes our baseline. The return is one of the most powerful of all narrative tropes: in myth, the hero-traveler magically undoes an undesirable change and restores an earlier desirable situation. But this is very conspicuously not what we experience anywhere in the world today if we return to the field from a baseline in the 1970s. During the first few days of every return, we catch up with gossip: who has died, who has eloped, have you heard what so-and-so did? But these are not simply repetitions of the stories one heard on an earlier visit, but stories of change: not just the succession of generations (in principle a device of timelessness), but the arrival of the first road, shop, school, or modern kind of crime. These are social and moral events that show history at work.

But there can be many ways of returning. The locations where I happen to have lived have given me two different kinds of returns, occasional or frequent, at long or short intervals. These in turn give me two very different senses of change. Among the Sora this seems sudden; among the Eveny, gradual. My perception of these contrasting paces is based in the first instance on accidents of my own biography, but uncannily seems to match the way in which local people in each place understand their own lives. In addition, there are differences inherited from preceding ethnographic traditions. The "tribes" of India were often interpreted in the British period as timeless aboriginals cut off from the Hindu world (see the biography of Elwin by Guha [1990]; similarly Prasad [2003, xv] writes: "The 'forest of joy' was Elwin's dreamland"), and it is only recently that they have been brought fully into the more gritty and developed tradition of Indian historiography (e.g., Sundar 1997). By contrast, Soviet ethnography emphatically set the "minority" peoples of the Siberian Arctic within a relentless and politically controlling historical framework extending back even to prehistory (e.g., Dolgikh 1960; Levin and Potapov 1964).

Independently of our coming and going, or of any scholarly writing, the people studied have their own quite separate concepts and experiences of time. These people outnumber the anthropologist and are at all stages of life. Indeed, it is this multiplicity that the anthropologist has come to study, with its span of ancestors and descendants, forms of naming and sometimes reincarnation, and cults to ensure social continuity and negate the finality of death. In this sense the anthropologist is insignificant, and everything runs as it would if we had never existed. Yet we did arrive at a specific moment in the lifespan of each person we meet, and their kinship system gradually expands to include us, emphasizing our relational and time-bound existence. For example, in relation to cohorts of active young Sora adults, I have graduated from *ubbang* (little brother) to *jojo* (grandfather or ancestor).

One of the main effects of long-term fieldwork is the deepening of friendships (Bell and Coleman 1999), as the anthropologist is normalized from a freak visitor into a recurrent presence. For a few local people who become our special friends, their closeness to us may profoundly change their lives as well as our own. We come to experience change together through the very process of changing each other's lives. For them, too, as we develop our joint quests and agendas and our mutual dependencies, there arises a certain mythic founding time from the beginning of our relationship. These individuals are often anomalous or extraordinary personalities, and I shall later suggest that their relationship with us is linked to a heightened capacity to objectify their own society.

SORA OF TRIBAL INDIA

For the Sora in the 1970s, every case of illness or death was caused by a person who had previously died under similar circumstances and was perpetuating their medical, emotional, and cosmological state onto the living. To fend off this attack, one would engage in dialogue with the deceased person (Vitebsky 1993). Together, living and dead would spend several years articulating the unspoken needs of both sides in order to negotiate a resolution, ultimately transforming each dead person into a benign ancestor and recycling the ancestor's name into a new baby, thereby undoing the pain of their death and perpetuating the patrilineage.

As a hill people living perpetually at the margin between shifting centers, it seems the Sora once corresponded to Scott's model (2009) of shrewdly independent peoples who evade the state in Southeast Asia (where incidentally the Sora are linked by their Austroasiatic language). But since the British conquest of their area in 1866, the Sora have lived under a system of governance that puts them at the bottom of every pile, ethnically, economically, and ecologically. Even when operating their un-Hindu tribal cosmology, Sora shamans gain their powers by marrying spirits in the underworld who are high-caste Hindu rajas, policemen, and government officers—that is, domesticated counterparts of the very people who oppress the Sora above ground. Though I did not see it in these terms during the 1970s, it now seems to me that much of Sora theology is about coping with the limits of agency; and this is leading me to interpret much of the change that I have witnessed, both here and in Siberia, in terms of fluctuations in agency and attempts to compensate for them.

After an intense immersion in Sora life for several years in the 1970s and early '80s, during which I served as a shaman's assistant, I did not return until 1992. No Sora ever visited me in England, nor did I receive letters from my nonliterate friends. In the meantime, Sora dialogues with the dead seemed from my account to be so fulfilling that they were even hailed by psychoanalysts (correctly I believe) as an inspired and powerful bereavement therapy.[2] However, I failed to foresee how this cosmology would so quickly cease to satisfy the Sora themselves, or to spot the time-bomb left by the Canadian Baptist missionaries who were being chased out by the government as I was arriving. Renewed visits since the 1990s have shown me how all young adults are becoming Baptists (or in neighboring areas less well known to me, fundamentalist Hindus)[3] as they are drawn more fully into the national political space of India through an influx of government "development" bringing roads, schooling, and literacy. Between them, the mutually hostile Christian and Hindu thrusts are squeezing out the shamanist worldview of the old-timers.

With my intense focus on shamans and their clients in the 1970s, I had failed to see this process developing—or at least to acknowledge it. As one of the last of the elders who wears a loincloth, converses with the Sora dead, and sacrifices animals to them within sight of bemused youths in Western dress, I am losing a world no human will ever see again. The effect for me has been of a sudden, cataclysmic change.

The Sora themselves share this sense of drastic change, through their evaluation of it is mixed. Rupture is inherent in the rhetoric and experience of evangelical conversion, where it intentionally cuts across a previous cosmology that strives for continuity through repetitive recycling: ancestral names distinguished by patrilineage are replaced by a repertoire of randomly distributed biblical names; funeral gatherings based on ritualized interaction between lineages and affines are replaced by congregations whose composition reflects the structure of parishes and church associations. Older people are afraid to die, since they know their children will not talk to them afterward; for younger people, it feels liberating as they give up animal sacrifice and "nakedness" (though also supposedly palm-wine and polygamy), and abandon subsistence agriculture to join the scramble for jobs as road laborer, pastor, or schoolteacher.

In a recent article (Vitebsky 2008) I discussed two people, Paranto and Taranti (both pseudonyms), whom I have known since they were children in the 1970s. Paranto grew up as a shamanist before becoming a Baptist, and he now has difficulty finding a way to mourn his dead father following a minimalist Christian funeral; Taranti became a shaman but has been forced by her Baptist children to give up. I gained a sudden insight into each of them when an interaction with me led them to break down in tears, in an unusual display of what I take to be unresolved grief: for Paranto this was when he projected his feelings for his father on to me as I was about to leave him; for Taranti it was when I provided an unexpected opportunity for her to go into trance and she discovered that she had lost the ability to do so.[4] I interpret the emotional distress of both my friends as an index of their inability to create a new kind of agency for themselves under new circumstances. However, their failure to become new, Christian persons has also helped me to understand the renegotiated agency of other, successful converts.

My friends are caught up in historical change, but they give their experience little if any "historical" interpretation. Sora has no terminology of historicity, instead placing past events within times such as *purban* (long ago) or genres such as *juana* (an account of an event witnessed by people we know) versus *kata* (myth, or events which happened before living memory). Taranti in particular frames her situation explicitly in mythic terms of her blocked relationship with her spirits.

Another Sora friend, by contrast, has played a more active role in historical change and has also developed a more reflective historical consciousness—perhaps too much for his own good, as we shall see. Mogana was born in the early 1930s. Though his father and sister were shamans, Mogana became one of the very few Sora Baptists in the 1940s. He traveled throughout India on church business, served as a linguistic advisor to the Canadian missionaries and Sora pastors translating the Bible, and was elected chairman (*sarpanch*) of the local council. Now, in a community where most die young (of disease), he has outlived almost all his contemporaries.

In my first years I hesitated to seek him out, since I assumed he would disapprove of my interests. But one day I took a chance and asked him to help me understand a tape of shamanic chants. Mogana had moved so far from his father's culture that at first he could not even work out the poetic syntax; but then he became enchanted by a recording of an exquisite incantation by the young Taranti. This epiphany changed Mogana's life. He begged me to bring him more tapes, and started accompanying me to rituals, his eyes opened to a world he had once shared and since forgotten.

One day, I took Mogana to see a special ritual in a remote mountain village. There he fell in love with a younger girl and eloped with her, despite being already married. I was seen by everyone as the catalyst of his affair, and was widely applauded for this by non-Christian men at drinking parties ("When are you going to find *me* a nice girl like that?"). But the Sora pastors made Mogana uncomfortable in church, and he was dropped from the team of Bible translators. For twenty-seven years, until his first wife died in 2005 and he ceased technically to be a bigamist, Mogana was not invited to speak at Christian meetings.

Throughout his years in disgrace, he held firmly to his faith; but he also spent ever more time around the shamanic rituals I was studying, making perceptive parallels between Sora and biblical ritual, a liberal comparative theologian trapped in a fundamentalist world. I started to wonder what he was really doing when he started to pose questions directly to the dead, ostensibly to help me fill gaps in my research data. His love for the words, sounds, and feelings of the shamanist world merged with his love for his father—and for me too, as the person he trusted to record and preserve it all. As each old shaman or ritual specialist dies with no successor, Mogana laments the loss of a great repository of the old culture, weeping and whispering to me, "I've still got his myths and chants in my liver!" I believe that Mogana is weeping not only for the loss of a world, but also for his active role in precipitating this loss.

EVENY OF ARCTIC SIBERIA

I arrived among the Eveny, speakers of a Tungus-Manchu language, in 1988. It was early in the period of reform called *perestroika,* and three to four generations after the start of the Soviet regime which perestroika was to unravel. Unlike my return to the Sora after a long gap, I have returned to Siberia almost every year for twenty years, witnessing the end of this regime and the start of postsocialist attempts at building a new life. In between trips I have received letters and Siberian visitors in England. The effect has been of a constant, all-round topping up of current information, a perpetual ethnographic present which develops in "real time."

To go back for brief but frequent visits, monitoring the minutiae of every political shift in these eventful years, seems to match the Eveny sense of historical time. Though individual events may be shocking (the mortality rate, especially through violent deaths among young men, is very high), there is little sense of *historical* shock. Indeed, and in striking contrast to the Sora, the Eveny have a strong discourse of lack of change. Twenty years after my first arrival, a return to a herding community, even when transformed from a state farm to a private cooperative, does not look or feel very different even though they have just passed through one of the greatest political shifts in world history.

When I first arrived, even the cautious, understated Eveny were nevertheless caught up in the euphoria that characterized the era of perestroika throughout the Soviet Union. Perestroika offered a rhetoric of rupture, a repudiation of past policies and their human cost. This quest for rupture as redemption seems analogous to evangelical Christian conversion among the Sora—except that what the Eveny had to break was not the mythic, spirit-given inequities of a cosmology, but the cruelty of a very human history. Eveny historical consciousness is so well developed that they see themselves as bit players at the edge of the most momentous global events, from Stalin's gulags (a white man's madness imposed on their territory), through Hitler's invasion of the Soviet Union (correctly prophesied by a local shaman, who was executed for his pains), to the nuclear bomb testing of the Cold War (which contaminated their reindeer pasture). Even among today's fairly educated Sora leaders, one could not find narratives positioning Sora political experience with such specific historical sensibility.

The most intimate family narratives of the Eveny are likewise very explicitly anchored in history. During the early Soviet period of the 1920s–1930s the reindeer that formed the foundation of their way of life were confiscated and put into collective farms, while indigenous leaders, shamans, and poets were killed. By the 1960s women were being moved to jobs in centralized villages and children institutionalized in harsh, distant, Russian-speaking boarding schools (many dying of starvation and exposure as they ran away); the herders were left behind on a lonely, all-male landscape.

So it turns out that there is indeed a discourse of shocking and cataclysmic rupture—but that this was long before my baseline moment of 1988. Rather than being present during a big change, I now feel I arrived thirty or even sixty years *after* the big change. Eveny discourse today is not simply about a lack of recent change, but about a *failure* to change now that this is needed. Even the impulse of perestroika has not proved strong enough to redeem this earlier trauma. During the 1990s there was a plunge from initial hope to great economic deprivation, with widespread disappearance of wages, social welfare, and helicopters or biplanes. On this landscape with no cash and no roads, many people no longer expected to go anywhere, ever, for the rest of their lives. Reindeer herders became even more isolated in their bachelorhood; the boarding schools had already produced two generations who did not know how to herd reindeer or parent their own children since they had not been parented themselves; and the terrible catalogue of young people's drunken accidents, murders, and suicides escalated. The discourse of failure to change for the better developed an undertone of a change for the worse: morality was declining, young people had no fear of stealing offerings from graves, and minority peoples like the Eveny were heading for extinction (Vitebsky 2002), as "endangered species." The general revival of Russia's economy in the 2000s, riding on the back of high world energy prices, has brought little comfort to the broken families of these communities.

My closest and most complex relationship here has been with a man of my own age called Tolya, some of whose adventures are recounted in detail (with his permission) in my book *The Reindeer People* (Vitebsky 2005). Tolya was born in a nomadic reindeer-herding camp and like all his generation fell victim to the boarding school. By the time I arrived he had become a member of the Communist Party and the elected chairman of the local council (by a strange coincidence, the same position that Mogana has held in India). Tolya has given me logistical support and valuable ethnographic commentary ever since we met on my first trip in 1988. In return, he has used me as a practical and symbolic resource in his many battles to reform the regional administration and improve the lives of herding families. But the experience of accompanying me on my research trips around the camps stimulated a new quest of his own, to document and analyze the "traditional" past of his people. As a result of knowing me, Tolya became an anthropologist himself, did a PhD at the regional university, and is now a lecturer there.

Tolya's new profession is closely tied to his devotion to the mother from whom he had been distanced by his boarding school. Our trips round the nomadic camps took us back to her, among many other elders. When the old lady finally died of liver cancer, he felt that he had lost one of his last living links with the generation who knew and lived the "real" culture. The moment of her death was marked by a dream. "I was in the city," he told me afterward, "and in my dream I saw the whole sky on fire above the village back home. The sky just exploded. The next day I received a telegram saying my mother had died." The dream echoed a childhood experience in which Tolya and some other children had been showered with fallout from an atomic bomb test. The other children died, though Tolya survived, and he later blamed radiation for the cancer which killed his mother. The dream felt like the end of the world in many senses—and with his mother, the end of the world he is dedicating his life to salvaging.

I interpret Tolya's anthropological quest as a parallel to his career as a political activist. Both follow a sequence of trauma and reparation, from his anger at his childhood boarding-school abuse, through his disillusionment with the Communist Party (with which he earlier colluded in its mission to destroy the previous culture), to the death of his mother. If all of this is not to become an irreparable loss, he must salvage the memory of his mother and perpetuate it in his anthropological writings. I am the trigger of this quest and his partial collaborator (my research grants pay for helicopters, and the front cover of his book uses my photo of the old lady).

HEART OF RUPTURE: MISSIONARY THRUST
AND RECONFIGURATION OF AGENCY

Change seems drastic among the Sora and sluggish among the Eveny. What should we make of this coincidence between their perception of the nature of change and mine? Perhaps my impressions, formed by the chance pattern of my returns, and theirs, formed by living their lives, coincide because this really is how it has been?

The first thing to say is that even though the timing is different, the processes seem related. In both places, there has been an intensification of a colonial presence that had hitherto been relatively light—and of its alien ideology. Where these people were previously neglected, it now suddenly matters to someone elsewhere to change them radically. The role of colonialism and the state, as well as the specific cosmologies of the Communist, Baptist, and Hindu evangelisms, may be different, but we can recognize a similar centralizing, totalizing thrust: where the local community's frame of reference is local it must be made universal, where their time is cyclical or non-destinational it must be made future-oriented, where their sense of morality comes from within it must be structured and validated by an outside source.

The missionary encounter makes some people experience a powerful rejection of their parents' view of the world. These people then become local leaders in the new idiom—Baptist pastors in Soraland, Communist Party officials in Soviet Siberia. Sometimes the militant combative ideology of the local converts becomes more extreme than that of the missionaries. In Soraland, I have watched the upsurge of this ripple into a wave from the early stages; among the Eveny, I have watched the backwash as the first ideological wave has failed. The arrival of the missionaries provides a new idiom for previous local tensions and factionalism, and amplifies them onto a larger stage. Whereas earlier, struggles would have taken place largely in a relatively closed realm of discourse (like disputes between litigants in a consensual legal universe), now competing positions are transformed into two radically conflicting worldviews. So instead of petitioning the dead to confirm their version of an inheritance, rival Sora heirs now take their dispute to court; Tolya's ideological struggle with the anti-reformist state farm director is a continuation in a new idiom of a conflict between their families in pre-Soviet times.

Though the landscapes, culture, politics, and personalities are very different, there are striking parallels between these two settings, and it seems their time-scales can be read off against one another within an overarching colonial and postcolonial trajectory. These are not simply two spaces, or even two stages in my own life, but also two local time zones within a wider global time. It seems the Sora are two or three generations behind the Eveny in a cycle of action and reaction, trauma and reparation, which all take place within a process of tighter incorporation into a large, multiethnic nation-state. Broadly, the Sora in the 1990s went through a process which corresponds to that undergone by the Eveny in the 1920s and '60s. From the 1920s, young Siberian native adults were selected and sent to a special college in Leningrad (now St. Petersburg), where they were trained to occupy administrative or Communist Party positions back home; from the 1960s all young children were taken into boarding schools from the age of seven. I remember many equivalent moments from my own time among the Sora, though these occurred decades later: how the first child who went to boarding school hanged himself in 1976 (and afterward spoke about his misery through the mouth of a shaman), or how power was configured through kin-groups and headmen with no presence of political parties at all (in the momentous general election of 1977 when Indira Gandhi was thrown out of power, no Sora I knew voted). Today, every Sora child spends years in school, and virtually all relations of power are routed through political parties.

The outcome of this rupture has been a radical reconfiguration of agency. But this agency, and its interpretation, have worked in a very different way in each location. In Sora awareness, whatever earlier ruptures there may have been (such as 1866, which imposed a feudal system of native headmen collaborating with the administration) were largely masked by their cyclical cosmology. Struggles with traders and officials were cast in an ahistorical scenario of helpless victims persecuted by demon-like outsiders and shielded by shamans who could summon familiar spirits who were themselves from the same social groups as the persecutors. This steady-state model was the main focus of my early study, and it is its final failure that has now overwhelmed both the old Sora and me. The shift to Baptist Christianity occurs as their humiliation (Robbins 2004, 15–16) ceases to be amenable to the mechanism whereby previous generations compensated for a lack of agency in the outside world with an elaborate interpersonal psychological agency inside the community. It allows young Sora to move beyond their parents' victimhood, in a rupture that is both the source and the product of a new kind of agency of their own. The pogroms recently conducted by Hindu fundamentalist groups against Christian Sora and other tribals can be interpreted as arising from a resentment at their growing assertiveness.

The Eveny had a rupture earlier, of a sort that made them highly conscious of the nature and limitations of their agency. We have seen how this has led them to locate themselves, humbly but insistently, in the greatest historical events of a wider world. I saw their sudden (externally introduced) opportunity to enhance their agency from 1988 into the early 1990s, and the subsequent failure of this. It now appears, both to them and to me, that this period was not a great celebratory transition at all, but a bruised aftershock from three generations of enforced rupture, and a confirmation that however sophisticated their historical awareness, their agency would remain extremely limited. If the 1970s really was an axial age among many of the world's indigenous peoples, as it may appear to a generation of their anthropologists, this is a reminder that those communities themselves may live with an infinite regress of meta-baselines (such as the traumatic Japanese invasion for the Ilongot; Rosaldo 1980) stretching beyond any lifespan and rendering the anthropologist's baseline contingent and distracting.

However, the anthropologist's baseline unavoidably colors the written ethnography. Looking back to the 1970s, I still believe that I correctly understood the theology and psychology of the Sora practice of holding dialogues with the dead. I also believe that its disappearance in front of my eyes is a loss of a great human intellectual and emotional achievement. But my historical understanding was undeveloped because I underestimated this practice's political inadequacy and denied the change that was growing around me. History was not going the way I wanted it to go, as I studied a cult of lineage continuity and looked back to ever more ancient ancestors and swashbuckling stories of their archaic doings.[5] Even if this vision was fed by an older British style of isolating "Tribals" from the Indian mainstream, it also matched the view of most Sora. The people I lived with complained vehemently about oppression, but had no exit strategy.[6]

My Eveny baseline experience in the late 1980s was historically better positioned. I was more mindful of history because when I started out, at least in those exhilarating and progressive first years of perestroika, history was on my side (and also—except for an antireformist old guard who were Tolya's enemies—on theirs). My book (Vitebsky 2005) can be read as a micro-barometer of twenty years of political change as this reached down to each family and brought them up sharply against the shifting possibilities and limits of their agency. My historical awareness was further reinforced by my experience of frequent returns, amounting for some periods almost to a constant presence.

ANTHROPOLOGIST AND FRIENDS

But it is not so easy to pinpoint the locus of agency, or of its absence. Unlike the revolutionary violence done to the Siberians, the change among the Sora at first sight appears spontaneous: nobody has physically compelled them to convert, nobody will kill or punish them if they do not. But coercion can blend into collusion. Some people are ready to welcome such a change, because their old world is crumbling from within (see also Tuzin 1997). I have briefly reviewed a range of Siberian personalities who variously embraced or subverted the Soviet system under pressure from Communist missionaries (Vitebsky 2002), and will explore motivations among Sora Christian enthusiasts in detail in Vitebsky (2012).

But what if we replace the external missionary with an anthropologist? The arrival and long-term residence of an anthropologist provides an unusual opportunity for local people to see their positions, processes and contradictions in a new light. Forestry Department, Revenue Department and missionaries in India; Communist Party in Siberia; police, administration, traders, moneylenders everywhere—all come to change people's vision or constrain their agency, and thus place them somewhere between cooperation and resistance. The anthropologist's intentions are different, and harder to fathom. But this person can also become an unusual resource, as an advocate who has greater social mobility than anyone rooted only in local relations. This mobility can give the anthropologist a trickster-like quality, as when the Sora believed I was immune to sorcery or sent me (successfully) to get a ban on forest shifting cultivation lifted, or when an Eveny village administrator entrusted me with an emergency petition on a scrap of paper to convey personally to the president of the Sakha Republic (which I did). A community with an anthropologist is better defended than a community without one.

Some local people become closely involved with this unusual kind of outsider. Our lives become intertwined, and there is a complicated interplay between our agendas and life changes. What does my presence do to my friends, and what do they want from our friendship?

In those first, archaic years, Sora used me repeatedly to give them protection by interceding with forest officers, traders, or police to block the endless catalogue of bribes, extortions and arrests that kept them intimidated and impoverished from generation to generation. At the time, I was elaborating my psycho-theological interpretation of their dialogues with the dead, and it was only later that I realized how their social and political subordination (which I understood well enough in those terms) was also a driving force behind their theology. Not only were their dialogues with the dead structured to deflect attack and transform victimhood; I now believe that as intercessor I was assimilated to the role of a shaman's familiar spirit, the high-caste official who is somehow miraculously on their side.

By contrast, Eveny have rarely wanted me to do any specific defensive work for them. They realistically exercise agency wherever they perceive an opportunity, and do not bother where it is pointless. They want to discuss archaeology, philosophy, history (using the Russian word *istoriya*), and even the philosophy of *istoriya*. They are also interested in strategy, and Eveny and other native groups have used me or my research students for various schemes of social and economic empowerment. But their most profound use of me has been to bear witness: "Write a book, tell the world how we live." This is a way of building on a very high respect for book learning, derived from Soviet education and amounting almost to a fetishisation,[7] to position themselves in history: a community that has not been described by a historian or anthropologist is a community that may as well never have existed. This is the gap in their agency that is called into visibility by their encounter with me—the ability to inscribe themselves in the record. Against a rhetoric of imminent extinction, they look to a future which may extend without them: "Your children should write a book in 2020 saying how they nomadized here with us, how we really did exist." In an uncanny echo of the gulag that the white man overlaid across their landscape, this recalls an urge well documented among inmates of prison-camps that even if they do not survive themselves, their stories and their suffering must be told: the worst thing of all is to disappear without trace.

Individuals like Mogana and Tolya guide my interpretation of time by means of a friendship that is perhaps made possible by their exceptional insight into their own social world, an orientation making them unusually comparativist or relativist. As curious, restless, anomalous personalities, they perhaps resemble an anthropologist: Tolya has actually become one, and Mogana might well have done so if he had had an education.

But there is a paradox. These progressive leaders are visionaries, and have suffered for their vision not only from political opposition but also from a conflict within themselves: they are caught, ambivalently, in a nostalgia for the past. Perhaps it is precisely because their impulse for social reform arises from deep local roots that they also somehow become selected as mourners for a disappearing way of life. They crystallize and perform a wider collective mourning, which is neglected in the community's rush toward the future. Contrast Taranti, whose mourning has less of an outlet: like several other Sora shamans undergoing torment from their abandoned spirits, she is very open with me about her emotional experience (more so than the secretive old shamans were in the 1970s—is this because these younger shamans have grown up with me?); but she is not able to place this experience in a wider frame or join me in a shared venture of social analysis. Though her failure to enter trance gave her a moment of intense feeling, which may reverberate till the end of her days, she is not able to develop her story, with or without me, as Mogana has done.

Mogana and Tolya were perhaps always predisposed to make this move, and this is why they were ready to form a life-changing friendship with an outsider. In this process, the anthropologist may not be so different from the (Christian or Communist) missionary, even though their agendas are so opposed. Both draw out confessions and other personal narratives that go beyond those current in the community. Our presence encourages or enables people with such a predisposition to objectify their lives in a particular way. For Tolya at least, the way was prepared through his Russian education, so that the past becomes "history" (*istoriya*) and his mother's way of life a "culture" (*kul'tura*). But even Mogana has come to feel that whatever I have been pursuing all these years is not just a way of being and doing, but some kind of entity that can be packaged. If he had access to the word "culture," he would probably use it.

In sharing, even serving, their nostalgia, my baseline is caught up with theirs in a shared mythicization—though I can also be drawn into further myths that predate my arrival. Mogana's nostalgia is for a way of life of his childhood, which he did so much to replace; Tolya's is for a more distant, pre-Communist past, the ethnographic present of his mother's youth, which gives him a personal baseline predating his own lifespan. Both men have been used by history to unleash more than they could have anticipated. For Mogana, his childhood vision of a Christian future has accelerated beyond his control and rendered his past irretrievable; for Tolya, who has passed through both Communist enthusiasm and its repudiation under perestroika, his reformist zeal has unraveled twice over, so that he has lost not only the past but also the future.

With Mogana at the author's home in England, 2010.

Having worked in their youth for a new social order, both men end up in later life using their community's outside anthropologist to help them salvage and reconstruct the past of their unconscious longing. Now that we are all growing old (Mogana's health is quite frail), both Mogana and Tolya are very concerned to archive all possible information about their old cultures, to provide documentation for future generations who are as yet uninterested. This fits the feelings of many Eveny, who are avid readers of ethnography, history, and archaeology, and Tolya is actualizing a widespread ideal on their behalf. But in seeking to document the past and approaching the witness-seeking position of the Eveny, Mogana is going very much against the Sora current. He is not only behind his time but also ahead of it, as he has been all his life.

Both men expect me to create something monumental out of my decades of note-taking and tape-recording. I believe they also want my help in providing themselves with the emotional release of closure, in scientizing the (obsolete but supposedly purer) ethnographic present of their baseline nostalgia, and in reconciling this morally and logistically with a continuing future-oriented program of reform. This is a duty I cannot shirk, and indeed, much of their agenda corresponds to a deep emotional urge in me. This urge is fueled by my own aging, and by the turnover of people within those communities, which now seems to me increasingly rapid. But my perspective is changing not just because I am growing older, nor because of other people's aging, but also because in these places the nature of time itself has been changing, as I realize from seeing generations experiencing its passage in different ways. Ultimately it is this that I am coming to grasp through being present all these years and being lucky enough to find such good lifelong friends.

NOTES

I am grateful to Signe Howell and Aud Talle for organizing the original workshop in Oslo and for comments from members of that workshop, as well as of seminars of the Magic Circle in Cambridge and the Czech Association for Social Anthropology in Prague; also to Igor Krupnik and Jean Comaroff for additional comments; and above all to my friends in the field, though I shall never be able to do justice to their life stories.

1. I was born in 1949 and was twenty-six when I first reached the Sora in 1975 and thirty-nine when I first reached the Eveny in 1988. When I met the Sora I was single and a student of low status; by the time I met the Eveny I had a professional title, family, and high-level official support.

2. In 1989, the American Psychoanalytic Association hosted a two-day Anthropology-Psychoanalysis Colloquium dedicated to the discussion of my account of Sora dialogues with the dead.

3. I have less familiarity with this neo-Hindu movement. It seems to be a movement of reform and purification that uses a rhetoric of continuity by appropriating the past, and thus offers the very opposite of rupture. But I think the destination is the same, though in different terms: working out an idiom for closer integration into wider Indian society.

4. For a video of Taranti discussing her situation the next day, see http://
n-topus.com/fivelang/taranti.xhtml.

5. I imagine this may apply to many anthropologists who started fieldwork
in the 1970s. For example, Paul Spencer writes of his youthful work among the
Samburu that it reflected "too close an identification with a widespread African
sense of tradition" (Spencer 1992, 60).

6. However, there is a long history of sporadic Sora uprisings (*fituri*) in
which they burn down the villages of nearby trading castes, and more recently
some presence of Naxalite (Maoist) guerillas.

7. One of my favorite literacy moments was seeing a young reindeer herder
relaxing in his tent with a Russian magazine serialization of Wittgenstein's commentary on Frazer's *Golden Bough*.

REFERENCES

Bell, J., and S. Coleman, eds. 1999. *The Anthropology of Friendship*. Oxford: Berg.

Dolgikh, B. O. 1960. *Rodovoy i plemennoy sostav narodov Sibiri v XVII veke* [The
clan and tribe composition of the peoples of Siberia in the 17th century].
Trudy Instituta Etnografii AN SSSR, vol 60. Moscow: Nauka Publishers.

Guha, R. 1990. *Savaging the Civilized: Verrier Elwin, his Tribals, and India*. Delhi:
Oxford University Press.

Levin, M., and L. Potapov. 1964. *The Peoples of Siberia*. Chicago: University of
Chicago Press [Russian original 1956].

Prasad, A. 2003. *Against Ecological Romanticism: Verrier Elwin and the Making
of an Anti-modern Tribal Identity*. Delhi: Three Essays Collective.

Robbins, J. 2004. *Becoming Sinners: Christianity and Moral Torment in a Papua
New Guinea Society*. Berkeley: University of California Press.

Rosaldo, R. 1980. *Ilongot Headhunting, 1883–1974: A Study in Society and History*. Stanford, Calif.: Stanford University Press.

Scott, J. 2009. *The Art of Not Being Governed: An Anarchist History of Upland
Southeast Asia*. New Haven, Conn.: Yale University Press.

Spencer, P. 1992. Automythologies and the Reconstruction of Aging. In J. Okely and
H. Callaway, eds., *Anthropology and Autobiography*, 50–63. London: Routledge.

Sundar, N. 1997. *Subalterns and Sovereigns: An Anthropological History of Bastar,
1854–2006*. Delhi: Oxford University Press.

Tuzin, D. 1997. *The Cassowary's Revenge: The Life and Death of Masculinity in a
New Guinea Society*. Chicago: University of Chicago Press.

Vitebsky, P. 1993. *Dialogues with the Dead: The Discussion of Mortality among the
Sora of Eastern India*. Cambridge: Cambridge University Press.

————. 2002. Withdrawing from the Land: Social and Spiritual Crisis in the Indigenous Russian Arctic. In C. Hann, ed., *Postsocialism: Ideals, Ideologies and Practices in Eurasia,* 180–195. New York: Routledge.

————. 2005. *The Reindeer People: Living with Animals and Spirits in Siberia.* Boston: Houghton Mifflin.

————. 2008. Loving and Forgetting: Moments of Inarticulacy in Tribal India. *Journal of the Royal Anthropological Institute* 14: 243–261 (the Henry Myers Lecture 2006).

————. 2012. *Living without the Dead: Religious Change and Emotional Loss in Tribal India* (provisional title). Chicago: University of Chicago Press.

8 | Compressed Globalization and Expanding Desires in Marovo Lagoon, Solomon Islands

EDVARD HVIDING

FROM HOME REEF TO HIGH COURT: CONTEXTS OF AN EXPANDING FIELD

I shall trace changes and continuities in my field locality, fieldwork contexts, and fieldwork strategies over some twenty-five years of continuous anthropological engagement with the people of the Marovo Lagoon, in the Western Pacific nation of Solomon Islands. As a regularly returning anthropological visitor to Solomon Islands since 1986, I have had the privilege of being allowed to follow closely the Marovo people and their expanding engagements with the world, a process that has continued to give me insights that have not always been of the expected kind.

A Commonwealth nation independent since 1978, Solomon Islands is remarkable for its population-to-language ratio: among an estimated population in 2010 of close to 600,000, between 75 and 85 languages (depending on linguistic definition) are spoken. Being resource-rich (in the form of fish, timber, and minerals) with a low population density, this nation of mainly large mountainous islands is also fraught with inter-island tension, and experienced armed civil unrest and almost complete government collapse in the period 1998–

2003. Located in the New Georgia islands in the western Solomons, Marovo Lagoon is a globally connected—yet by most world standards still remote—tropical place of internationally renowned high marine and terrestrial biodiversity. The lagoon area also exemplifies Melanesian cultural and linguistic diversity, with 13,000 people and five languages, and a complex history of migrations, inter-island raiding and trading, colonial intervention, and missionary enterprise (Hviding 1996a; Hviding and Bayliss-Smith 2000; Hviding 2005).

When I first arrived in Solomon Islands in 1986, rural life was still dominated by elements of British colonial legacy, a three-tiered system of government with some rural outreach (including vestiges of a "headman" system), and mainstream modernist agendas promoting "development"—rather inefficiently pursued by the national government. Meanwhile the rural majority of the population retained overall control over everyday life through a robust subsistence economy based on customary ownership of land, sea, and the resources there. As I carried out my first, and longest, period of fieldwork during 1986–1987, I was allowed to participate in this tropical village life where people lived and worked with close kin, and managed—through a very modest cash income from copra, marine products such as shark fins and pearl shell, and the local marketing of food crops—to cover their households' equally modest needs for cash, mainly for school fees and the proverbial consumption goods quartet of "soap, salt, kerosene, and sugar." Intruding on this quiet post-independence period typical of life in the rural Solomons were a few international actors, both concentrating their resource extraction efforts in the western parts of the nation: Solomon Taiyo, a Solomons-Japanese venture in industrial tuna fishing, which exploited lagoons such as that of Marovo for live baitfish, and Lever's Pacific Timber, a subsidiary of the giant Unilever corporation, which carried out large-scale logging mainly on land obtained as "forest estate" by the colonial government (Barclay 2008; Bennett 2000).

In the early 1990s things started changing rapidly, as large-scale timber extraction by Asian logging companies accelerated throughout Solomon Islands, as the reform (and later decline) of government virtually abolished the state's rural presence, and as conservation-oriented nongovernmental organizations began defining villages as "communities" and aspired to intervene in what they saw as a decline of customary leadership and the ravages of logging. The late 1980s and early 1990s also saw a boom in rural desires for the new concept of ecotourism. For the Marovo Lagoon, the sudden growth of eco-tourism was fueled by the rapid decline of copra prices and the rise of international conservation-oriented attention—including an unsuccessful New Zealand–funded move to have the lagoon added to UNESCO's World Heritage list. While I traveled and worked throughout the lagoon area during this period of intense economic (and moral) reorientation, I observed, and helped write a number of funding applications for, the building of many small ecotourism resorts consisting of a thatched house or two and an outhouse over the water. The desires of all these new village-based ecotourism operators were hardly fulfilled. The explosive growth of arrivals by adventurous tourists projected by the New Zealand tourism consultants never materialized. By 1996 most had already given up, and in their capacities as customary land owners many made swift transitions to a very different type of internationally connected enterprise: large-scale logging of the rainforest by Asian companies, which gave landowning kin groups windfall profits in the form of timber royalties and exceeded the horizon of any previously existing economic ambition in the rural Solomons.

Meanwhile the nation slid into a period of armed conflict between the Isatabu Freedom Movement (representing aggrieved land owners of Guadalcanal) and the Malaita Eagle Force (representing a large diaspora of laborers and dependents from the island of Malaita resident on Guadalcanal). The capital, Honiara, became a Malaitan-controlled enclave, and government decayed toward bankruptcy and retreated from its already restricted rural reach. In June 2000 the conflict on Guadalcanal escalated into a coup d'état that removed the elected prime minister Ulufa'alu and replaced him with a government supported by the Malaita Eagle Force (Fraenkel 2004; Kabutaulaka 2001b; Moore 2004). In this context of government collapse, the situation in the western parts of the nation, including the timber-rich New Georgia Group where the Marovo Lagoon is located, was dominated by an unstable diversity of connections between the local and the global, involving intense interaction with Asian logging companies (which saw little need to close down their operations in a situation of national collapse), and a continuing but diminishing activist presence of Anglo-European conservation organizations. The situation in the Western Solomons was complicated even more by violent spillover from Guadalcanal, by a presence of armed irregulars from the Bougainville Revolutionary Army, which had long operated just across the border with Papua New Guinea, and by a unilateral declaration by the Western Solomons as a state-in-federation on national independence day, 7 July 2000.

Against this chaotic background, everyday life among the village households in Marovo Lagoon and the rest of the Western Solomons continued in quiet ways, buffered by local resource ownership as all sources of cash except timber royalties disappeared. Meanwhile court cases over land rights and royalties escalated rapidly. The expansion from 1990 to 2000 of the scale of events, relations, and connections in Marovo Lagoon was truly remarkable, and the retreat of the state from about 2000 did little to shrink the scale of local engagements with the global as the contested scenes of logging and conservation continued to unfold and develop, now in ever more unpredictable ways (Hviding and Baines 1994; Hviding 2003a, 2006).

Of particular interest for understanding this expansion of scale, not yet sufficiently studied, are the accelerating, diversifying, and increasingly mutualist relations in rural Solomon Islands between customary land owners and timber-hungry Asian companies. These companies, largely subsidiaries of Malaysian, Indonesian, and Korean corporations, are difficult to study ethnographically, since they make little documentation available about their activities in the Solomons, and since rural logging camps and company offices in town do not welcome any visitors not themselves involved in logging (Hviding and Bayliss-Smith 2000, 206–209; see Kabutaulaka 2001a for a rare example of fieldwork in the logging industry). The parallel but much less successful "community-oriented" engagements by international NGOs, including major players like WWF, are easier to study, given their copious reporting (mainly in "grey" literature and on the internet) and their emphasis on open "workshop"-type activities (Hviding and Bayliss-Smith 2000, chapters 11–12; Hviding 2003a). The representatives and reports of the conservation organizations tend to view the active local agents in rural locations like Marovo Lagoon as passive victims of global political economy, with foreign logging companies as a particularly evil force. This simplified and paternalistic representation of rural Solomon Islanders has dominated much international discourse, has informed countless conservation project proposals and development policy documents, and ignores the complex processes of intense mutual engagement in Solomon Islands between customary landowning groups and the logging industry.

Considering the long history in Island Melanesia of large-scale social, economic, and political inter-island relations (Spriggs 1997), it comes as no surprise that rural Melanesians should be capable of understanding and influencing the power games of outside worlds. The first decade of the twenty-first century has indeed seen a remarkable reconfiguration of power in the Western Solomons, through the rise of a once obscure prophet movement—the Christian Fellowship Church—into a major actor in politics and rural development in this part of the country, with close connections to politics on the national level (Hviding, forthcoming). These twists and turns of indigenous leadership in Marovo Lagoon indicate a form of *longue durée* that conceptually connects the postcolonial and precolonial as two historical stages when local politics drive larger-scale systems in unpredictable ways disconnected from "the moral certainties that colonialism . . . simultaneously enforced and enabled" (Thomas 1997, 23). My recurrent fieldwork has shown me how events in the Marovo Lagoon over the past few decades have striking elements of unpredictability.

In the final scenes of *Chea's Great Kuarao* (Hviding et al. 2000), a documentary film produced with a Bergen-based team from footage we filmed in Marovo Lagoon in 1996, the two hundred or so people of a village in central Marovo called Chea are seen celebrating their successful completion of a remarkable communal fishing effort, carried out over the period 9–11 September. More than an act of practical fishing, the very special method called *kuarao* requires several days of labor-demanding tasks and the participation at various stages of young and old, male and female. First the old men examine signs of moon, tide, and wind and decide when to commence. On the initial day the adult men gather several hundred meters of a climbing vine (*Flagellaria indica*) from the coastal forest and produce three tight coils from it. The following dawn sees these coils unrolled as a large circle in a few meters of water over ocean-facing reefs, with the participation of the entire village (except menstruating women, and those too old). During the early morning hours the circle of vines is gradually tightened as the tide goes down. By about nine o'clock a large catch of reef fish should be confined in a narrow space that can be encircled by a gill net, after which a plant poison is used to paralyze the fish, which can then be gathered and gutted. While ideally resulting in a large catch that can be used for a feast or sold, the kuarao of the Western Solomon Islands is also a communal ritual that demonstrates the customary rights over reefs and displays the ability of the village to organize large-scale work under proper leadership.

The third day puts all this social effort and moral communication on display, and so on 11 September 1996 the people of Chea and their neighbor village (with which they share a school) held a bazaar, organized to maximize the monetary income from the kuarao and the public demonstration of its success. Intense participation by all over several days had produced an income to the village school of about 700 Solomon Islands Dollars (SBD, a shaky currency which then stood at about four to one USD—and by 2010 has fallen to more than eight to the USD). About this time, what became known as the Melanesian logging boom was affecting many villages in the vicinity of Chea with its full force. However, as so-called saltwater people, with customary ownership mainly of lagoon and reefs, the people of Chea had not yet engaged this contested scene of timber royalty income and environmental devastation. Unlike the "bush people" of the Marovo Lagoon, groups with customary entitlement to vast inland tracts of uninhabited rainforest, the people of Chea had no trees to sell. Nevertheless, like virtually all rural groups of Solomon Islands at the time, they were pondering ways in which even they might "land a company" (*vahore kabani,* a pervasive vernacular term in the 1990s) and reap the monetary benefits that they saw—or believed—neighboring timber-rich groups were receiving.

For many Melanesians, the final years of the twentieth century were a time when aspirations and desires expanded beyond the wildest imagination. With customary rights to land, sea, and the resources there constitutionally underwritten, kin-based groups in Papua New Guinea and Solomon Islands found themselves able to convert their ancestral entitlements into fast cash by allowing logging operations to take place on their lands. Although no royalties paid by any logging company to Melanesian land owners have ever represented more than a fraction of the global market value of prime tropical hardwood, the money has continued to be seen as substantial by rural people, who have for so long lived without much assistance from national governments and have been largely deprived of alternative income opportunities. In the legal context of land ownership in Solomon Islands, where the state has relatively little influence over customary land (and sea) tenure grounded in ancestral entitlements conferred through kinship, court cases over contested claims to land, forest, and royalty incomes exploded during the 1990s. In ways that surpassed all previous material aspirations among rural Solomon Islanders, the logging boom of the 1990s generated an almost immediate, spectacular leap in the scale of economic concerns from ranging in the hundreds or perhaps thousands of Solomon Islands dollars to dealing with millions.

And so in 2002, six years after they had joyfully celebrated a community income of SBD 700, the leaders of Chea were entangled in legal cases about land rights and millions of dollars in timber royalties, notably focused on a place not close to home. The court cases concerned a timber-rich, uninhabited island much farther west in the

New Georgia Group, to which the Chea people claimed historical genealogical connections through two women of their kin group whom that group's headhunter ancestors had abducted as young girls from the vicinity of the uninhabited island, in the late nineteenth century. In this, the claimants of Chea, who (like nearly all groups of the Marovo and wider New Georgia area) follow principles of cognatic descent sometimes with patri- or matrilineal bias, invoked firm matrilineal connections to the contested land. This close focus on kinship and descent has been typical of logging-related court cases in the High Court of Solomon Islands since the 1990s, and there has been a resurgence of attention to fine-grained genealogical knowledge. The conflict that the Chea people engaged in concerned the control over a major share of more than SBD 2 million paid by an Asian company as timber royalties. The leaders of Chea won, and most of their huge royalty share was immediately channeled into building the biggest village church anywhere in the Marovo area.

In 1996, a community effort raising SBD 700 was celebrated. In 2002, stakes were in the order of SBD 2 million, obtained not through hard communal work. Instead, this colossal and unprecedented income prospect came through the signing of a logging agreement by village leaders, their active engagement in heated debates about the complexities of matrifiliation, patrifiliation, and cognatic kinship, and their appearance between 1999 and 2002 in at least four cases in the High Court of Solomon Islands. The financial scope of local ambition had, it seemed, multiplied by three thousand over those few years—local desires had indeed expanded as global connections had accelerated. Meanwhile, social disruption and inequality had grown, not only in relationships between men and women, but among kinship groups, too, in patterns closely connected to traditional hierarchical patterns in the Western Solomons of former times, when the large-scale predatory polities of coastal dwellers exploited local inland dwellers and less powerful overseas populations. Large-scale economic concerns and inter-island preoccupations with kinship and genealogy had reappeared, and had connected postcolonial New Georgia with the precolonial.

CUMULATIVE FIELDWORK AND THE MULTIPLICITY OF SITES

I was led to fieldwork in Solomon Islands as a graduate student, from my interest in cultural and social contexts of maritime practice, especially how local seas were territorialized. Benevolent correspondents within anthropology and fisheries management directed me toward Island Melanesia. South Seas dreams had not formed part of my anthropological plans, but after this initial inspiration from senior scholars I wrote a few letters in 1985 to suggested contacts in Solomon Islands government ministries. One of my letters found its way to the desk of Graham Baines, an Australian-Fijian environmental scientist who then worked as an adviser to the Solomon Islands government (and who was connected to the scholars who had advised me to look toward the Solomons), just when he was dealing with another request, from the Marovo Area Council and a gathering of local chiefs. Their request was for an anthropologist who could document "the importance of the Marovo Lagoon to the people of Marovo Lagoon." A few telexes and telegrams were exchanged, and when I arrived in Honiara in April 1986 I had a research permit in hand, the first to be issued to an anthropologist for quite a few years (there had been some high-level distrust of the anthropological profession). The permit instructed me to write, upon completion of up to eighteen months of field research, a substantial report in a form of English intelligible both locally, to government, and to multinational companies. That report (Hviding 1988) should document the Marovo people's uses of and rights over the lagoon and its resources. An expectation of further written products of local usefulness was also expressed.

Since then I have remained in a relationship of reciprocity to this far from static or secluded Melanesian society. Some old shell valuables (exported to Norway with permission from the Solomon Islands National Museum) are in my custody in Bergen and remind me that, in the words of the late chief of the people of Chea, "We have gained access to your work and to you so that you know that

Author with his fishing canoe and 9.9HP outboard motor, 1989.

we may at any time ask you for assistance." Over the years I have
completed three multilingual books in the Marovo language and
English, with materials from several other vernaculars of the area
(Hviding 1995a, 1995b, 2005). These books, distributed to all schools
of the Marovo area (in the case of the most recent one as part of a
UNESCO-funded project in vernacular education), have been among
the most challenging works I have ever completed for publication.
I hazard to call them not just multilingual but also multiepistemo-
logical. But the persisting local insistence that I must remain preoccupied with activities deemed useful "for Marovo" has in no way
been a barrier against more conventional (and academically more
meriting) writing and publishing on such anthropological topics as
people's knowledge, use, and tenure of sea, reefs, and rainforest, kinship, space/place, epistemology, resistance, globalization, headhunting, and so forth (e.g., Hviding 1993, 1996a, 1996b, 2003b, 2003c; Hviding

and Bayliss-Smith 2000). And an evolving engagement in anthropological film (Hviding et al. 2000; Hviding and Scott 2006) has also contributed, like my first field report completed "on behalf of" Marovo leaders in 1988, to the Marovo people's continuous efforts in positioning themselves and their concerns in a wider world.

From the beginning I have carried out my fieldwork from a main base in the village of Chea, located in the central lagoon area on the small island that itself is named Marovo. In the mid-to-late nineteenth century early European navigators gave that name to the entire lagoon. Living in Chea among "salt-water people" who are historically sea-oriented and lay claim to large areas of lagoon but little land, I pursued my study of sea tenure and maritime practice. This was complemented by a second fieldwork base at the village of Tamaneke in northern Marovo, some 30 kilometers' sea travel from Chea. Tamaneke is regarded even among Marovo people as remote and inaccessible, and is a traditional abode of "bush people," historically land-oriented, with scarce sea holdings but with ancestral rights to a vast hinterland of rainforest hills. In this, my fieldwork strategy from 1986–1987 onward, and the sea- or forest-related participant observation it involved, depending on which of the two villages I was in, mirrored the well-known distinction in the history of Island Melanesia between salt-water (or sea) and bush (or land) people, a contrast that implies complementarity and reciprocity as much as distance and conflict (see, e.g., Ivens 1930 and Hocart 1922, 76–77, on Solomon Islands; Sahlins 1976, 32–42, on Fiji).

My tale of expanding rural horizons is a far from atypical example of the increasing scale of local concerns in Solomon Islands. It is also a good background from which to reflect on contemporary crosscurrents in Island Melanesia and their bearings on the engagements of anthropology with this extraordinarily complex and culturally diverse region. My own research in and on Solomon Islands has taken place over the past twenty-five years (of which about three and a half were in the field), and it remains a dialogue between fieldwork and field, supplemented by further dialogues with other locations in Melanesia through reading the work of colleagues, some of whom have become increasingly preoccupied with tracing, and understanding, massive recent changes across the region, perhaps nowhere so much as in remote inner New Guinea. In *Exchanging the Past: a Rainforest World Before and After,* Bruce Knauft states the following about his understanding of the Gebusi of the Papuan Plateau of inner New Guinea which he revisited in 1998, sixteen years after his first fieldwork:

> I am fully convinced that had I studied the Gebusi only in 1998 there is little way I could have reconstructed the depth and character of indigenous culture that was present just sixteen years earlier. Conversely, there is no way I could have extrapolated the extent and character of change based on my understandings of 1980–82, however accurate these were at the time. (2002, 23)

The fieldwork strategy I have followed is a different one, where short-interval field visits over a long, continuous time span have taken place from grounding in an initial long period of what may now be viewed by many as the classic fieldwork genre of a bygone age. I first worked eighteen months in Marovo in 1986–1987. This was followed by five months in 1989–1990, six months in 1991–1992, four months in 1996, and six brief visits of up to a month each, most recently in May of 2008. Fieldwork with the Marovo people has also become multi-sited far beyond the place itself through a week in London in 2005 that centered on two very famous institutions of empire: Buckingham Palace (where a powerful rural leader of Marovo received his knighthood from Queen Elizabeth), and the British Museum (where that leader and his entourage examined old objects from home).

Such a fieldwork strategy, cumulative and multitemporal at short intervals, makes for close observation of gradual change. I see "the field" in Marovo as expanding across the temporal horizon of my engagement with it—an expansion being caused not primarily by shifts in my own focus of research interest, but in large measure by the intensifying presence of an increasing number of foreign agents and by the diversification of Melanesian responses and initiatives. Let me explain why I believe that Solomon Islands, and the Western Solomons in particular, have had a somewhat problematic position in relation to mainstream anthropological agendas in Melanesia.

In mainstream Melanesianist anthropology, which even today is far more interested in spectacular and surrealist scenes of mining and evangelist mission in inner New Guinea (e.g., Golub 2006; Robbins 2004), Solomon Islanders are not seen as nearly as exotic as many groups of New Guinea. Anthropology never found entirely "pristine" cultures in the Solomons. Today just about every adult Solomon Islander is a Christian in the second or third generation, and the major parts of the archipelago were well cultivated by Protestant missionaries already in the latter half of the nineteenth century—to the degree that scholarly reports based on observations from the late 1930s dismissed whatever remained of local customs in the heavily missionized Western Solomons as "particularly drab and mediocre" (Capell 1944, 22). As I set out for fieldwork in the mid-1980s, among the very small number of senior colleagues then doing anthropology in Solomon Islands there were those who expressed their opinion of the Western Solomons as rather unpromising.

So I never started my first personally formative fieldwork with the assumption of going there to get immersed in "traditional culture." Yet I soon realized that everyday life in the Marovo Lagoon, seemingly dominated by the Methodist and Seventh-day Adventist churches (both established there since around 1915), was full of references to and discussions about the Melanesian domain of *kastom* (Keesing 1982), including everyday magic and rampant sorcery. My initial interest in sea tenure and maritime practice—the ways in which these Melanesians related to and interacted with the sea—proved relevant and rewarding in its own right but also led me to unexpectedly deep investigations of regional cultural and linguistic history, and far into the classic anthropological topic of cognatic kinship, a somewhat unfashionable topic in the mid-to-late 1980s, yet of considerable fame in Solomon Islands anthropology (consider the influential work by Scheffler [e.g., 1965] and Keesing [e.g., 1968] on Choiseul and Malaita). It was not difficult to realize that the people of Marovo were extraordinarily preoccupied with issues of kinship in relation to rights in land and sea and the resources there, issues that bilaterality and rules of exogamy reaching to fifth cousins rendered infinitely complicated. At the time, it seemed to me that an empirically based critique of the study of kinship (Schneider 1984) could be carried out without dismissing the anthropological viability of kinship, since it was so privileged and viable in its own ways among the Marovo people themselves. I have mentioned how the logging boom of the 1990s caused so many disputes over land and royalties that local preoccupations with kinship only expanded.

Over the years, when asked by colleagues why I always go back to the Marovo people and continue to write about them, my answer is first that I do it because their kind hospitality and interest in my work enable me to, and second that I do it because they continue to have exciting developments ready for me. There's always something new, and often something astonishing. I am now completing another book on Marovo, about the Christian Fellowship Church (or CFC), a powerful indigenous social movement whose leader is seen by many followers as a living god (and who is the one knighted by the Queen in London in 2005). The CFC combines ancestor worship, apparently occult practices, and strong ideas of unity, compassion, and peaceful coexistence with large-scale economic development. The church leadership uses accumulated timber royalties gained from a twenty-year involvement with Asian companies to fund its own rural infrastructure, and during 1998–2003 effectively replaced the defunct national government in the Western Solomons (see Hviding, forthcoming). The spectacular ascendance of the CFC could not have been predicted from my initial fieldwork in 1986. But neither could I have understood the dynamics in the rapid, massive buildup of its financial and political force had I not started living among them in their home village of Tamaneke some twenty-five years ago—when the man referred to these days by his followers as "living god" was a somewhat baffled, uneducated forty-two-year-old trying to figure out what to do about the job just bestowed upon him at his death of his father, the CFC's founder known as the Holy Mama.

Despite widespread stereotypic notions, fieldwork in what may seem "classical" anthropological locations should in no way be seen as confined to the "village." While I have myself maintained the same fieldbase by the Marovo Lagoon, dividing my time between the villages of Chea (Seventh-day Adventists) and Tamaneke (spiritual headquarters of the Christian Fellowship Church), grasping the ongoing dynamics of everyday life here in seaboard Melanesia requires mobility obtained through the ownership or hire of canoes with outboard motors, since local social life itself—concerning fishing, land use, marriage, church activities, funerals, and whatever else—is so inherently mobile, echoing the maritime mobility of precolonial times (Hviding 1996a). Outboard motors are themselves a visible sign of expanded economic horizons in Marovo. While in 1986 the normal range was 9.9–25HP, that of today is 40–80HP—and this in a place where everyday life is still firmly anchored in subsistence gardening, fishing and gathering.

The analytical scope I continue to aspire to as such encompasses about 13,000 people referring to themselves as Marovo (they were about 6,000 back in 1986), their fifty villages or so along almost 100 kilometers of lagoon shore from southeast to northwest, and their five related Austronesian languages, of which I have learned to speak and write the dominant one. Much time has also been well spent over the years in provincial centers, at rural marketplaces, airfields, and seaports, and in the exceedingly complex national capital Honiara. I have allowed events and relationships to lead me out and about. This, of course, is no sensational fieldwork strategy. It only illustrates Bruce Kapferer's argument that assumedly "village-based" and thus per definition myopic fieldwork believed to dominate the history of anthropology is but an illusion, well suited for postmodern critiques but far from a reality generally reflected in anthropological practice (Kapferer 2000, 19–20 and n10). The "multilocal" scope of my own fieldwork in over the years, beyond the village and between villages, has simply resulted from following very active Melanesians around in extra-local arenas and localities where their everyday activities have led them. To paraphrase Kapferer (2000, 28): "The 'village' [is] more a place to reside and a point from which the anthropologist [moves] out along the lines of social relations." And conversely: when and where big things happen quickly in the rural Solomons and ac-

Author with chartered fiberglass boat and 80HP outboard motor, 2007.

tivate far-reaching and dispersed connections and "systems"—but with agency represented by few participants on the ground—the village itself may well be that very place where global connections are made visible.

COMPRESSED GLOBALIZATION IN MELANESIA

I suggest here that some striking developments in Melanesia during the most recent years pose interesting challenges to the long-term anthropology and ethnographically grounded microhistory of the region. Repeated fieldwork over a long time span but at rather short intervals seems to me to be a useful cumulative strategy for grasping the continuous flow of processes of encounter and engagement that I have referred to as "compressed globalization" (Hviding 2003a). By this I mean that a diversity of large-scale connections of a global nature are initiated, engaged in, even performed, locally—by very few participants on the ground, and often in unexpected or unpredictable ways. This line of argument concerning both repeated fieldwork and the attempt to observe globalization relates to the observation by Gewertz and Errington (1997, 127), two well-known re-visitors to their Melanesian fields, of "Papua New Guinea as a place where the global intersects the local in axiomatically condensed form." This statement, implying general validity for the current situation in Papua New Guinea, can be extended to the Melanesian region more widely, and certainly reflects my experiences over the years in Marovo.

My old friend and continuous collaborator Vincent Vaguni (b. 1950) exemplifies the complexities that have developed since he was on the committee that in 1985 invited me to come and do research in Marovo. Vincent is a trained teacher, reads any book that may turn up in his remote village at Tamaneke, and is known for sharp rhetoric in four New Georgian vernaculars, Solomon Islands Pijin, and English. Vincent's life career (which may not be as unique in comparative Melanesian terms as one might think) has included work as elected politician on provincial level; as environmental activist on occasion employed by international NGOs; as chairman of his own "develop-ment" NGO; as the right-hand man of his group's customary chief; as spokesman of land- and sea-owning kin groups in matters of log-ging, mineral prospecting, and commercial fishing; as local liaison officer for various Australian mining companies; as member of the board of directors of a local landowners' corporation dealing with logging licenses; as educational secretary for the Christian Fellow-ship Church, and more.

This colorful and globally well-connected career, in continuous expansion over thirty years, has introduced Vincent to conference venues, hotels, meeting rooms, shopping malls, and cities in Aus-tralia, New Zealand, and other Pacific Islands countries, and has given him temporary employers such as the Commonwealth Sci-ence Council and the World Wildlife Fund. Vincent has met Queen Elizabeth II in Honiara, and has engaged in negotiation and confron-tation with transnational counterparts of Japanese, Korean, Indone-sian, Malaysian, Philippine, Australian, British—sometimes, appar-ently, even bewilderingly global—origin. In 2007 he was observed in the capital, Honiara, on a dedicated search for several million Solomon Islands dollars of missing timber royalties, and in 2009 his career experienced a full circle of sorts when he was contracted by an Australian university to promote environmental awareness in Marovo villages. But through all these years Vincent has also lived a conventional rural family life, with the weekly highlight being the Saturday hunt for feral pigs with a pack of dogs and a spear made from a World War II American bayonet. Vincent and his wife, Amina Kada, are the main protagonists in a documentary film we have pro-duced in Bergen (Hviding and Scott 2006), where the two of them engage in a long, betelnut-infused conversation with me about all the strange things that have been going on over the years with all these new arrivals in the Marovo Lagoon.

Melanesian village people such as my friends in Marovo still insist on maintaining locally distinct ways of life, often defined by *kastom*. But they also engage in new relationships with expanding surrounding worlds, a fact that creates new types of situations where villagers appear to pursue agendas that seem unfamiliar to long-lived anthropological perception of the region. As Marshall Sahlins observed more generally, in his call for the continued legitimacy of the concept of culture, against certain implications of postmodernism, postcolonialism, and the like (subsumed by him under the concept of "afterology"): "These people have not organized their existence according to what has been troubling us lately" (Sahlins 1999, 406). Melanesianist anthropologists who have so far taken the rapid swirl of local-global connections seriously have commented on how today's Melanesia is a world where "crucial processes concerning colonial and . . . postcolonial changes can be remembered and locally discussed with considerable clarity . . ." (Gewertz and Errington 1997, 129), and where "the temporal compressions of late modernity—including the tensions between indigenous dispositions and newer institutions, social networks, and technologies—are particularly striking" (Knauft 1999, 243). Situations on the ground are dense, and contemporary Melanesianist anthropology is challenged to apply fieldwork-based perspectives toward understanding how local life-worlds engage in some of the great global questions of our time.

Close and continuous connections between the complexity of events in Melanesia and the adaptation of fieldwork strategies make for ethnographically grounded understandings of important continuities and discontinuities, ranging from precolonial to postcolonial. For Marovo, I do not necessarily assume conditions of a "before" and an "after," a radical scenario more applicable to inner New Guinea locations of recent first encounter with Christianity and cash. The Marovo people have been dealing with the wider world for far too long to see their life-world as being disrupted or to engage in the development of dual or competing ontologies. They have flexible cultural frameworks for handling and incorporating new social, cultural, or material arrivals. Events of transcultural encounter in New Georgia were and are characterized by open-ended categorization based on relational schemes, varieties of which are known from throughout the

Austronesian world. Central to this is the dualist notion of "side" (referred to in Marovo as *kale*, a cognate of proto-Austronesian **mpali*, see Blust 1981). It refers to people, objects, or circumstances as standing in a complementary, ideally reciprocal, interactional relationship with each other. In terms of social life, the resultant, reciprocal process of *varikale* (side-making) refers to a somewhat ideal state of proper relations. In this kind of worldview, neither the events of the past nor those of the present can be interpreted as emerging from stable, stringent, and consciously structured designs. Rather, the procedure of social life is driven by processes of indigenous categorization of prototypical kinds that allow for a wide range of relationship scenarios. New people, new things, new ways of being, and new ideas are identified, then, in terms of something or somebody already known. But the new is not a fixed representation of a preconceived structure—the basic notions of proper relationships and expected social categories allow for a wide range of encounters to be meaningful. Stability in the unstable, so to speak; order in non-order— far into the potentially confusing and fragmented discontinuities offered by today's world.

As islanders and seashore dwellers in a region whose cultural history is grounded in mobility, migrations, and regional systems of warfare and trade, Island Melanesians, like the Marovo people, have been used to creating some sense of order relatively quickly in their understanding of, and relationships with, more or less unexpected arrivals coming in from the ocean. Their extendable schemas for creating new forms out of others already in existence (Strathern 1992) enabled them to be relatively unsurprised when the first European sailing ships arrived in the archipelago, and to make quick sense of who their crews really were. They were Ship Men—as white people still are in Marovo Lagoon and elsewhere in the New Georgia islands. In comparison, the captain's logs of some of these ships indicate that the Europeans who came to this or that corner of New Georgia were much surprised—even disappointed—that these black "savages," armed to the teeth, were not surprised to see them, but instead quickly initiated trade (Jackson 1978, 46–47). As reported by an early anthropological observer, it also appears that the New Georgians of early colonial times had a rather low (one might say realist) opinion of white men, who "were mad . . . and were always after women" (Hocart MSS, 30:2).

MULTITEMPORAL METHOD: RETURNS TO THE FIELD

In the enduring and intensifying situation in Marovo Lagoon of temporally and socially compressed situations and processes, a strategy of continued fieldwork with regular follow-up visits allows for tracing the continuous expansion of repertoires of agents, encounters, engagements, and desires. This promotes a focus on local ways of handling all these overseas agents—some of whom are, admittedly, quite spectacular (such as Asian logging company negotiators arriving in the village carrying cash-stuffed briefcases [referred to locally by the succinct Melanesian pidgin expression konman keis])—as elements of a continuous cumulative process. The present does not appear as a radical rupture with a "traditional" past. The practice of return visits up to every second year after the long initial fieldwork has allowed me to suggest, for Marovo, an analytical picture where a major characteristic of the anthropological field is a typically Melanesian relational expansion (after Wagner 1986, 31) of local understandings and interpretations into frames of reference of ever-increasing diversity and scale.

In recent years I have increasingly combined ethnographic material from my own continuing fieldwork throughout this expansive era with other sources. Materials from archives give compelling insights into Marovo people's encounters over more than two hundred years with European explorers, North American whalers, gun vessels, and survey ships of the Royal Navy, missionaries from Australia, New Zealand, and the islands of Polynesia, and various other agents of colonialism as the British Empire fastened its grip over the Solomons from the establishment in 1893 of a protectorate. This scope allows for an analysis of a certain *longue durée* of encounters where distinctions between such concepts as first, past, subsequent, and present are disturbed and even erased.

Being able to return over and over again to the same small and remote corner of the world is a true privilege for an anthropologist. Needless to say, anthropologists who are themselves indigenous to their field may obtain this privileged situation more easily—a pattern I recognize also from my Norwegian colleagues who work in Norway. In any event, and whoever the anthropologist, and wherever the field, the continuous process of long-term repeated fieldwork— very different from a revisit after a long time of absence—offers cumulative, close observations of escalating encounters and intensifying relations between the people in the field, the actors and structures of the nation, and (as in Marovo) diverse Western and Eastern representatives of capital, moral, and adventure. In my enduring engagement with the Marovo people, this gives me inspiration to search back in time in order to develop an ethnographically grounded anthropological microhistory of far-reaching processes through which Melanesians have engaged, and continue to engage, with worlds beyond the local, while striving to maintain local control over desired ways of everyday life.

Perhaps anthropology today is challenged significantly by the unpredictable presence, just about anywhere and most conspicuously in locations believed to be remote and "traditional," of far-reaching relations among the most diverse persons, objects, and ideas. In this sense, that which is the anthropologically comparative project exists right where the anthropologist is located. Comparison is not necessarily to be carried out between places, but within places: in the field itself, in a multitude of "ethnographic presents," encountered most meaningfully during regular returns to the field.

The people of Chea village did obtain their big money from logging, and they have continued the task of completing their enormous church—but they also continue to carry out their kuarao fishing. In September 2007, when I last participated in the high excitement and cross-generational engagement of this communal ritual, things once more went the way they ought to: the kuarao, they said, "was *mana.*" Ancestral rights to reefs and present-day strengths in village organization were soundly demonstrated. The direct material reason for the fishing expedition was the need to properly feed several hundred visitors due to arrive the following day of from other parts of Marovo, to be hosted on the Seventh-day Adventist Sabbath by the people of Chea—right in their huge royalty-funded church. And so the divisions between old and new desires, the subsistence-oriented and the monetary, the local and the global, faded on that day in that corner of modern Island Melanesia. The past was in the present, and the anthropologist reflected upon his many years of engagement in and amazement at the twisted trajectories of compressed globalization, expanding desires, and the long run of everyday life in the Marovo Lagoon.

NOTES

I am grateful to Signe Howell and Aud Talle for their initiative and dedicated follow-up of this exciting collaborative project, and to the authors of the chapters in this book for inspiring discussion. In the process of transforming conference paper into book chapter, a particularly important contribution was given by the audience at the anthropology colloquium of the University of Hawai'i at Mānoa, to which Geoffrey White invited me to present an advanced version.

For continuously and so very generously offering me the opportunity and the circumstances of long-term fieldwork involving so many returns, my gratitude to the people of Marovo Lagoon knows no bounds. In particular, I wish to express my thanks to Harold Jimuru and Vincent Vaguni, close friends, partners at sea and in forest, and eminent educators from the time I was new in the field. Their families, the good people of Chea and Tamaneke villages, and chiefs Kata R. Ragoso and Jonathan Evu have hosted me, fed me, taught me, and in the proper Marovo way "kept" me since the first time in 1986. Four elderly gentlemen no longer with us contributed greatly to my education in the ways of New Georgia: Dyson Kiko Jimuru and his brother Kuloburu Liligeto, first-generation Seventh-day Adventists who had been raised in the old ways, taught me the Marovo language and so much about the ways of the past. On the remote weather coast of Vangunu, the worldly traditionalists Mapeli Jino and David Livingstone Kavusu led me into strange and wonderful experiences.

As for lessons about what was once the future, the Reverend Ikan Rove KBE (Spiritual Authority of the Christian Fellowship Church) and his brother the Hon. Job D. Tausinga (Member of Parliament) allowed me from the start to follow the extraordinary development of their social, religious, and political movement. Among the educated Marovo elite of more or less my own generation, Beraki Jino, Wilson Liligeto, Sam Patavaqara, and Aseri Yalangono have been particularly consistent discussion partners, always with challenging news and probing interpretations on how the rural and local relate to the national and the global. For permission to carry out research over the years I am grateful to the Solomon Islands Government represented by the Ministry of Education, the National Museum, the Western Province, and the onetime Marovo Area Council.

Funding for fieldwork over the years has had a number of sources, most importantly the Research Council of Norway, the University of Bergen, and UNESCO (SC/CSI/LINKS). Graham Baines originally introduced me to fieldwork in Solomon Islands, and our respective engagements with the people of the archipelago have since been intertwined. Tim Bayliss-Smith and the late Bob Johannes have allowed me to deepen my understanding through interdisciplinary horizons involving their perspectives from human geography and marine biology. Cato Berg has been transformed from onetime student to a colleague with whom I can meaningfully discuss and develop just about any matter of the Solomons. And finally: to share both life and fieldwork is a true privilege, which has been granted me by my wife and fellow anthropologist Karen Leivestad, who has shared Marovo with me for the last twenty years.

REFERENCES

Barclay, Kate. 2008. *A Japanese Joint Venture in the Pacific: Foreign Bodies in Tinned Tuna.* London: Routledge.

Bennett, J. A. 2000. *Pacific Forest: A History of Resource Control and Contest in Solomon Islands, c 1800–1997.* Leiden: Brill.

Blust, R. 1981. Dual Divisions in Oceania: Innovation or Retention? *Oceania* 52:66–79.

Capell, A. 1944. Notes on the Islands of Choiseul and New Georgia. *Oceania* 17:310–326.

Gewertz, D., and F. Errington 1997. Why We Return to Papua New Guinea. *Anthropological Quarterly* 70 (3): 127–136.

Fraenkel, J. 2004. *The Manipulation of Custom: From Uprising to Intervention in the Solomon Islands.* Canberra: Pandanus Books.

Golub, A. 2006. Who Is the "Original Affluent Society"? Ipili "Predatory Expansion" and the Porgera Gold Mine, Papua New Guinea. *The Contemporary Pacific* 18:265–292.

Hocart, A. M. MSS. Manuscripts and fieldnotes on Eddystone and New Georgia, on deposit at the Turnbull Library, Wellington, New Zealand.

———. 1922. The Cult of the Dead in Eddystone of the Solomons. *Journal of the Royal Anthropological Institute of Great Britain and Ireland* 52:71–112, 259–305.

Hviding, E. 1988. Marine Tenure and Resource Development in Marovo Lagoon, Solomon Islands: Traditional Knowledge, Use and Management of Marine Resources, with Implications for Contemporary Development. Honiara: South Pacific Forum Fisheries Agency. FFA Reports 88/35.

———. 1993. Indigenous Essentialism? "Simplifying" Customary Land Ownership in New Georgia, Solomon Islands. *Bijdragen tot de Taal-, Land-en Volkenkunde,* 149:802–824.

———. 1995a. *Of Reef and Rainforest: A Dictionary of Environment and Resources in Marovo Lagoon.* Bergen: Centre for Development Studies, University of Bergen, in collaboration with Western Province Division of Culture.

———. 1995b. *Vivinei tuari pa Ulusaghe: Stories and Legends from Marovo, New Georgia, in Four New Georgian Languages and with English Translations.* Recorded, translated, and edited by Edvard Hviding, with assistance from V. Vaguni and others. Bergen: Centre for Development Studies, University of Bergen, in collaboration with Western Province Division of Culture.

———. 1996a. *Guardians of Marovo Lagoon: Practice, Place, and Politics in Maritime Melanesia.* Pacific Islands Monograph Series, 14. Honolulu: University of Hawai'i Press.

———. 1996b. Nature, Culture, Magic, Science: On Meta-languages for Comparison in Cultural Ecology. In P. Descola and G. Pálsson, eds., *Nature and Society: Anthropological Perspectives,* 165–184. London: Routledge.

———. 2003a. Contested Rainforests, NGOs and Projects of Desire in Solomon Islands. *International Social Science Journal* 55 (4): 439–453.

———. 2003b. Between Knowledges: Pacific Studies and Academic Disciplines. *The Contemporary Pacific* 15:43–73.

———. 2003c. Disentangling the *Butubutu* of New Georgia: Cognatic Kinship in Thought and Action, in I. Hoëm and S. Roalkvam, eds., *Oceanic Socialities and Cultural Forms: Ethnographies of Experience,* 71–113. Oxford: Berghahn Books.

———. 2005. *Reef and Rainforest: An Environmental Encyclopedia of Marovo Lagoon, Solomon Islands / Kiladi oro vivineidi ria tingitonga pa idere oro pa goana pa Marovo.* Knowledges of Nature Series, No. 1. Paris: UNESCO.

———. 2006. Knowing and Managing Biodiversity in the Pacific Islands: Challenges of Conservation in the Marovo Lagoon. *International Social Science Journal* 58 (1): 69–85.

———. Forthcoming. Replacing the State in the Western Solomon Islands: The Political Rise of the Christian Fellowship Church, in E. Hviding and K. M. Rio, eds., *Made in Oceania: Social Movements, Cultural Heritage and the State in the Pacific.* Oxford: Sean Kingston Publishing.

Hviding, E., and G. B. K. Baines. 1994. Community-based Fisheries Management, Tradition and the Challenges of Development in Marovo, Solomon Islands. *Development and Change* 25 (1): 13–39.

Hviding, E., and T. Bayliss-Smith. 2000. *Islands of Rainforest: Agroforestry, Logging and Ecotourism in Solomon Islands.* Aldershot: Ashgate.

Hviding, E., and R. Scott. 2006. *Vincent and the Rainforest: Global Conversations in Rural Melanesia.* Documentary film. DVD, 73 minutes, Hoava and Pijin with English subtitles. Produced by SOT-Film and University of Bergen.

Hviding, E., R. Scott, and T. Tollefsen 2000. *Chea's Great Kuarao.* Documentary film, DVD and VHS, 57 minutes. Marovo with English narrative and subtitles. Produced by SOT-Film and University of Bergen, in collaboration with the Solomon Islands National Museum.

Ivens, W. H. 1930. *The Island Builders of the Pacific: How and Why the People of Mala Construct Their Artificial Islands, the Antiquity & Doubtful Origin of the Practice, with a Description of the Social Organization, Magic & Religion of Their Inhabitants.* London: Seeley, Service. (Reprinted 1978, New York: AMS Press).

Jackson, K. B. 1978. *Tie hokara, Tie vaka: Black Man, White Man. A Study of the New Georgia Group to 1930.* PhD diss., Australian National University, Canberra.

Kabutaulaka, T. T. 2001a. *Paths in the Jungle: Landowners and the Struggle for Control of Solomon Islands' Logging Industry.* PhD diss., Australian National University, Canberra.

———. 2001b. *Beyond Ethnicity: The Political Economy of the Guadalcanal Crisis in Solomon Islands. State, Society and Governance in Melanesia Project,* Working Paper 01/1. Canberra: Australian National University.

Kapferer, B. 2000. Star Wars: About Anthropology, Culture and Globalisation. *Journal of Finnish Anthropological Society* 26 (3): 2–29.

Keesing, R. M. 1968. Nonunilineal Descent and the Contextual Definition of Status. *American Anthropologist* 70:82–84.

———. 1982. Kastom in Melanesia: A Theoretical Overview. *Mankind* 13:297–301.

Knauft, B. M. 1999. *From Primitive to Postcolonial in Melanesia and Anthropology.* Ann Arbor: University of Michigan Press.

Knauft, B. 2002. *Exchanging the Past: A Rainforest World of Before and After.* Chicago: University of Chicago Press.

Moore, C. 2004. *Happy Isles in Crisis: The Historical Causes for a Failing State in Solomon Islands, 1998–2004.* Canberra: Asia Pacific Press.

Robbins, J. 2004. *Becoming Sinners: Christianity and Moral Torment in a Papua New Guinea Society.* Berkeley: University of California Press.

Sahlins, M. D. 1976. *Culture and Practical Reason.* Chicago: University of Chicago Press.

———. 1999. Two or Three Things I Know about Culture. *Journal of the Royal Anthropological Institute* 5:399–421.

Scheffler, H. W. 1965. *Choiseul Island Social Structure.* Berkeley: University of California Press.

Schneider, D. M. 1984. *A Critique of the Study of Kinship.* Ann Arbor: University of Michigan Press.

Spriggs, M. 1997. *The Island Melanesians.* Oxford: Blackwell.

Strathern, M. 1992. The Decomposition of an Event. *Cultural Anthropology* 7:245–254.

Thomas, N. 1997. *In Oceania: Visions, Artifacts, Histories.* Durham, N.C.: Duke University Press.

Wagner, R. 1986. *Symbols that Stand for Themselves.* Chicago: University of Chicago Press.

9 |

Widening the Net

Returns to the Field and
Regional Understanding

ALAN BARNARD

My main field research has been with a group of people called the Naro, or Nharo, who live mainly in central-western Botswana. Some live in Namibia. I first visited Botswana and Namibia in 1973 and began fieldwork proper in 1974. Since then I have visited Naro country many times, and in 2008 a group of Naro and !Xoõ from Namibia visited me at my home in Scotland. I have also worked with related Bushman or San groups. My argument here is that one does not truly know one's own ethnography until one goes back to it after an absence, and that equally one does not know it until one has studied not only one's "own" people but the people next door.

Each return to the field yields both new empirical data and new insights to what was there before. Both the ethnographer and the field change, and in my case geographical moves, from one part of the Kalahari to another, yield new insights not only to new places but also to where I was before. Thus, one area of exploration in this chapter is what I call latitudinal research, which adds geographical and cultural breadth. This is conveniently contrasted to longitudinal research, which was more or less the original brief when the authors of this book first met in Oslo in 2006. Here I examine this contrast, but not only with regard to the long term; rather, with at least equal regard to what happens when we return to the field time and time again—in other words, specifically with multitemporal field research. People change; the population shifts, and settlements are abandoned and started up again; the developmental cycle in domestic groups creates new social situations; and our individual changing theoretical perspectives, along with wider changes in the discipline, including new fashions, give us new ways of looking even at whatever might not have changed.

Latitudinal field research is multisited. Terence Turner (this volume) makes the point that multitemporal field research tends to entail visits to more than one site, and that this, in turn, creates a deeper understanding and presumably a test for the typicality of one's impressions based on early fieldwork at just one site. My own, latitudinal, research is multisited in a rather different sense than Turner's. I have not gone back to the same group so much as widened my definition of "the field" to include the region: Khoisan southern Africa. This is a result of many factors: personal circumstances, new research opportunities, political changes in southern Africa, and so on. But it is also to some extent a result of my desire to put into practice the theoretical perspective I developed in my early fieldwork. My first steps in "regional structural comparison" were simply attempts to explain my ethnography of one group, the Naro, in terms of wider, regional structures, and to search for deeper, underlying structures that generated surface cultural representations. That 1970s plan changed, and certainly the language did, when I was able to return not just to my original fieldwork sites but to other sites in southern Africa where related groups lived. What had at first been an attempt to fit Naro into a wider pattern developed into an attempt to understand the breadth of that pattern through repeated visits to Ts'aokhoe, ≠Haba, G/wikhoe, G//anakhoe, Deti, !Xoõ, !Xū, Ju/'hoansi, ≠Au//eisi, Kxoe, N/u, Hai//om, Nama, Damara, and so on, as well as to the Bantu-speaking neighbors of these Khoisan peoples.

Thus for me, "my people" became, in a sense, "the Khoisan," not one people or ethnic group but a cluster of related groups. I could never understand the Khoisan as a whole in quite the same way I

Botswana, 1975.

could understand the small group whose language I learned and with whom I lived closely, but I could understand something different. That, at least, became my goal. It could never have been a goal had I not returned to the field, nor had I not returned to slightly different "fields," both temporally and spatially.

THE RESEARCH MILIEU I ENCOUNTERED

Some thirty years ago, Richard Lee (1979a) published a paper called "Hunter-gatherers in Process." It appeared in an edited volume, *Long-Term Field Research in Social Anthropology*. At that time, it was still the notion of "hunter-gatherers" that attracted attention in most writings on San or Bushmen. The group Lee worked with was then called the !Kung, but they have since become known in ethnography as the Ju/'hoansi (singular, Ju/'hoan). At the time of Lee's paper, the generic name for the larger ethnic unit of southern African hunter-gatherers had recently changed from Bushmen to San. Preferences varied, but later the term Bushmen became popular again, and later still San returned—though many so-called San despise that name and prefer traditional generic labels like Ju, Kua or N/oa-khoe. These changes reflect several things: the growing involvement of anthropologists with regional politics, especially the politics of subjugated minorities; the increasing awareness of a wider readership in southern Africa; a wish to call people something that is not derogatory, but more akin (if not identical) to what they call themselves; and simply changing anthropological fashion.

In the early years of my research I had an interest in issues of ethnic labels. However, the repeated to-and-fro of political correctness, corrections of political correctness, and debates among San or Bushman activists themselves, for me put paid to the idea of developing my career as one in "correct" terminological usage (but see Barnard 2007, 129–142). Scientific debates, if they may be called that, hinged on the true meaning of words like San (Khoekhoe *sān* or *saan*, food-gatherer, vagabond, rascal, etc.) or the gender implications of a word like Bush*man*, while debates among Bushmen themselves considered the appropriateness of foreign and possibly benign words like Bushman (from seventeenth-century Dutch *Bosjesmans*), versus equally foreign and usually derogatory words like San, Masarwa (the Tswana equivalent), or the Tswana neologism Basarwa (intended as more respectful because of its *human* noun-class prefix). At present I usually use either San or Bushmen, sometimes interchangeably, and sometimes according to context: Bushmen among those who prefer to call themselves that, and San in government circles. San is the usual government term in both Namibia and South Africa, although not in Botswana, where Basarwa is the norm. San is also much more usual among archaeologists, whereas many cultural anthropologists who specialize in the study of these peoples use Bushmen.

From the early 1970s to the early 1980s, I did fieldwork with the group just to the south, called Naro, then usually spelled Nharo and later spelled without the H. By the 1990s linguists had developed a Naro orthography and thrown out the H (previously indicating initial low tone and breathy vowel), and I accepted their new spelling. In fact, the new spelling was a re-creation of one used in the 1920s. As with Ju/'hoansi, it was generally acknowledged that what was important about Naro was that they were, or had until recently been, hunter-gatherers. Yet the meaning of the category hunter-gatherers was also to change rapidly and in complex ways through the 1980s and 1990s. Before the 1980s, "hunter-gatherers" was a concept often defined very narrowly. Many anthropologists used it in a way that excluded anyone who engaged in any other subsistence pursuits at all. "Part-time hunter-gatherers," as they were called, were not quite "real" hunter gatherers, but something else (see Barnard 1989). The Naro were part-time hunter-gatherers, with goats of their own, and some with jobs as cattle herdsmen for members of other ethnic groups. Although I considered myself more and more a hunter-gatherer specialist, it was hard at first to escape the notion that "my" people were not the real thing. The fact that I specialized also in kinship, a conservative aspect of social organization, perhaps allowed me some scope that anthropologists interested in, say, economic activities would not have.

Gradually two theoretical positions emerged, and Kalahari ethnographers were split into two camps. Traditionalists, like Lee (e.g., 1979b), seemed to want a kind of purity in their peoples that was almost impossible to find. Revisionists, like Edwin Wilmsen (e.g., 1989), rejected the notion of hunter-gatherer purity. They recognized that it is always elusive, or at least has been for two thousand years throughout much of southern Africa. Others, and I include myself in this category, held a wider definition of the hunter-gatherer and were happy to include people who hunted, gathered, looked after someone else's livestock, or kept their own, and even people who did occasional wage labor. We had discovered that Naro, some Ju/'hoansi, and members of other groups did not cease to be "real" Bushmen when they took on other subsistence pursuits. The drought years, from the late 1970s to the early 1990s, forced many to engage in other pursuits, and anthropology came gradually to accept them still as hunter-gatherers, due in part to the growing revisionist critique, but due at least as much to the revelation that traditional religion, kinship practices, consensus politics, and the sharing ethos all remained intact. The elements of culture that Julian Steward (1955) had called "core," those that were related most closely to environment, subsistence, and technology, turned out not to be "core" at all, but in fact peripheral to these deeper elements, which persisted in spite of economic change. In the first decade of the current millennium there have been changes in the deeper aspects of culture, what Marxists of the 1970s (e.g., Godelier 1975) called "superstructure," as opposed to "base" or "infrastructure," but that is another matter. My initial feelings in the 1970s were that Naro were resisting outside pressures and that a reversal of both dominant hunter-gathererist paradigms of the time, Stewardian and Marxist, was needed. The following two decades, if possibly less so the decade after those, confirmed this hypothesis.

Lee's 1979 paper documents the changes in natural environment, outside political influences, and internal change, including demographic changes in Ju/'hoan society. Lee also comments on the variety of personnel, no fewer than fourteen individual researchers who from 1963 to 1976 made up the Kalahari Research Project. But to my mind, in spite of the extraordinarily detailed and rich ethnography of that research group, something is missing in Lee's account. It is what is missing, a wider regional understanding, that I want to explore through my own work in the remainder of this chapter.

REGIONAL STRUCTURAL COMPARISON

My first encounter with regional structural comparison was in 1975. I was nearing the end of a year-and-a-half stint of fieldwork with Naro when I decided to revisit a Naro community I had spent some time with earlier in the period. They were living on the eastern edge of the Ghanzi (Gantsi) cattle-ranching area, some working as laborers on the ranches and living with ranch workers and squatters from other parts of the western Kalahari. Nearly all these people were of minority status and mainly linguistically related to Naro: Ts'aokhoe,

≠Haba, G/wi and G//ana. A few living nearby were from the quite different ≠Au//ei or southern Ju/'hoan group. I was mainly interested in kinship, and I noticed that these two groups had intermarried, and that they knew each other's kinship terminologies, rules of marriage, naming systems, and kinship etiquette. They explained it all to me, in the Naro language. I have never learned to speak Naro very well, but I could speak fluent kinship theory, and so could they.

At the time, I was a PhD student at University College London, a large college of the University of London. From Botswana I wrote to my supervisor, Adam Kuper, who was then on sabbatical at Gothenburg University in Sweden. At exactly the same time, he wrote to me, saying that he had sorted out Southern Bantu kinship and particularly patterns regulating marriage and bridewealth. He had done this through a new perspective he was to call "regional structural comparison" (see, e.g., Kuper 1980, 1987). This is essentially a structuralism similar to that practiced some years before in the Netherlands, based on the region as the unit of analysis, rather than the human mind (as in the work of Lévi-Strauss) or the specific society (as in that of Leach or Needham). Our letters crossed in the mail. He had found this theoretical approach through years of ethnographic thinking, with reading and earlier ethnographic fieldwork. I had come to exactly the same approach through fieldwork discussion, with Bushmen who knew each others' systems—and knew them *as systems,* and indeed as systems comparable and commensurable with their own.

However, it took me many years, with more field trips, much more reading of the works of my colleagues in Khoisan studies, and considerable reflection before things really fitted together. Kinship was easy, as was another early topic, settlement patterns. Very soon after my initial sixteen-month stay with the Naro I had noticed what no one else seemed to have, that four different patterns occurred among Bushmen, and that these were related to microenvironmental differences (Barnard 1979). Relatively speaking, Naro were permanently aggregated and !Xoõ permanently dispersed, while Ju/'hoansi aggregate in the dry season and disperse in the wet season, and G/wikhoe aggregate in the wet season and disperse in the dry season. It is a bit more complicated than that, of course, but that simple model emerged in my mind when I was able to escape the detail of field observations and place my own findings among those of others in a growing literature on seasonal movements.

However, other aspects of culture, like religious belief, proved more elusive. They key was that differences between one group and the next could be explained in terms a common, deep regional structure. In some realms, like kinship, individuals knew the systems and could explain them with comparative knowledge. In others, like settlement patterns, I had to piece together the patterns. Does a group aggregate in the wet season (like the Ju/'hoansi) or in the dry season (like the G/wi)? And why? On that issue, my earliest inclination was to assume cultural difference, but further research, more in the library than the field, led me to that conclusion of microenvironmental causal factors (see, e.g., Barnard 1992, 223–236). Further work on religion, worldview, and so on, led to attempts to apply these ideas much more widely, and returns to the field were accompanied by returns to the literature in what became really a long-term career development, to understand Khoisan cultures as permutations of a larger entity than the single band, people, or small-scale society (see also Barnard 1988, 1996).

LONGITUDE AND LATITUDE: MULTITEMPORAL
AND MULTISITED FIELDWORK

Long-term fieldwork often enables comparison by giving us time to reflect, to read, and to move from group to group. For me, long-term fieldwork obviously has a spatial as well as a temporal dimension. In the original Oslo workshop on which the AAA session titled Returns to the Field was based, the organizers used the term longitudinal rather than long-term fieldwork. Longitudinal, long-term, multiple-visit, multitemporal, and so on all connote different imagery, and the meanings of these words are not quite interchangeable. Nevertheless, it is worth reflecting on what the opposite of longitudinal fieldwork might be, and in that context I offer latitudinal fieldwork, which is multisited in a very wide sense. It is multitemporal field research where the boundaries are not those of a single community, but those of an ethnographic region.

Our individual accumulated expertise gives us the ability to understand regional issues, as well as historical change. In comparative studies within a region we might find, for example, historical trajectory, relations with outsiders, seasonality, diverse cultural factors, environmental factors, and so on. Regional specialization entails some degree of retreat from the discipline of social anthropology into specialist, regional studies. In my own case, I read more South African archaeology and Namibian history these days than I do general social anthropology. The issue is complicated by the fact that anthropology itself has changed over these decades, as structuralism all but disappeared, indigenous voices emerged, and postmodernism came and went. Thus, even if the Naro had remained the same (which they have not), new generations of anthropologists would certainly see them differently. And even though my own theoretical approach has remained fairly consistent, I have not been immune from changing fashions. Developments in kinship, in hunter-gatherer studies, and so on, have changed the way I have seen them, and the way I see other Khoisan groups on each return visit to southern Africa.

But what is a "region"? My notion of region, like Kuper's, has usually meant something akin to what used to be called a "culture area," in other words, linguistically and culturally related peoples who together possess a cultural configuration larger than the ethnic group (Barnard 1992, 1996; Kuper 2002). An alternative is the notion of region that comprises the majority as well as minority populations, and this is the way Kalahari revisionists have seen the relevant "region." Yet in my own work, what draws out things in Naro society is setting Naro against a framework of Bushman or San, or even Khoisan, kinship, myth, ritual, botanical knowledge, ideology of exchange, environmental understanding, and so on. The meaning of "minority" culture and social life comes out most fruitfully seen against a collection of related minorities: Naro, G/wi, G//ana, Ju/'hoansi, the historical / Xam, and the cattle- and sheep-herding Khoekhoe peoples. Whatever a region is, it is not simply a geographical entity, but a complex of interrelations of cultures, culture contact, or indeed cultural structures or forces of domination and subjugation. Both these regional understandings, revisionist and comparativist, are useful, and usually more meaningful than worldwide comparison. Yet both take a very long time to develop.

In the United Kingdom the generic term for someone who teaches in a university is "lecturer," while the word "professor" is reserved for the most senior rank of academics. I went through the ranks of lecturer, senior lecturer, reader, and professor, achieving my personal chair in 2001. There are two ways of becoming a professor: personal chair (by promotion from a lower rank within the same university) and established chair (by competition, normally coming from another university). Personal professors usually bear quite specific titles, rather than ones that merely indicate their academic discipline. Thus, my own job title now happens to be, not Professor of Anthropology, nor Professor of Social Anthropology, but Professor of the Anthropology of Southern Africa. I am quite pleased with the title, not least because southern Africa is quite big enough a field to occupy a full career's concern. Anything bigger, like "anthropology," would be too much.

As an anthropologist of southern Africa, my expertise should be about that really quite complex subcontinent. Such an expertise cannot be merely a matter of returning to a small piece of ground and seeing what has changed, with individuals coming and going, acquiring material possessions, being pushed around by their immediate neighbors, or whatever. The changes are much more profound. There have indeed been enormous historical changes since 1972, when I started working in southern Africa. For example, the transformation of Botswana from a poor to a relatively rich country, then the coming of HIV and AIDS, and then the long legal battle of G/wi and G//ana for rights to their own land, settled in court (if not yet on the ground) in 2006. Or the great struggle to end apartheid, with the achievement of South African democracy in 1994 and subsequent land grants in that country. Related to this is the "rediscovery" of "forgotten" Khoisan minorities there, like the ≠Khomani, long denied ethnicity and classified under apartheid as "Coloureds." There has also been Namibia's long war of liberation, with independence in 1990, and the transformation of some local economies, at least for quite a number of Ju/'hoansi or "!Kung of Nyae Nyae," from hunting, to herding, to small-scale entrepreneurship and other things. I gave a lecture at the University of Namibia in 2007 and was delighted to find in the audience a Kxoe law student from northeastern Namibia, and a G/wi public policy student originally from the Central Kalahari Game Reserve in Botswana. That would have been impossible, indeed almost unimaginable, even ten years before.

I do not reject now any major aspect of the regional structural approach I pursued in the 1970s to the 1990s; I simply have moved on to other questions. However, if I were to formulate a regional structural approach today, I would most certainly configure it more dynamically, with a view to explaining both regional and temporal dimensions in a single framework. Such a project, though, is better done in retrospect than with anticipation. Thus it could never really have formed a great part of my initial research design. I would also try to engage with a more complex understanding of "culture," more specifically, a notion to do with cultures less as bounded entities like languages, and more as internalized entities like idiolects, but subject too to random and unstructured change. Bushmen, anthropology (in the hands of each new generation), and our own individual theoretical understandings are all subject to change. The best anthropological theory, if the most difficult, would be one that comprises explanation across both space and time, and through history, structure, and agency in equal measure. And it would be one that predicts as well as explains the past and the present. That last part, if not the whole idea of a comprehensive theory of culture, is in my view not merely illusive, but impossible. That does not mean that we should not seek it, but rather simply that we will not find it.

THREE EMPIRICAL "DISCOVERIES"

If grand theories of culture remain elusive, at least we can, occasionally, make new discoveries. Let me comment here on three of my discoveries, if they can be called that, all of which were made not in return visits, but in my earliest main period of field research. The significance of later visits to the field was in the building of stronger theoretical apparatuses around these discoveries. Thus discovery, at least for me, is an early phenomenon, with a fuller understanding coming rather later. The three discoveries I shall touch on here are the diversity of settlement patterns, universal kinship classification, and the existence of *hxaro* beyond the Ju/'hoansi.

I have already mentioned the diversity of settlement patterns, but let me elaborate here in light of the process of ethnographic discovery. Before fieldwork I read some of Meyer Fortes's work on the developmental cycle in domestic groups (e.g., Fortes 1958). In the 1940s Fortes had made the extraordinary discovery among Tallensi and Ashanti (in modern Ghana) that what might appear to a fieldworker to be diverse, randomly organized units (some small and centered on a married couple, some large and centered on a polygamous man, and so on) might all be products of a single social structure when seen through time. The fieldworker will only be there for a year or two and thus will see homesteads of different sizes, but if he or she were to remain for forty or sixty years, it would become evident that the small homestead expands as children are born, and then fission occurs, followed by what he calls replacement, as people die and the next generation replicates the pattern of the one before. Large and small units are part of a single cycle. I went to the Kalahari with this in mind, and sure enough, as other ethnographers were describing band membership in terms of (apparently) random movements of people, Bushmen themselves were seeing things quite differently. Bushmen told instead of going back to join bands where they had residence rights through their parents. It might take sixty years to see and confirm the pattern on the ground, but just sixty seconds to "see" it in the mind.

Another tool I came armed with was a skepticism about the role of environmental factors in determining social organization. When I noticed, both through reading and through fieldwork observation, that different Bushman groups had different sizes of groups and different seasonal patterns, I assumed it was because of cultural factors. In fact, further analysis, really what might be called "mental ethnography," led me to see that environmental differences, like the location of water resources or availability of melons for water in the dry season, enabled different uses of land, and therefore different patterns of settlement (Barnard 1986). The abundance of resources, in turn, was reflected culturally in the degree of territoriality groups maintained, with well-off groups usually being less territorial and less-well-off groups usually more territorial (Barnard 1979, 1991). The further visits to the field, and to the literature, enabled me not only to confirm my suspicions (of which I was glad) but also to develop a deeper appreciation of how such principles worked and to provide examples, although without necessarily ever witnessing a complete developmental cycle or verifying all my suppositions.

My main concern through most of my field studies has been in one way or another with kinship. Most of my findings are probably of interest only to specialists, but one that I still hope someday will be of wider interest is the idea of universal kinship classification (or what I at first called universal kin categorization). Others had commented before on the phenomenon, but no one had given it a name or really thought much about it as something found in some societies but not others. It is found in those societies with prescriptive alliance structures, but also in hunter-gatherer societies that lack such structures, like Bushmen, for whom each member of society is placed in a kinship category in relation to every other (Barnard 1978). This is necessary for Naro and other Bushmen because without it they will not know who is marriageable and who is not, whom one can joke with and whom one cannot, and even how close to each other any two people may sit. There is no such thing as non-kin, as all Naro (or Ju/'hoansi, or G/wikhoe, etc.) are kin to each other. The question is not "Are we related?" but "How are we related?" It follows that ethnographers must be fitted into the system, and in some groups, including both Ju/'hoansi and Naro, personal names are used as if names occupied genealogical positions, both for any Ju/'hoan or Naro outside close kin and for outsiders. Since I bear the Naro name

!A/e, any Naro can place me in his or her genealogy according to the nearest person also called !A/e and address me accordingly by kin term. If for example a man's nearest relative called !A/e is his cross-cousin, then he will call me "cross-cousin" and I will reciprocate the classification. I have recently returned to the phenomenon, this time not on the ground but very much in the mind, with my present work in the social anthropology of human origins and a theory of the co-evolution of language and kinship (Barnard 2008).

Hxaro was discovered by Polly Wiessner among the Ju/'hoansi and first described comprehensively in her PhD dissertation (Wiessner 1977). Wiessner visited me in the field among the Naro and told me of her discovery, and I very soon found the same among the Naro. Naro use the verb //aī to describe this exchange action, or say that two people are //aī-ku (in exchange with each other). Very briefly, this relationship entails the giving of movable, nonconsumable material goods, with the right of the giver to demand, at a later date, a return "gift." Those in such a relationship have rights to hunt in each other's territories or use their resources, and the hxaro or //aī relationship itself serves to redistribute the meager material goods in these materially simple societies. Yet it was not my discovery of this identical relationship among the Naro that was important, but rather my discovery of similar phenomena among other Khoisan peoples. Having seen how it worked among the Naro, in the 1980s and 1990s I was able to visit and interview members of Khoekhoe-speaking communities. I found, for example, that Damara pastoral-ists have a custom called mā!khunigus (!khuni being the root, plus mā, to give, gu, a reciprocal suffix, and s, the feminine-singular suffix of an abstract noun). Unlike Ju/'hoan hxaro, this practice includes the exchange of consumable items. It involves the giving of things in delayed exchange; like may not be exchanged for like, but the goods may be similar. A brown shirt may be given today, and reciprocated with a white shirt next month or next year. This practice is con-ceptually distinguished from simply asking for something without any expectation of a return (see Barnard 2004, 11–13). I have seen similar but slightly different customs among Nama and Hai//om too, but what is important is that these exist in a complex of different kinds of exchange. There is variation among Khoisan that crosses the hunter/herder boundary. Thus, while hxaro may be a useful practice for hunter-gatherers to engage in, it is not only hunter-gatherers who have such practices. The recognition of this is a discovery not only about Khoisan who are not hunter-gatherers, but also about those that are. Again, I believe that my regional approach and multisite as well as multi-visit methodology has given me insights into such systems which would otherwise have been impossible.

MORE RECENT CONCERNS

There is a natural tendency for return visitors to the field to move into contemporary history and allow the boundary between ethnography and history to blur (see Widlok 2004). Incidents take over from generalization. But, strangely, time and space can move in more than one direction. In 2006 I attended a conference with a small number of colleagues in archaeology, linguistics, history, genetic, and so on, to reanalyze aspects of Khoekhoe society in the Cape before Dutch colonization. The processes I had observed in contemporary southern Africa, together with my decades of reflection, proved a useful entry for me into issues such as whether pottery and livestock were brought to southern Africa two thousand years ago though migration of herders, or through diffusion among existing hunter-gatherer populations. Thus, accumulated knowledge from the field, both in the sense of fieldwork and in the sense of an ethnographic field of study, may increase our abilities to provide insight into questions posed in allied disciplines.

Long-term work with a population, either at one long stretch or with return visits, as a whole can also build both close engagement and a feeling of deep understanding. For me, the latter—an increasing understanding, which I hope is deep—is primarily what has come about, since I no longer engage in long field studies but try instead to build on a depth of knowledge that is sympathetic but attuned too to a greater awareness of complex national and international issues than in my youth. Does it matter that Khoisan are in the minority? Yes, in that (1) that is what makes them interesting to the outside world, and (2) it is how they perceive themselves. It is also what makes them vulnerable. It has been the cause of their mistreatment for centuries, and therefore what lies behind, for example, the Kalahari debate, the "indigenous peoples" debate, and the legal battle over rights of access to the Central Kalahari Game Reserve.

There is an interesting contradiction here for the Khoisan peoples as a whole. On the one hand they are minorities. On the other hand, they embody the New South Africa. President Thabo Mbeki chose the new motto !Ke e: /xarra //ke (roughly, "People who are different, coming together"), and chose to have it in the /Xam language, which, like the Latin of the previous motto, is extinct and therefore represents no linguistic community more than any other (see Barnard 2003). But there are /Xam genes in the gene pool of the so-called "Coloured" population and also in that of Zulu, Xhosa, and so on. Taking another angle, while they may be a small minority, the Khoisan themselves are diverse. There is far greater linguistic variation among the Khoisan than among the peoples of most of Europe and South Asia put together. This makes the Khoisan peoples more interesting to anthropology, I believe, and also more studyable to me than they might be if they were more uniform or even larger in population.

For me, it is not simply a matter of returning to the same small group of people that brings awareness, but returning to a changing political climate, and to diverse but related groups, each with slightly different circumstances. Nor can environmental change be ignored. I have mentioned the drought years of the late 1970s, 1980s, and early 1990s. Had I not seen the green Kalahari of 1974 and 1975, I would not know how bad things had become in 1979. But equally, had I not been there in 1979 or later I would never have realized how good things had been in 1974. Through the 1980s and 1990s a generation of children grew up who did not known how or where to gather wild plants, and this occurred in several parts of the Kalahari. Likewise, settlements change radically, although the pattern is not always irreversible. ≠ā, a Naro place in Botswana where I had lived in 1974 and 1975, had been abandoned completely when I returned in 1979. When I next visited it in 1982, it was reoccupied by Naro, many of whom I knew, but none of whom had lived there in 1975. For me personally all this was unsettling, but nevertheless strangely calming, too, in that the happy field situation I had known earlier was not something I should miss because it was not there any more. Most of the people of ǂā had by 1982 settled some miles to the south at the relatively large settlement of Hanahai, where there were members of other San groups, some attempts at growing maize and vegetables, peripheral hunting and much food-gathering when possible, and food subsidies, as well as a school and permanent water. They were undoubtedly better off there, but their lives would be different from then on.

In 2007 Namibia's minister of foreign affairs asked me to serve, in the words of my commission, as "Honorary Consul of the Republic of Namibia with the Consular Seat in the city of Edinburgh and jurisdiction over Scotland." The United Kingdom's Foreign and Commonwealth Office duly granted exequatur, and now I had an unpaid job to serve (part of) Africa to complement my paid job to teach about Africa. Conventional wisdom would say that I was a strange choice: neither Namibian nor ethnically Scottish, an anthropologist rather than a business person or retired politician, and, being an anthropologist, not a specialist on some large population group but on southern Africa's minorities. There is also the irony of an apparent Scottish "chief" like me representing Namibia through reports to the High Commissioner of the Republic of Namibia in London. (Some honorary consuls in Scotland really are clan chiefs, and Commonwealth countries exchange not "ambassadors," but "high commissioners"—previously the title of senior colonial officials in the times of "indirect rule" in the British Empire.) My new role has given me opportunities to learn and to reflect more on the complex history of Namibian ethnic relations, and among other things to try to establish educational and cultural exchanges for the benefit of Namibians of all ethnicities, including San or Bushmen. It has even given me the chance, for example, to receive the !Gubi Family,

Scotland, 2008.

a group of six San musicians and dancers, at my home (which is also the Namibian consulate) near Edinburgh. Thus, after years of my returning to the field, "the field" returned to me.

Neither the duration of my own fieldwork nor my written accounts of San custom can compete with those of several of my more illustrious colleagues. Yet I think what I have done is useful in a different way. The rewards of long-term engagement with individuals and social groups are obvious, but the rewards of decades of accumulated knowledge, analysis, and reanalysis in a regionally focused framework cannot be underestimated either. It remains relatively rare for one to make explicit the importance of both *time* and *intraregional comparison,* but for me this dual methodological interest is crucial. After Namibia's war of liberation, many Bushmen who had fought on the South African side, against Namibian independence, were resettled in South Africa. When I visited their camp at Schmidtsdrift, South Africa, in 1997, I could tell instantly which half was !Xū and which half was Kxoe, because I could see traditional patterns of settlement in the way !Xū and Kxoe there arranged their army tents.

A novice in Khoisan studies, however good a fieldworker, might possibly have missed that. For that reason, I prefer to define my "fieldwork site" not as a specific point on the landscape, but rather as a whole subcontinent. For me, this blend of metaphorical longitude (which in a wide sense could be either long-term or multitemporal) and latitude provides the best chance for ethnographic understanding.

REFERENCES

Barnard, Alan. 1976. *Nharo Bushman Kinship and the Transformation of Khoi Kin Categories.* PhD diss., University College London.

———. 1978. Universal Systems of Kin Categorization. *African Studies* 37:69–81.

———. 1979. "Kalahari Bushman Settlement Patterns." In Philip Burnham and Roy F. Ellen, eds., *Social and Ecological Systems* (A.S.A. Monographs 18), 131–144. London: Academic Press.

———. 1986. Rethinking Bushman Settlement Patterns and Territoriality. *Sprache und Geschichte in Afrika* 7 (1): 41–60.

———. 1988. Structure and Fluidity in Khoisan Religious Ideas. *Journal of Religion in Africa* 18:216–236.

———. 1989. The Lost World of Laurens van der Post? *Current Anthropology* 30:104–114.

———. 1991. Social and Spatial Boundary Maintenance among Southern African Hunter-Gatherers. In Michael J. Casimir and Aparna Rao, eds., *Mobility and Territoriality: Social and Spatial Boundaries among Foragers, Fishers, Pastoralists and Peripatetics,* 131–151. New York: Berg.

———. 1992. *Hunters and Herders of Southern Africa: A Comparative Ethnography of the Khoisan Peoples.* Cambridge: Cambridge University Press.

———. 1996. Regional Comparison in Khoisan Ethnography: Theory, Method and Practice. *Zeitschrift für Ethnologie* 121:203–220.

———. 2003. !Ke e: /xarra //ke—Multiple Origins and Multiple Meanings of the Motto. *African Studies* 62:243–250.

———. 2004. Mutual Aid and the Foraging Mode of Thought: Re-reading Kropotkin on the Khoisan. *Social Evolution and History* 3(1): 3–21.

———. 2007. *Anthropology and the Bushman.* Oxford: Berg.

———. 2008. The Co-evolution of Kinship and Language. In N. J. Allen, Hillary Callan, Robin Dunbar, and Wendy James, *Early Human Kinship: From Sex to Social Reproduction,* 232–243. Oxford: Blackwell Publishing.

Fortes, Meyer. 1958. Introduction. In J. R. Goody, *The Developmental Cycle in Domestic Groups*, 1–15. Cambridge: Cambridge University Press.

Godelier, Maurice. 1975. Modes of Production, Kinship, and Demographic Structures. In Maurice Bloch, ed., *Marxist Analyses and Social Anthropology* (A.S.A. Studies 2), 3–27. London: Malaby Press.

Kuper, Adam. 1980. *Wives for Cattle: Bridewealth and Marriage in Southern Africa*. London: Routledge and Kegan Paul.

———. 1987. *South Africa and the Anthropologist*. London: Routledge and Kegan Paul.

———. 2002. Comparison and Contextualization: Reflections on South Africa. In Andre Gingrich and Richard G. Fox, eds., *Anthropology by Comparison*, 143–166. London: Routledge.

Lee, Richard B. 1979a. Hunter-gatherers in Process: The Kalahari Research Project, 1963–1976. In George M. Foster, Thayer Scudder, Elizabeth Colson, and Robert Van Kemper, *Long-Term Field Research in Social Anthropology*, 303–321. New York: Academic Press.

———. 1979b. *The !Kung San: Men, Women, and Work in a Foraging Society*. Cambridge: Cambridge University Press.

Steward, Julian H. 1955. *Theory of Culture Change: The Methodology of Multilinear Evolution*. Urbana: University of Illinois Press.

Widlok, Thomas. 2004. (Re-)current Doubts on Hunter-Gatherer Studies as Contemporary History. In Alan Barnard, ed., *Hunter-Gatherers in History, Archaeology and Anthropology*, 217–226. Oxford: Berg.

Wiessner, Pauline Wilson. 1977. *Hxaro: A Regional System of Reciprocity for Reducing Risk among the !Kung San*. 2 vols. PhD diss., University of Michigan, Ann Arbor.

Wilmsen, Edwin N. 1989. *Land Filled with Flies: A Political Economy of the Kalahari*. Chicago: University of Chicago Press.

Afterword

Reflecting on Returns to the Field

BRUCE KNAUFT

As commentator, I begin with a pang of humility with respect to these essays by long-term fieldworkers. I have spent just two and a half years stretched over three decades among the Gebusi people of Papua New Guinea, who have been my primary focus of ethnographic fieldwork. This is paltry compared to the many trips and longer periods of time that most presenters in the current volume have spent conducting fieldwork. Indeed, the combined duration of ethnographic returns represented in this book are something on the order of three centuries. So compared to the present company my own experience of long-term fieldwork is limited. Partly as a way out of this limitation, I begin with a few general remarks about time and temporality in relation to fieldwork and in relation to modernity.

As has often been noted, and as Reinhart Kosselleck (1985) has stressed, modernity, since the late eighteenth century in Europe and the United States—and increasingly in other nations as well—has championed a distinct relationship to time. On the one hand, in contrast to many other worldviews, modernity emphasizes knowledge of and learning from the past not for its own sake but to shed light on the present and improve upon it in the future. The *bildungsroman* of accumulated personal and collective enlightenment is key to modernity, not just drawing on the past but auguring the potentials of

new time ahead, a *neuzeit,* a never-before-experienced and potentially better future. This notion is distinctive to Euro-American and
now global varieties of modernism.

Such modern temporality also informs the willful destruction and
sweeping away of the past in favor of hoped-for progress in the future. In modernity, these are linked; the modern emphasis on the
newer and ever-new, not on the repetition of the past, links to the
transcendence of previous ways of life—much as Haussmann leveled the rabbit warrens of nineteenth-century Parisian communities to make way for broad new modern boulevards. In modernity,
as Marshall Berman (1982) has emphasized, destructive creation and
creative destruction are fundamentally linked.

This working of modern time is evident in both the object and
the method of the chapters in this volume. As they aptly illustrate,
larger forces and agents sweep away or threaten to sweep away customs and traditions in favor of the newer and more modern, however
these are locally or regionally defined. What is more, being modern
her- or himself, the ethnographer tries to use personally observed
history to build up increasing knowledge and wisdom that can gain
greater purchase not only on processes of change but on how local
experiences and sensibilities are or may be refractory to plans or ideologies of wider modernity. As the chapters of this volume underscore, destruction seldom produces the desired progress.

In a larger sense, then, an ironic relationship often pertains in the
long term of repeated field visits—between the hoped-for progress of
increasing knowledge and greater understanding of destructive ten-
dencies, and the uncovering if not critique of overblown hopes or expectations or ideologies of progress among the people we study with.

It is perhaps revealing that almost all the chapters in this volume
pertain to decentralized rural populations and now-marginalized
peoples—groups that in our older anthropology were labeled foragers, tribes, or perhaps, in Edvard Hviding's case, chiefdoms. This
is significant not just topically but in terms of our sociology of long-
term ethnographic knowledge. Longitudinal ethnography dates itself self-consciously by the general location and communities of its

founding fieldwork decades before. To assess the future trajectory and potentials of long-term field returns, then, one needs to take the current locational and topical trends of social and cultural anthropology and project them into the future. A newer generation of fieldworkers is now engaging sites of ethnographic research that include international governance and humanitarian aid agencies, the ethnography of myriad institutions and of public culture, and, in the mix, highly urban experience—from cyberspace to business and unemployment, widespread migration, and a wide range of security, health-related, educational, governmental, commercial, and environmental forms and formations. These are the tip of the iceberg of new topical and location venues. How will or could or should these communities or networks look longitudinally in twenty or thirty years, in 2030 or 2040? Are such restudies possible or likely? Are they thinkable? I anticipate that they are—and that this is not just a curious speculation but an important possibility to cultivate. The peoples studied in projects undertaken by new generations of anthropologists will ramify in their own distinct ways and with their own networks over time, as those of erstwhile tribal or chiefly or forager populations have done. In the process, the terms used to describe and conceptualize these communities will probably change; present notions may seem diluted or outdated within a decade or two. Both of these changes—in the communities we study and in how we conceive of and understand them—are important not just to mark but to emphasize and reflect on over time. For these reasons, longitudinal studies are likely to be highly important in the future for anthropology's own developing notions of time and space as well as its relation to changing world circumstances and contexts. This importance echoes Alan Barnard's trenchant comments in his chapter concerning the use of repeated fieldwork to increase our comparative understanding of continuities and variations across geographic, social, and cultural space.

Arguably, the search for the ever-new that is the hallmark of modernity has intensified in anthropology itself during the past three decades. During the 1980s and '90s, much of this development traveled under the signs of postmodernity, postcolonialism, reflexivity,

With a senior Gebusi
man, 1981. PHOTOGRAPH
BY EILEEN KNAUFT.

cultural studies, and/or experimental ethnography (see Knauft 1996).
These emphases intensified the anthropological search for and expression of not the long-standing, the depth of history, or the privilege of temporal wisdom, but pastiche, hybridity, the multisitedness
of the new, and the appearance of change in the present—along with
new genres of ethnographic writing and presentation.

Against this, earlier emphases in anthropology and specifically
American ethnography, from at least Boas through Kroeber, emphasized long-term research commitment through repeated seasons
of return fieldwork. During the 1960s, '70s, and '80s, however, this
emphasis became less important and, eventually, deprivileged amid
greater emphasis on the ever-new in culture and in representation. As
Signe Howell notes in her introduction, this trend is thrown into relief by the fact that despite much reflexivity in ethnography and ethnographic writing during the last quarter-century, there have been
very few considerations of fieldwork in longer duration—of repeated
returns to the field.

In national terms, this volume includes a significant Norwegian
emphasis, represented by the editors and three of its ethnographic
chapters. This reflects the contributing importance of long-term field
research facilitated by Norwegian anthropology programs at univer-
sities such as Oslo and Bergen. In much of continental Europe, including Germany and France, emphasis on repeated seasons of anthropological field research, extending over many years or decades,

is arguably more frequent in relative terms than in American anthropology. This tendency is worth noting amid the growing understanding of and emphasis on the complementary contribution of different anthropologies in different world areas (see Ribeiro and Escobar 2006).

At one level and on prima facie grounds, repeated returns to the field provide greatly increased ability to appreciate and understand dynamics and parameters of social and cultural change. From the chapters of the present volume, this awareness of change seems especially pertinent in two seemingly different but complementary ways.

On one hand is the *structural* worsening plight of marginal peoples in many places. Peter Metcalf emphasizes this: many of the chapters document and underscore the increasing subordination of the people we study to outside agents, organizations, and policies. Vitebsky (this volume) writes that "since the British conquest of their area in 1866, the Sora have lived under a system of governance that puts them at the bottom of every pile, ethnically, economically and ecologically." More generally, in comparing his long-term understanding of the forest-dwelling Sora of tropical India with his decades of research with the Eveny of Russian Siberia, he writes:

> The role of colonialism and the state, as well as the specific cosmologies of the Communist, Baptist and Hindu evangelisms, may be different, but we can recognize a similar centralizing, totalizing thrust: where the local community's frame of reference is local it must be made universal, where their time is cyclical or non-destinational it must be made future-oriented, where their sense of morality comes from within it must be structured and validated by an outside source.

Increasingly, however, such disempowerment is not so much in spite of but in direct relation to people's increasing interconnection with—and positive valuation of—regional, national, and international actors and agencies. Persons like Vincent Vaguni, in Edvard Hviding's account, have themselves been provincial politicians, environmental activists, liaison officers to mining companies, director of landowners' corporations, officers of powerful church organizations, and active travelers to international conferences—as well as right-hand men to customary chiefs—and yet living, in many ways, "a conventional rural family life, with the weekly highlight being the Saturday hunt for feral pigs with a pack of dogs and a spear." But for all this engagement and partial success and in many ways because of it, there often grows an increased sense of *relative* deprivation vis-à-vis actors and agents of a larger world.

At the same time, as Edvard Hviding's chapter also suggests, the personal resilience, adaptability, and potential of persons as individuals is profound and striking across almost all of the contributors' descriptions. Against either a dismal view of the life of marginal peoples going downhill in a global handbasket, or a modernity-at-large view of increasing interconnection, progress, and benefit, the presentations of this volume provide a more nuanced and richer view. In some cases, including those in the chapters by Turner and by Morphy and Morphy, both relative subordination and creative response increase at the same time, as if in direct or dialectical relation. On the one hand, structural disempowerment of marginalized peoples grows relative to larger economic, national, and international pressures and forces. But at the same time and sometimes for this very reason, people's engagement with these forces can be surprisingly strong, adaptable, and creative.

The various chapters of this volume play across both ends of this spectrum and combine them. Terence Turner's contribution is perhaps the most positive, documenting the ability of Kayapo to engage effectively with outside intrusion in the Amazon on and through their own terms. Turner has played a role not only in documenting but as an activist in their resistance against state pressure and outside forces. Peter Metcalf, at the other extreme, is more pessimistic, with little apparent hope for increasingly marginalized and peripheral peoples, or for helping them. But to the extent that the chapters bring the experiences and practical engagement of actual persons and friends to light, these dynamics are often significantly intertwined.

Alan Barnard's chapter speaks of how Khoisan are a disparaged minority and yet ideological embodiments of then-President Mbeki's new South Africa. Signe Howell describes how even with the increase of a money economy, Chewong sociality is still embedded in punén moral exchange. Terence Turner suggests how longstanding connections of kinship and domestic organization continue to inform moral suasion amid a host of changes in Kayapo politics and economy—at the same time that new and more modern forms of internal as well as external status differentiation and exploitation also increase.

In the mix, unanticipated or unintended consequences both complicate and accentuate features of change—and of tradition. A prime case in point are the Yolngu mortuary rituals described over decades by Morphy and Morphy. On the one hand, a time traveler from seventy years ago would find the sounds of a Yolngu burial ceremony very familiar, as if little had changed. As the Morphys put it, the guiding spiritual objective—to ensure that the person's spirit returns to the ancestral dimension—has never altered. On the other hand, one now finds refrigerated morgue units being bought and Yolngu bodies transported in them at great and in some cases exorbitant expense, including by air, for highly protracted funerary journeys and rites. The large nearby bauxite mine and Australian welfare payments have both greatly increased the Yolngu death rate from injury, accident, suicide, and illness associated with alcohol and substance abuse— while also significantly increasing the funds available for funerals, in one case even the planting of giant aluminum flag poles around the grave. Yolngu increasingly spend much of their lives as well as their resources going from funeral to funeral to funeral. This is poignantly traditional/modern and modern/traditional at one and the same time. Both disempowerment vis-à-vis outside forces and creative responses from within increase.

Many of the chapters focus quite aptly on the specific implications of long-term returns to the field, both for the ethnographic encounter and for the ethnographer—as well as for the people with whom the ethnographer is studying. Often, over time, our subjects become friends and deeper parts of our ongoing lives, and vice versa.

This perspective provides a distinctive vantage point on ethnographic fieldwork more generally. Most primary ethnography provides the life-position perspective of a twenty-something (or early-thirty-something) researcher, often single and sometimes newly married, usually without children (or at least ones who are grown). The strength of this ethnographic subject position is also its weakness; it provides a narrow life cycle window from which to view alternative peoples and cultures. As young adults, first fieldworkers often take on the childlike status of often not knowing the local language, not to mention the culture, at the same time that they are often perceived in local terms to be quite wealthy if not powerful. A complement to and counterbalance against this bias in ethnographer–subject positioning is the perspective of older anthropologists who return over years and decades, time and again. The understanding gained from this longer perspective is important to cultivate if anthropology is to provide a rounded view of changes, not just over time but from different points in our own life cycles, and as accumulated over the professional life course. With time, most ethnographers are afforded new and sometimes more intimate cultural status as a mature person or elder. As Vitebsky recounts concerning his decades of contact with the Sora, "I have graduated from *ubbang* (little brother) to *jojo* (grandfather or ancestor)."

Often, if not typically, as these chapters reveal, this maturity is accompanied by increased expectations the local community placed on the returning ethnographer. In some ways, long-returning ethnographers become like the growing number of diasporic returnees around the world who come home sporadically from points distant. Like such long-term émigrés, returning anthropologists are often expected to bring back and share their wealth; the returning ethnographer becomes a distinctive kind of a long-lost relative. Long-term returns to the field are thus easily associated both with joy, appreciation, and intimacy, and with high expectations and costs. Aud Talle shows us the strange and in some ways wonderful twists of this process as they reciprocate and complement each other in fieldwork over time. The woman she knows from the late 1970s as only a nameless girl who screamed and fought mightily to avoid being genitally cut, becomes, years later, a mother with children of her own. Met later by Talle, the woman seems neither shy about, enamored of, nor psychologically scarred by her former apparent act of gendered resistance or by the process of being genitally cut itself. Professor Talle is forced to put her own earlier categories of understanding about the significance of genital cutting into question. And yet, this same woman has now joined a Christian church to "handle the problems [she] faced due to the husband's excessive drinking and squandering of livestock property on alcohol and other women." Along with her sons, she has made a concerted effort to pray to God for her husband's misbehavior, which has started to improve. When Talle asked the woman what she had thought of the long-lost ethnographer when she had initially returned to the field, she said, "I prayed and prayed for help and you came along as my helper . . . you are my 'angel.'" In this case, it could be said, gendered support in the face of patriarchy appears, at least in our own terms, to be confirmed after all and in cross-cultural perspective. This illustrates how the wheel of anthropological perception changes over time, turning in newly surprising, enriching, and also humbling ways.

As these chapters reveal, the long-term ethnographer often accumulates not just increasing status as an aficionado or historian of the people she or he studies among, but increasing potentials for friendship and for supporting local communities. At turns loving, moral, humanitarian, stressful, and demanding, these ties are often both very rich and refractory to comparative assessment. They go beyond being professional connections, within-culture friendships, humanitarian interventions, or even familial, much less contractual, obligations. Often, our relations with our long-term friends in the field tie several of these features together. The chapters by Turner and Talle reveal these long-term personal relations with particular care and nuance. As Signe Howell suggests, with benefit of time and contextual understanding, tacit understanding even silences in fieldwork can speak volumes.

This brings me finally to Piers Vitebsky's chapter, which is pertinent in relation to these issues. His long-term nuance and understanding in the field—both among the Eveny in Siberia and the forest-dwelling Sora in India—has made him a sounding board and

With friends at a Gebusi
garden hamlet, 1998.

facilitator if not a target for some of the deepest expressions of local people's search for meaning in both societies. The very inarticulacy of their selected moments of poignant remembering of their longer-term past—Paranto's remembering his dead father, Taranti's remembering the spirit familiar of her previous shamanic experience, and Tolya's becoming a PhD and Siberian anthropologist in reverence to the lost past of his mother—reveals the deep power of personal and cultural meaning across years and decades of change. In these cases, expressions of meaning are catalyzed not only for us but for selected persons in these societies themselves by means of the ethnographer's long association and supportive personal relationship. In addition to being an aficionado, a repository, and even a personal icon of tradition, the mature returning ethnographer is easily, and sometimes inadvertently, a sounding board or lightning rod for the transduction of meaning between the present and the past. I have experienced this myself, for instance, when I inadvertently revealed secrets of male-male sexuality and insemination to young Gebusi men who did not know of these customary practices (Knauft 2010, ch. 10).

Lest I close with a view of ethnographic maturity that is too beneficent or hagiographic, I must also note the final stages and ultimate personal insignificance of returns to the field. As Vitebsky suggests for the Sora and the bygone Eveny, the aging elders easily pine for acknowledgment—and the same goes for long-standing ethnographers. Eventually, as Vitebsky describes elsewhere (2008), Sora ancestors eventually stop visiting those they have been associated with, lose their voice, and become inarticulate. Eventually they take the form of silent butterflies. For the Sora, butterflies are the lonely residue of persons who are beyond the reach of dialogue. Often it is the fate of long-term ethnographers to go back and forth between being at turns lovingly ancestor-like, on the one hand, and beyond dialogue, on the other. Ultimately, of course, the latter holds sway. As Vitebsky says of Sora butterflies, when there are fewer and fewer people to remember them, they ultimately become memories without rememberers. This is the fate of most, if not all, ethnography and ethnographers.

This is ultimately also the fate of all books, and indeed of all people. But in the bargain, and even more so because of impermanence, is the enduring importance of understanding the challenge and sometimes the beauty of human connections over time, passing on as much as we can from our generation to the next.

REFERENCES

Berman, Marshall. 1982. *All That Is Solid Melts into Air: The Experience of Modernity.* New York: Penguin.

Knauft, Bruce M. 1996. *Genealogies for the Present in Cultural Anthropology.* New York: Routledge.

———. 2010. *The Gebusi: Lives Transformed in a Rainforest World,* 2nd ed. New York: McGraw-Hill.

Kosselleck, Reinhart. 1985. *Futures Past: On the Semantics of Historical Time.* Cambridge, MA: MIT Press.

Riberio, Gustav Lins, and Arturo Escobar, eds. 2006. *World Anthropologies: Disciplinary Transformations within Systems of Power.* London: Berg.

Vitebsky, Piers. 2008. Loving and Forgetting: Moments of Inarticulacy in Tribal India. *Journal of the Royal Anthropological Institute* 14:243–261.

CONTRIBUTORS

ALAN BARNARD is Professor of the Anthropology of Southern Africa at the University of Edinburgh. His books include *Hunters and Herders of Southern Africa; History and Theory in Anthropology; Anthropology and the Bushman;* and *Social Anthropology and Human Origins.* He is co-editor of the *Routledge Encyclopedia of Social and Cultural Anthropology.*

DAVID HOLMBERG is Professor of Anthropology and Asian Studies at Cornell University. He has published extensively on the Tamang of Nepal, including *Order in Paradox: Myth, Ritual, and Exchange among Nepal's Tamang.*

SIGNE HOWELL is Professor of Social Anthropology at the University of Oslo. Her books include *The Kinning of Foreigners: Transnational Adoption in a Global Perspective; The Ethnography of Moralities; Societies at Peace: An Anthropological Perspective;* and *Society and Cosmos: Chewong of Peninsular Malaysia.*

EDVARD HVIDING is Professor and Chair of Social Anthropology at the University of Bergen. Among his books are *Guardians of Marovo Lagoon, Islands of Rainforest* (with T. Bayliss-Smith), and *Made in Oceania: Social Movements, Cultural Heritage and the State in the Pacific* (co-edited with K. M. Rio).

BRUCE KNAUFT is Project Director, States at Regional Risk Project (SARR), and Samuel C. Dobbs Professor of Anthropology at Emory University. His books include *Critically Modern: Alternatives, Alterities, Anthropologies* (edited; IUP, 2002); *Exchanging the Past: A Rainforest World of Before and After;* and *The Gebusi: Lives Transformed in a Rainforest World.*

PETER METCALF is Professor of Anthropology at University of Virginia. His books include *The Life of the Longhouse: an Archaeology of Ethnicity; They Lie, We Lie: Getting On with Anthropology;* and *Celebrations of Death: The Anthropology of Mortuary Rituals* (with R. Huntington).

FRANCES MORPHY is Fellow at the Centre for Aboriginal Economic Policy Research (CAEPR) at the Australian National University. She is editor of *Agency, Contingency and Census Process: Observations of the 2006 Indigenous Enumeration Strategy in Remote Aboriginal Australia* and the *Macquarie Atlas of Indigenous Australia* (with W. Arthur).

HOWARD MORPHY is Professor at the Research School of Humanities College of Arts and Social Sciences at the Australian National University. His books include *Ancestral Connections: Art and an Aboriginal System of Knowledge* and *Becoming Art: Exploring Cross-Cultural Categories.*

AUD TALLE (1944–2011) was Professor of Social Anthropology at the University of Oslo. Her books include *The Power of Culture: Female Circumcision as Tradition and Taboo* (in Norwegian) and *Women at a Loss: Changes in Maasai Pastoralism and Their Effects on Gender Relations.*

TERENCE TURNER is Professor of Anthropology at the University of Chicago (Emeritus) and at Cornell University (Adjunct). He has published on Kayapo social organization and culture. He has also made films with the BBC and Granada International about Kayapo culture and political struggles in defense of their environment, and he founded the Kayapo Video Project to train and assist the Kayapo to use video to document their own culture

PIERS VITEBSKY is Head of Anthropology and Russian Northern Studies at the Scott Polar Research Institute, University of Cambridge. His books include *The Reindeer People: Living with Animals and Spirits in Siberia; Dialogues with the Dead: The Discussion of Mortality among the Sora of Eastern India;* and *Shamanism.*

INDEX

Warner, W. Lloyd, 49, 54

wealth, 33–35, 38, 42, 88, 123–124, 147, 159, 163, 166, 257; commodity, 36–37, 42

whitemen, 123–124

whites, 88, 125, 129, 131, 142, 146, 189, 197, 222–223

Wilson, Monica, 1, 8

women, 13, 14, 37, 39, 41–42, 46, 57, 64, 77–80, 83–87, 89, 92nn5,6, 114, 126, 165–168, 189, 208, 210, 223, 258; young, 8, 36, 119n3. *See also* gender; rights, women's

World War II, 176n2, 220

Yirrkala, 55–56, 58–60, 64

Yolngu, 13, 49–51, 53–67, 69–70, 256